ECONOMIC POLICIES IN THE PACIFIC AREA DEVELOPING COUNTRIES

Economic Policies in the Pacific Area Developing Countries

Bela Balassa
Professor of Political Economy
The Johns Hopkins University

New York University Press
Washington Square, New York

© Bela Balassa 1991

All rights reserved

Manufactured in Great Britain

First published in the U.S.A. in 1991 by
NEW YORK UNIVERSITY PRESS
Washington Square
New York, N.Y. 10003

Library of Congress Cataloging-in-Publication Data
Balassa, Bela A.
Economic policies in the Pacific area developing countries / Bela
Balassa.
　p. cm.
Includes bibliographical references and index.
ISBN 0–8147–1169–3
1. East Asia—Economic policy.　2. Asia, Southeastern—Economic
policy.　3. East Asia—Commerce.　4. Asia, Southeastern—Commerce.
5. Economic forecasting—East Asia.　6. Economic forecasting—Asia.
Southeastern.　I.Title.
HC460.5.B25　1991
338.99—dc20　　　　　　　　　　　　　　　　　　　　　91–6929
　　　　　　　　　　　　　　　　　　　　　　　　　　　　　CIP

Contents

Preface	vi
1 Economic Developments in the Pacific Area Developing Countries since 1963	1
2 Hong Kong	30
3 Korea	46
4 Singapore	73
5 Taiwan	96
6 Indonesia	121
7 Malaysia	142
8 The Philippines	164
9 Thailand	183
10 Conclusions	202
Index	207

Preface

The developing countries of the Pacific Area have attracted much attention in recent years. These countries have attained rapid rates of economic growth and, apart from the Philippines, avoided the debt crisis. They have also assumed considerable importance in world trade and are poised to maintain their outstanding growth record.

These considerations point to the need to improve our understanding of the factors determining the economic performance of the Pacific Area developing countries. Such is the purpose of the present volume which examines both the newly industrializing countries (NICs), comprising Hong Kong, Korea, Singapore, and Taiwan, and the newly exporting countries (NECs), including Indonesia, Malaysia, the Philippines and Thailand, in that area.

The volume begins with an analysis of economic developments in the Pacific Area developing countries in a comparative framework. The first chapter covers indicators of economic growth, domestic savings and the efficiency of investment, the role of exports, the policies applied, social indicators and trends in international trade.

Next follow chapters concerning each country. These examine government policies, economic growth, international trade and prospects for the future in the individual countries. While the overall structure of these chapters is similar, the treatment varies to a considerable extent depending on the characteristics of the particular countries.

The conclusions restate the main findings of the volume and summarize the policies that need to be followed by the Pacific Area developing countries in order to maintain high economic growth rates. Further attention is given to the future role of these countries in the world economy.

The research and writing of this volume were financed by the Pew Charitable Trusts under a grant to the Institute for International Economics. I am indebted for the support of both of these organizations. The Institute's publication 'Pacific Area Developing Countries: Prospects for the Future' used material from the tables and the text of this volume.

BELA BALASSA

1 Economic Developments in the Pacific Area Developing Countries since 1963

INTRODUCTION

The developing countries of the Pacific Area have had an outstanding economic record over the past twenty-five years. This conclusion applies to the East Asian NICs, including Hong Kong, Korea, Singapore and Taiwan; with the exception of the Philippines, it also applies to the group of NECs which includes Indonesia, Malaysia, the Philippines and Thailand (the ASEAN member countries other than Singapore and Brunei).

In the following discussion, the economic performance of the Pacific Area developing countries will be contrasted with that of a 'comparator' group of countries. The East Asian NICs will be compared with the Latin American NICs, including Argentina, Brazil, Chile and Mexico. In turn, the economic performance of the East Asian NECs will be contrasted with that of a group of Latin American countries at similar levels of development, including Colombia, Jamaica, Peru and Venezuela.

The classification scheme reflects not so much income levels as the level of industrialization, and it pertains to the present situation rather than to that prevailing a quarter of a century ago. The share of manufacturing industries in the gross domestic product (GDP) is in the 25–30 percent range in the NICs except that it is 43 percent in Taiwan and 20 percent in Hong Kong; it is in the 20–25 percent range in the NECs except for 14 percent in Indonesia, where industry is relatively undeveloped and oil accounts for a large share of GDP.

INDICATORS OF ECONOMIC GROWTH

The Pacific Area developing countries had relatively low income levels in 1963. Apart from Hong Kong and Singapore, they had lower

Table 1.1 GDP per caput (US$)

	At purchasing power parities in 1980 prices					At exchange rates
	1963	1973	1981	1988	1988/1963	1988
Hong Kong	2 247	4 552	7 751	11 952	5.32	8 249
Korea	747	1 553	2 457	4 094	5.48	2 849
Singapore	1 777	3 838	6 308	11 693	6.58	7 623
Taiwan	980	1 976	3 028	4 607	4.70	4 804
Argentina	2 949	4 157	3 935	3 474	1.18	2 563
Brazil	1 400	2 338	3 252	3 424	2.45	2 305
Chile	3 231	3 502	4 443	3 933	1.22	1 492
Mexico	2 312	3 403	4 576	3 649	1.58	1 749
Indonesia	463	706	1 155	1 348	2.91	409
Malaysia	1 233	2 146	3 281	3 643	2.95	1 886
Philippines	965	1 209	1 565	1 460	1.51	603
Thailand	537	761	1 096	1 627	3.03	887
Colombia	1 364	2 010	2 582	2 844	2.09	1 217
Jamaica	1 554	2 455	1 873	1 797	1.16	1 189
Peru	1 973	2 362	2 494	2 102	1.07	2 178
Venezuela	6 123	5 735	4 194	3 814	0.62	2 716

Sources: 1963–81 figures from R. Summers and A. Heston, 'A New Set of International Comparisons of Real Product and Price Levels Estimates for 130 Countries', *Review of Income and Wealth*, vol. 34, no. 1 (March 1988). The 1987 estimates were updated from 1985 figures by utilizing national data on economic growth rates.

per caput incomes than any of the Latin American countries under consideration. Even Hong Kong and Singapore were behind Argentina, Chile, Mexico and Venezuela in terms of income per head in 1963 (see Table 1.1).

The situation changed dramatically in the following twenty-five years. By 1988, all four of the East Asian NICs surpassed the per caput incomes of every Latin American country. Also, Malaysia surpassed all the Latin American NICs other than Argentina and Brazil; and Indonesia and Thailand reduced the distance that separated them from the Latin American NECs. Only the Philippines remained behind.

These changes occurred as the per caput incomes of the four East Asian NICs increased between $4\frac{1}{2}$ and $6\frac{1}{2}$ times during the 1963–88 period. The next best performers were Malaysia, Thailand and Indonesia, with incomes per head rising more than $2\frac{1}{2}$ times. Per caput incomes increased by less than half in the Philippines, however, and growth rates were lower than in the Latin American countries under consideration other than Jamaica, Peru and Venezuela. In the last-mentioned country, incomes per head declined; this contrasts with a doubling in Colombia, the champion among the Latin American NECs. Among the Latin American NICs, per caput incomes increased by a factor of $2\frac{1}{2}$ in Brazil but much less in the other countries of the group.

Further interest attaches to intercountry differences in increases in per caput incomes over time. Table 1.1 provides data for the benchmark years of the 1963–73 period of world economic boom, the 1973–81 period of two oil shocks, and the 1981–8 period of the debt crisis.

It appears that the Pacific Area developing countries had already started gaining on the comparator countries by 1963–73. In particular, per caput incomes doubled in the East Asian NICs, far surpassing the performance of any of the other countries under consideration.

The Pacific Area developing countries increased their lead during the period of the oil shocks, with the East Asian NICs again doing extremely well, notwithstanding their reliance on imported petroleum. In the same period, Argentina, Jamaica and oil-exporting Venezuela suffered declines in per caput income.

Differences in economic performance increased further in the period of the debt crisis. Apart from the Philippines, all Pacific Area developing countries experienced increases in per caput incomes, with the East Asian NICs being again in the lead. By contrast, apart from small gains in Brazil and Colombia, all the Latin American countries under consideration experienced declines in incomes per head.

The differences observed in the 1981–8 period may be explained by reference to the foreign debt situation. There is a contrast between the high degree of foreign indebtedness of Latin American countries and the Philippines and the low external debt of developing countries of the Pacific Area (see below).

DOMESTIC SAVINGS AND THE EFFICIENCY OF INVESTMENT

With the exception of the Philippines, then, the Pacific Area developing countries experienced much larger increases in per caput incomes than the comparator countries in the 1963–88 period. In this connection, reference may be made to differences in domestic saving ratios and investment efficiency on the one hand, and the changing relative importance of exports on the other.

A comparison of the East Asian and Latin American NICs does not show regional differences in domestic saving ratios in the 1963–73 period, and there were also considerable differences within each group. The superior growth performance of the East Asian NICs is thus explained by their higher investment efficiency which is measured, however imperfectly, by incremental capital–output ratios (ICORs). Among Latin American NICs, Brazil and Mexico had relatively low ICORs (see Table 1.2).

The situation changed in the 1973–81 period. All East Asian NICs increased their domestic saving ratios to a substantial extent while the increases were smaller, or domestic saving ratios declined, in the Latin American NICs. At the same time, the East Asian NICs maintained higher levels of investment efficiency than their Latin American counterparts. An apparent exception is Mexico where newly-found oil raised GDP growth rates, thereby reducing the ICOR.

Nevertheless, except for Hong Kong, the East Asian NICs experienced increases in their very low ICORs of the first period. In 1981–7, ICORs increased further in Hong Kong and Singapore while declining slightly in Korea and Taiwan. Korea, together with Singapore, also experienced considerable increases in domestic saving ratios.

In the 1981–7 period, negative GDP growth rates in Mexico and very low growth rates in Argentina and Chile do not allow us to derive meaningful estimates for the ICOR. Negative growth in Mexico occurred despite the rise in domestic saving ratios while growth rates in Brazil continued to fall behind those of the East Asian NICs.

Except for Malaysia, the East Asian NECs generally had lower domestic saving ratios than the Latin American NECs in the 1963–73 period. Apart from the Philippines–Colombia comparisons, however, this was more than offset by higher levels of investment efficiency.

Table 1.2 GDP growth rates, domestic savings ratios, and the ICOR

Country	1963–73 GDP growth rate	1963–73 Domestic saving ratio	1963–73 ICOR	1973–81 GDP growth rate	1973–81 Domestic saving ratio	1973–81 ICOR	1981–7 GDP growth rate	1981–7 Domestic saving ratio	1981–7 ICOR
Hong Kong	8.9	24.3	3.6	9.1	29.0	3.4	7.2	28.3	4.0
Korea	9.3	13.0	2.1	7.8	23.6	4.2	8.9	29.8	3.5
Singapore	10.3	16.5	3.1	7.8	32.8	5.0	5.3	42.0	8.4
Taiwan	11.1	24.4	1.9	8.0	32.8	3.7	7.6	33.7	2.9
Argentina	5.0	20.5	4.2	1.1	24.2	20.2	0.4	16.0	31.4
Brazil	8.2	26.3	2.2	5.8	21.2	4.4	3.8	20.5	4.4
Chile	2.8	14.3	7.5	3.7	14.2	4.5	0.6	14.5	24.8
Mexico	7.4	19.2	2.7	6.7	22.1	3.4	−0.2	25.5	−81.9
Indonesia	6.7	11.1	1.3	7.2	29.1	2.4	3.2	29.0	8.7
Malaysia	7.0	24.4	2.8	7.3	31.8	3.6	4.2	32.1	7.8
Philippines	5.3	18.1	3.9	5.8	24.3	4.7	−0.0	20.0	−452.4
Thailand	7.9	19.2	3.0	6.9	22.0	3.6	5.6	21.8	4.0
Colombia	5.9	17.1	3.1	4.6	19.9	4.1	3.2	19.9	6.1
Jamaica	5.3	25.6	5.1	−2.2	14.4	−9.1	0.8	14.9	18.8
Peru	4.6	23.1	6.8	3.7	20.0	6.8	1.7	25.6	12.7
Venezuela	4.5	35.3	4.3	2.1	36.7	13.9	0.6	24.9	27.9

Source: World Bank.

Domestic saving ratios increased to a considerable extent in 1973–81 in the East Asian NECs whereas little change occurred or a decline was experienced in the Latin American NECs. And while ICORs increased in the East Asian NECs in the 1981–7 period, the Philippines apart, these countries had higher levels of investment efficiency than the Latin American NECs, the exception being Colombia.

THE ROLE OF EXPORTS

The East Asian NICs attained high rates of economic growth in an open economy as shown by their high export–GDP ratios (see Table 1.3). These differences cannot be explained by disparities in country size: while Brazil and Mexico have large economies, Korea's population and GDP are greater than Argentina's, and Taiwan's population and GDP are greater than Chile's.

In Korea and Taiwan, the export–GDP ratio increased greatly between 1963 and 1987, indicating the leading role of exports in the growth process. This was also the case, to a lesser extent, in Hong Kong and Singapore which already had high export–GDP ratios at the beginning of the period. At any rate, the figures for these countries are much affected by entrepôt trade. The results are further affected by the importation of inputs for processing to export which raised the ratio for Singapore above 100 percent (in any case, export values and value added (GDP) are not strictly comparable).

Export–GDP ratios increased much less in the Latin American NICs than in Korea and Taiwan; they declined in Argentina. In Mexico's case, the oil finds raised the export–GDP ratio; in Chile, an even larger increase occurred as economic policy shifted in an outward-oriented direction after 1973.

Export–GDP ratios for Indonesia are distorted by fluctuations in the price of petroleum. In the other three East Asian NECs, a fairly steady increase is shown throughout the period, with the largest rise occurring in Thailand. This contrasts with declines in the Latin American NECs, the exception being Colombia. Still, Colombia's export–GDP ratio falls behind that of the East Asian NECs.

Export expansion in the Pacific Area developing countries involved an increasing shift towards manufactured goods. In Korea, the share of manufactured goods in total exports rose from 45 percent in 1963 to 92 percent in 1987; in Taiwan, the corresponding figures

Table 1.3 Export and import shares

	Export/GDP ratio				Import/GDP ratio			
	1963	1973	1981	1987	1963	1973	1981	1987
Hong Kong	NA	66.7	73.9	104.1	NA	74.4	83.9	104.1
Korea	2.3	24.2	30.8	39.0	14.6	31.2	37.9	33.8
Singapore	124.5	88.0	151.0	143.7	153.4	123.5	198.5	163.3
Taiwan	15.3	42.1	47.6	56.6	16.7	35.6	44.7	36.5
Argentina	10.1	8.4	7.3	18.5	7.2	5.7	7.6	17.0
Brazil	5.7	12.8	8.2	8.2	5.2	14.5	8.5	5.1
Chile*	10.4	11.4	12.1	25.0	11.2	10.2	19.5	18.6
Mexico*	6.2	4.1	8.1	13.2	8.0	6.9	9.2	19.0
Indonesia	NA	19.7	25.9	23.8	NA	16.8	14.4	14.7
Malaysia	44.6	39.8	47.1	56.0	43.0	32.0	46.3	39.6
Philippines	12.9	17.6	14.8	16.6	13.5	16.8	21.9	20.2
Thailand	14.1	14.9	19.5	24.0	19.1	19.5	27.6	27.6
Colombia	9.2	11.4	8.1	14.8	10.5	10.3	14.3	12.6
Jamaica	25.8	20.6	32.9	30.5	28.9	35.8	49.8	53.1
Peru[+]	21.1	12.4	16.0	20.7	21.1	11.4	16.9	9.9
Venezuela	24.4	27.5	30.1	21.4	12.7	16.5	18.2	18.3

* Latest figures are for 1986.
[+] Latest figures are for 1985.

Sources: GDP and exchange rate data are from the International Monetary Fund (IMF), *International Financial Statistics*, various issues. Merchandise import and export figures are from IMF, *Direction of Trade Statistics*, various issues. All data for Taiwan from Council for Economic Planning and Development, Republic of China, *Taiwan Statistical Data Book, 1988*.

were 38 and 91 percent (see Table 1.4). Smaller changes occurred in Hong Kong, which already had a 92 percent manufactured export share in 1963, and in Singapore, where entrepôt trade in primary products is of importance.

The share of manufactured exports increased also in the Latin American NICs, but it remained much lower than in the East Asian NICs. The relevant shares for 1963 and 1986 (1987 for Argentina) are: Argentina, 6 and 32 percent; Brazil, 3 and 47 percent; Chile, 4 and 8 percent; and Mexico, 17 and 47 percent.

Manufactured exports were slower to develop in the NECs. But in these countries, too, much faster progress was made in the Pacific Area than in Latin America. Thus, between 1963 and 1987 (1986 in Indonesia and the Philippines) the share of manufactured goods in

Table 1.4 Commodity composition of exports (percent)

	1963 Fuels	Nonfuel primary	Manufactures	Other	Total	1973 Fuels	Nonfuel primary	Manufactures	Other	Total
Hong Kong	0.0	7.8	91.7	0.5	100.0	NA	3.3	96.5	0.2	100.0
Korea	3.0	51.8	45.1	0.2	100.0	1.1	14.7	84.0	0.2	100.0
Singapore	16.7	52.3	27.8	3.3	100.0	19.8	33.8	44.3	2.1	100.0
Taiwan	0.9	61.0	38.0	0.0	100.0	0.3	16.0	83.6	0.1	100.0
Argentina	0.8	93.4	5.7	0.1	100.0	0.2	77.4	22.4	0.0	100.0
Brazil	0.7	96.1	3.0	0.2	100.0	1.3	77.1	19.6	2.0	100.0
Chile	0.0	95.9	3.9	0.2	100.0	0.2	96.1	3.7	0.0	100.0
Mexico	4.5	78.4	17.0	0.1	100.0	0.9	57.1	41.9	0.1	100.0
Indonesia	38.5	61.2	0.3	0.0	100.0	50.1	47.8	1.9	0.2	100.0
Malaysia	4.1	90.3	4.7	0.9	100.0	5.4	82.6	11.4	0.6	100.0
Philippines	0.4	94.9	4.6	0.1	100.0	0.9	83.1	16.0	0.0	100.0
Thailand	0.0	96.5	2.5	1.0	100.0	1.3	78.6	16.0	4.0	100.0
Colombia	18.3	77.9	3.3	0.5	100.0	5.3	68.4	26.1	0.2	100.0
Jamaica	0.0	92.8	7.2	0.0	100.0	2.4	90.7	6.9	0.0	100.0
Peru	1.8	97.1	0.9	0.2	100.0	1.2	95.9	2.7	0.2	100.0
Venezuela	92.6	5.7	1.6	0.1	100.0	93.1	5.5	1.4	0.0	100.0

	1981				1987			
Hong Kong	0.1	96.5	0.4	100.0	0.3	95.6	1.3	100.0
Korea	0.7	90.0	0.5	100.0	1.5	92.4	0.0	100.0
Singapore	27.3	48.2	7.7	100.0	15.8	56.1	5.5	100.0
Taiwan	1.9	88.7	0.1	100.0	0.8	91.6	0.2	100.0
Argentina	6.8	19.6	0.0	100.0	1.3	31.6	0.1	100.0
Brazil	5.1	39.1	1.5	100.0	4.8	46.7	0.0	*100.0
Chile	1.8	7.7	0.3	100.0	0.9	7.6	0.0	*100.0
Mexico	57.7	24.7	2.0	100.0	38.1	46.7	0.0	*100.0
Indonesia	79.8	3.0	0.3	100.0	48.4	27.3	0.0	*100.0
Malaysia	26.6	19.6	0.5	100.0	19.9	39.3	0.2	100.0
Philippines	0.7	44.7	0.0	100.0	1.2	63.7	0.0	*100.0
Thailand	0.0	25.5	1.8	100.0	0.7	51.6	0.9	100.0
Colombia	1.5	27.3	1.1	100.0	32.5	19.4	2.2	100.0
Jamaica	2.7	5.9	0.0	100.0	1.6	30.7	0.0	*100.0
Peru	25.9	16.5	0.1	100.0	23.1	18.4	0.0	*100.0
Venezuela	92.8	2.4	0.0	100.0	81.7	8.3	0.0	*100.0

* Data refer to 1986. Some figures may not sum to 100 percent due to rounding.

Source: UN, *Commodity Trade Statistics,* various issues.

Table 1.5 Per caput exports of manufactured goods (US$, current)

	1963	1973	1981	1985	1986	1987
Hong Kong	179.7	866.9	2664.7	2891.9	3414.6	4273.1
Korea	1.5	79.2	492.8	673.4	767.3	1035.3
Singapore	175.0	730.0	4139.0	4563.7	5136.2	7243.0
Taiwan	10.8	237.7	1110.8	1444.9	1848.5	2456.8
Argentina	3.7	29.4	62.6	58.7	58.0	63.8
Brazil	0.5	12.2	73.4	82.8	75.3	86.6
Chile	2.6	4.7	25.5	21.0	28.0	31.6
Mexico	3.7	19.6	28.5	59.1	89.6	120.4
Indonesia	0.0	0.5	4.5	14.8	17.1	28.4
Malaysia	5.6	30.6	163.1	270.9	318.1	424.7
Philippines	1.1	5.5	26.8	22.5	26.0	63.5
Thailand	0.4	6.2	36.6	52.0	72.9	111.9
Colombia	0.9	13.8	30.5	21.0	25.5	32.7
Jamaica*	8.3	13.5	26.9	62.0	78.3	NA
Peru	0.4	2.0	21.7	32.3	28.4	24.0
Venezuela	5.3	5.9	26.9	35.4	43.5	47.8

* Aluminum excluded.
Source: UN, COMTRADE data base.

total exports rose from 5 percent to 39 percent in Malaysia, from 5 percent to 64 percent in the Philippines, from 3 percent to 52 percent in Thailand, and from almost zero to 27 percent in Indonesia, whose exports are dominated by petroleum.

Among the Latin American NECs, Jamaica reached a manufacturing export share of 31 percent in 1987 from 7 percent in 1963. In the years 1963 and 1987 (1986 in Colombia) the corresponding shares were: Colombia, 3 and 19 percent; Peru 1 and 18 percent; and Venezuela, 2 and 8 percent.

Data on manufactured export shares are affected by the availability of natural resources, in particular oil. At the same time, per caput manufactured exports provides an indication of a country's success in these export products.

Table 1.5 shows the rapid expansion of manufactured exports in the East Asian NICs. These exports were negligible in Korea and Taiwan in 1963 but reached $1035 per head for the former and $2457 per head for the latter in 1987. The rate of expansion was slower in Hong Kong and Singapore, which started from a higher base (nearly $180 per head in both cases in 1963). The absolute figures, however, are much higher ($4273 in Hong Kong and $7243 in Singapore in 1987), although a substantial portion of the total represents re-exports.

The per caput manufactured exports of the Latin American NICs are dwarfed by those of the East Asian NICs. In 1987, these exports were $120 in Mexico, $87 in Brazil, $64 in Argentina and $32 in Chile.

Among the East Asian NECs, Malaysia and Thailand reached higher levels of per caput manufactured exports than the Latin American NECs in 1986. Malaysia is in the lead with manufactured exports per head surpassing $400, followed by Thailand ($112). In turn, these exports were $64 per head in the Philippines and $28 per head in Indonesia.

THE POLICIES APPLIED

The data show that, for the 1963–87 period as a whole, superior Pacific growth performance was associated with high domestic saving ratios and high levels of investment efficiency. At the same time, exports played an important role in the growth process, contributing to the efficient use of investment funds.

The differences in the results may be explained by reference to the policies applied. These will be considered in the following sections, for the East Asian and Latin American NICs first, and then for the East Asian and Latin American NECs.

The NICs

Apart from Hong Kong, all developing countries passed through the first stage of import substitution, involving the replacement by domestic production of the imports of nondurable consumer goods and their inputs. The manufacture of these products, including clothing and textiles, shoes and leather, and furniture and wood, conform to the production possibilities of the developing countries. They utilize in large part unskilled labor, involve the use of simple production processes, are not subject to important scale economies, and do not require the existence of a sophisticated industrial structure.

Once the first stage of import substitution has been completed, however, the rate of growth of industrial production cannot continue to exceed that of consumption. At this point countries face two choices: embarking on the exportation of nondurable consumer goods and their inputs or moving to the second stage of import substitution through the replacement by domestic production of the imports of producer and consumer durables and intermediate products.

Among present-day NICs, the first alternative was chosen by Korea, Singapore and Taiwan in the early 1960s. These countries also carried out financial reforms to permit the raising of domestic saving ratios.

Negative real interest rates (nominal interest rates exceeded by the rate of inflation) led to financial repression in the Latin American NICs which was not conducive to increasing domestic saving and to the efficient allocation of the amount saved. These countries shifted to the second stage of import substitution which proved costly as the commodities in question did not conform to the production possibilities of the countries concerned. The manufacture of producer and consumer durables requires the existence of a sophisticated industrial structure to provide parts, components and accessories made to precision. Also, such vertical specialization needs a large domestic market for manufactured goods (as does horizontal or product specialization).

Large domestic markets are also necessary for the production of many intermediate goods, where traditional economies of scale obtain. Furthermore, the manufacture of producer and consumer durables relies to a considerable extent on skilled and technical labor while intermediate products are highly capital-intensive. At the same time, the margin of transformation for intermediate products is often small and can be squandered through poor organization of production.

The resulting high domestic costs reduced the efficiency of investment in countries pursuing a strategy of continued import substitution. In order to compensate for the higher costs, these countries also increased import protection, thereby discriminating against exports.

As the costs of continued import substitution became apparent, leading to declines in export expansion and economic growth, the three large Latin American NICs undertook reforms aimed at providing improved incentives to exports in the mid-1960s. The most far-reaching reforms were carried out in Brazil. By contrast, Mexico's favorable balance-of-payments position, due to workers' remittances, tourism and border industries, hampered its reform effort, and the opposition of urban interests obstructed the course of economic reforms in Argentina.

The reforms undertaken in the mid-1960s permitted reducing the bias of the incentive system against exports in Brazil, to a lesser extent in Mexico, and even less in Argentina. But not even Brazil provided equal incentives to exports and import substitution, as was the case in the East Asian NICs. Finally, after initial efforts, reforms were jettisoned by the Allende government in Chile in the early 1970s.

Policies changed again following the oil shock of 1973–4. The quadrupling of oil prices, together with the ensuing world recession, imposed a considerable cost on the economies of the NICs. This cost, shown in Table 1.6, was the largest in the East Asian NICs that were most exposed to foreign trade. (The cost of external shocks is measured as the balance-of-payments effects of the deterioration of the terms of trade and the export shortfall, resulting from the slowdown of the world economy.)

Table 1.6 further shows the balance-of-payments effects of the policies applied in response to external shocks, including additional net external financing, export promotion, import substitution and deflationary policies. Additional net external financing has been established as the difference between actual financing and that estimated on the assumption that past trends in exports and imports continued. The effects of export promotion have been calculated in terms of changes in export market shares. Import substitution has been defined as savings in imports associated with a decrease in the income elasticity of import demand compared with the preceding period. Finally, the effects on imports of changes in GNP (gross national product) growth rates in response to the macroeconomic policies followed have been estimated on the assumption of unchanged income elasticities of import demand.

The East Asian NICs accepted an initial decline in the growth rate of GNP to limit reliance on external financing. Economic growth accelerated subsequently, however, as the countries in question continued with outward-oriented policies. At the same time, maintaining realistic exchange rates helped not only exports but also import substitution.

Among the Latin American NICs, Chile shifted to outward-oriented policies in response to the external shocks it suffered. These policies led to considerable gains in export market shares while reliance on external financing was reduced. In turn, Brazil and Mexico relied to a considerable extent on external borrowing to finance the adverse balance-of-payments effects of external shocks. Argentina, self-sufficient in petroleum, experienced practically no external shocks.

Table 1.6 External shocks and policy responses to external shocks

		External shocks (% of GDP)	Additional net external financing	Export promotion (% of external shocks)	Import substitution	Deflationary policies
1974–8	Hong Kong	NA	NA	NA	NA	NA
	Korea	10.5	−88	90	128	−30
	Singapore	20.9	42	11	−24	70
	Taiwan	7.2	−92	14	96	82
	Argentina	0.5	−168	−13	146	136
	Brazil	3.3	30	15	66	−11
	Chile	6.0	−48	71	18	60
	Mexico	1.2	123	−70	33	14
	Indonesia	−22.2	−95	17	−20	−2
	Malaysia	NA	NA	NA	NA	NA
	Philippines	10.9	113	6	−13	−6
	Thailand	5.8	12	42	39	7
	Colombia	−0.9	45	−14	−127	−3
	Jamaica	14.9	−19	−29	47	101
	Peru	2.9	145	−32	−14	2
	Venezuela	NA	NA	NA	NA	NA

1979–81	Hong Kong	NA	NA	NA	NA
	Korea	9.4	−18	8	116
	Singapore	30.4	39	−59	31
	Taiwan	13.1	−40	91	22
	Argentina	1.2	423	−281	67
	Brazil	2.5	−33	49	47
	Chile	3.9	257	−133	−74
	Mexico	−0.5	309	−756	−64
	Indonesia	−7.4	−119	7	−5
	Malaysia	NA	NA	NA	NA
	Philippines	6.4	69	−13	−5
	Thailand	6.2	73	−29	19
	Colombia	4.5	149	−102	0
	Jamaica	16.5	44	23	61
	Peru	0.9	−379	143	48
	Venezuela	NA	NA	NA	NA

Source: World Bank.

Table 1.7 External debt ratios (gross)

Country	External debt/exports				Debt service/exports			
	1973	1978	1981	1987	1973	1978	1981	1987
Hong Kong	.	.	.	.	.	.	.	.
Korea	121.7	100.6	107.1	65.9	14.8	16.1	24.3	26.3
Singapore	17.6	12.7	9.6	14.6	7.8	8.0	8.3	7.4
Taiwan	.	.	.	.	.	.	.	.
Argentina	196.8	153.9	248.7	851.6	22.8	50.5	61.3	76.4
Brazil	208.7	367.7	279.3	419.7	32.8	58.8	60.4	81.8
Chile	266.1	253.2	324.4	382.4	41.9	59.7	90.8	56.9
Mexico	397.9	516.7	271.4	488.7	39.5	85.1	57.2	58.9
Indonesia	204.2	139.1	87.4	269.1	3.5	9.5	5.3	35.7
Malaysia	29.3	45.3	64.1	120.9	3.0	5.0	5.9	15.7
Philippines	107.6	204.5	200.4	443.1	22.6	40.7	37.5	78.1
Thailand	57.7	71.8	112.8	154.7	18.5	22.9	28.1	32.2
Colombia	197.1	105.7	201.0	330.7	28.4	20.1	50.4	60.4
Jamaica	309.1	161.2	226.6	654.4	10.3	52.8	53.0	135.1
Peru	290.4	391.6	205.3	566.8	44.1	74.7	71.6	95.8
Venezuela	57.3	93.3	72.2	389.8	6.1	18.4	22.1	56.3

Sources: World Bank, *World Debt Tables*; IMF, *International Financial Statistics* and *Balance of Payments Statistics*.

The three large Latin American NICs also increased the extent of inward orientation of their incentive system, thereby promoting the replacement of imports by domestic production. Only Brazil, which continued with the export subsidies introduced in the preceding period, made some modest gains in exports; Argentina and Mexico lost export market shares.

The effects of the policies followed in regard to foreign borrowing are apparent in Table 1.7, which shows considerable increases in the external indebtedness of Brazil and Mexico between 1973 and 1978. By contrast, Korea and Singapore experienced a decline and Taiwan's external debt remained very small.

Having found oil that led to rapid export expansion, the ratio of external debt to exports declined in Mexico after 1978. Brazil reduced its reliance on borrowing and adopted a mixture of policies aimed at increasing exports and import substitution, and slowing the economy. Argentina and Chile experienced considerable capital inflows as a result of the overvaluation of the exchange rate which was intended to reduce inflation.

The East Asian NICs again accepted a slowdown in economic growth after 1978 to limit reliance on foreign borrowing while maintaining their outward-oriented policies; this led to the subsequent acceleration of economic growth. Only Korea engaged in some foreign borrowing but its debt–export ratio hardly changed.

The results of alternative policies are apparent in the debt situation of the NICs on the eve of the debt crisis. While in Korea the debt–export ratio was 1.1 in 1981, this ratio reached 3.2 in Chile, 2.8 in Brazil, 2.7 in Mexico and 2.5 in Argentina. Also, the ratio of debt service to exports ranged between 90 percent (Chile) and 57 percent (Mexico) in the Latin American NICs, compared with 24 percent in Korea. These high ratios necessitated corrective action on the part of the Latin American NICs, contributing to a decline in their per caput incomes after 1981. By contrast, growth continued in the East Asian NICs, where Singapore and, in particular, Taiwan accumulated a net asset position abroad.

The NECs

The NECs have remained one step behind the NICs in terms of industrial development. They continued with the first stage of import substitution until the early 1970s, when they came to face the choice between the second stage of import substitution and export promotion. By and large, the first option was chosen by the Latin American NECs and the Philippines, while in the other East Asian NECs a mixture of policies was applied. At the same time, the external shocks the countries in question suffered and their policy responses to these shocks influenced the results to a considerable extent.

Colombia is self-sufficient in petroleum and did not experience external shocks in the 1974–8 period. It also adopted policies that favored exports, leading to gains in export market shares. In turn, Venezuela benefited from higher petroleum prices but failed to use the increased earnings to advantage. It undertook inefficient investments in highly capital-intensive industries and maintained a constant exchange rate in the face of rapid inflation, which not only discriminated against exports but also engendered capital flight. Thus, Venezuela's external debt came to increase while its per caput income declined.

Jamaica suffered large external shocks not only through increases in petroleum prices but also through the shortfall of its alumina exports. Moreover, it lost export market shares and suffered a decline in GNP while limiting reliance on external borrowing. By contrast, Peru maintained past growth rates by financing the adverse balance-of-payments effects of external shocks abroad.

In contrast to Venezuela, Indonesia devalued the exchange rate to bolster the nonpetroleum sector. It also avoided capital flight and its exports increased more than its foreign debt. Thailand and Malaysia also limited reliance on external borrowing while promoting economic growth through exports.

Among the East Asian NECs, the Philippines provides an exception, with its policies resembling those of Latin American countries. Continuing import substitution and the overvaluation of the exchange rate adversely affected exports. The Philippines financed the adverse balance-of-payments effects of external shocks through foreign borrowing, considerably increasing its external debt.

The pattern of policy responses to external shocks and, in particular, of foreign borrowing changed in the Latin American NECs after the second oil shock. Benefiting from higher petroleum prices, Venezuela reduced reliance on foreign borrowing after 1978. Peru did the same as it found new oil deposits that permitted increasing exports to a considerable extent. By contrast, Colombia and Jamaica borrowed abroad to finance in full or in part the adverse balance-of-payments effects of external shocks. Jamaica, however, continued to lose export market shares and experienced a decline in GNP.

After 1978, the debt–export ratio declined in Indonesia while increasing in Thailand. Nevertheless, Thailand's external indebtedness remained at low levels (1.1 of export value in 1981), permitting the continuation of growth-oriented policies in the period of the debt crisis. Similar conclusions apply to Malaysia, whose debt level was only 0.6 of exports in 1981. The debt-service share did not exceed 6 percent in Indonesia and Malaysia, but it was 28 percent in Thailand.

By contrast, the ratio of the external debt to exports in the Philippines (2.0) exceeded that for Venezuela (0.7), matched the figure for Colombia (2.0) and was only slightly behind those for Peru (2.1) and Jamaica (2.3). A similar picture emerged in regard to debt-service ratios. Along with the Latin American NECs, the Philippines had to apply deflationary policies after 1981 to cope with their external debt.

Economic Developments since 1963

Table 1.8 Employment and unemployment

	Index of manufacturing employment (1975=100)				Unemployment rate*			
	1963	1973	1981	1986	1963	1973	1981	1986
Hong Kong	NA	85.8	133.4	135.5	NA	NA	4.6	2.8
Korea	28.6	80.5	130.2	181.0	8.1	4.0	4.5	3.8
Singapore	NA	87.1	155.0	133.0	NA	4.5	2.9	6.5
Taiwan	36.3	93.5	141.4	172.2	4.3	1.3	1.4	2.7
Argentina[+]	NA	NA	NA	NA	5.7	5.6	4.5	4.4
Brazil[‡]	NA	81.7	191.3	198.5	NA	NA	7.9	5.3
Chile[§]	NA	NA	113.0	116.3	NA	3.1	11.3	8.7
Mexico	NA	NA	NA	NA	NA	NA	4.2	4.9
Indonesia	NA	NA	NA	NA	NA	NA	NA	NA
Malaysia	NA	NA	NA	NA	NA	NA	NA	NA
Philippines[§]	77.6	90.9	115.1	119.5	6.3	4.8	5.4	6.1
Thailand	NA	88.6	128.5	NA	NA	NA	NA	NA
Colombia	NA	NA	NA	136.5	NA	NA	8.1	13.0
Jamaica	NA	107.6	114.6	155.8	NA	21.9	25.6	23.6
Peru	NA	90.5	111.1	NA	NA	4.2	6.8	8.2
Venezuela	NA	NA	141.2	168.2	NA	NA	6.4	10.3

* Pertains to nonagricultural employment.
[+] First unemployment rate is for 1964.
[§] The latest employment and unemployment figures are for 1985.
[‡] Second unemployment figure is for 1972.

Sources: International Labor Office, *Yearbook of Labor Statistics*, various issues. Taiwanese data from Council for Economic Planning and Development, Republic of China, *Taiwan Statistical Data Book, 1988*.

SOCIAL INDICATORS

Information on economic growth rates should be complemented by data on social indicators, such as employment and unemployment, health and education. Data on overall employment are scarce and even data on manufacturing employment are available for a relatively few countries. Table 1.8 shows that manufacturing employment increased approximately fivefold in Korea and Taiwan between 1963 and 1986, leading to a decline in the unemployment rate by approximately one-half.

Table 1.9 Health indicators

	Life expectancy		Infant mortality		Population per physician	
	1965	1987	1965	1987	1965	1984
Hong Kong	66	76	28	8	2 460	1 070
Korea	57	69	63	25	2 700	1 170
Singapore	66	73	26	9	1 900	1 310
Taiwan	67	73	24	7	1 819	1 260
Argentina	66	71	58	32	600	370
Brazil	57	65	104	63	2 500	1 080
Chile	60	72	107	20	2 100	1 230
Mexico	60	69	82	47	2 020	1 240
Indonesia	44	60	138	71	31 740	9 460
Malaysia	58	70	55	24	6 220	1 930
Philippines	56	63	72	45	NA	6 700
Thailand	56	64	88	39	7 230	6 290
Colombia	57	66	96	46	2 500	1 190
Jamaica	65	74	49	18	1 990	2 060
Peru	51	61	131	88	1 650	1 040
Venezuela	63	70	65	36	1 210	700

Sources: World Bank, *World Development Report*, 1989; Taiwanese data from Council for Economic Planning and Development, Republic of China, *Taiwan Statistical Yearbook, 1988*.

In 1986, the rate of unemployment was 2.7 percent in Taiwan and 3.8 percent in Korea; it was 2.8 percent in Hong Kong and 6.5 percent in Singapore. Apart from Singapore, where the high rate of unemployment remained temporary, these results compare favorably with those for the Latin American NICs, where the unemployment rate was lowest (4.4 percent) in 1986 in Argentina. But the figures for the Latin American NICs underestimate the actual unemployment rate to a considerable extent. Also, there is substantial underemployment in Latin America which has no parallel in the East Asian NICs.

Apart from the Philippines (6.1 percent in 1986), data on unemployment are not available for the East Asian NECs. Unemployment is very high in the Latin American NECs, reaching 23.6 percent in Jamaica, 13.0 percent in Colombia, 10.3 percent in Venezuela and 8.2 percent in Peru in 1986.

Health indicators (see Table 1.9) show improvements in all the countries under consideration. Among the NICs, life expectancy

Economic Developments since 1963

increased the most in Hong Kong, Korea, and Chile between 1965 and 1987. By 1987, life expectancy was highest in Hong Kong (76 years), followed by Singapore and Taiwan (73 years); it was lowest in Brazil (65 years) and Mexico (69 years).

Infant mortality rates are the most favorable in Taiwan (7 per 1000), followed by Hong Kong (8) and Singapore (9), having declined by two-thirds during the preceding two decades. They are followed by Chile (20) and Korea (25); at the other extreme, infant mortality rates are 47 per 1000 in Mexico and 63 per 1000 in Brazil.

Differences in the number of people per physician are considerable among the NICs. The rate varied between 370 (Argentina) and 1310 (Singapore) in 1984, having declined by about half in the previous sixteen years.

Life expectancy rates were relatively high in the Latin American NECs in 1965 and increased further over the next two decades. In 1987, Jamaica was in the lead (74 years), followed by Venezuela (70 years). These two countries also had the lowest infant mortality rate (18 and 36 per 1000) in 1987.

Among the East Asian NECs, Malaysia leads in terms of life expectancy (70 years) and infant mortality (24 per 1000); it also had the lowest number of people per physician (1930) in the group. Life expectancy is the lowest (60 years) and infant mortality the highest (71 per 1000) in Indonesia, where there were 9460 people per physician in 1984.

Educational indicators are shown in Table 1.10. Argentina and Chile traditionally had high literacy rates and maintained this advantage during the period under consideration; Brazil is, however, surpassed by all the East Asian NICs.

The East Asian NICs are ahead of the Latin American NICs in terms of secondary school enrollment ratios. In the first group, the range is between 95 percent (Korea) and 69 percent (Hong Kong); in the second group, it is between 74 percent (Argentina) and 36 percent (Brazil).

Secondary school enrollment is of importance for the training of technical and highly-skilled labor, while higher education may include an element of conspicuous consumption. Among the NICs, Argentina leads in terms of higher education enrollment ratios (39 percent), followed by Korea (33 percent), with Brazil at the bottom (11 percent).

The Harbison–Myers index is a weighted average of secondary school enrollment and higher education enrollment ratios, with the

Table 1.10 Educational indicators

	Literacy rate (percent)*		Enrollment in secondary schools (percent)		Enrollment in higher education (percent)		Harbison–Myers Index		Psacharopoulos Index[+]	
	1960	1980	1965	1986	1965	1986	1965	1985	1965	1985
Hong Kong	70.4	77.3	29	69	5	13	54	134	1145	1943
Korea	70.6	87.6	35	95	6	33	65	254	854	2166
Singapore	49.8	82.9	45	71	10	12	95	131	1001	1167
Taiwan	72.9	89.7	44	88	7	21	79	191	912	1926
Argentina	91.4	93.9	28	74	14	39	98	250	911	1371
Brazil	61.0	74.5	16	36	2	11	26	90	512	1006
Chile	83.6	94.4	34	70	6	16	64	149	1062	NA
Mexico	65.4	83.0	17	55	4	16	37	135	410	959
Indonesia	39.0	67.3	12	41	1	7	17	74	237	797
Malaysia	22.3	69.6	28	54	2	6	38	83	467	1201
Philippines	71.9	83.3	41	68	19	38	136	255	923	1853
Thailand	67.7	88.0	14	29	2	20	24	130	159	858
Colombia	62.5	85.2	17	56	3	13	32	115	NA	NA
Jamaica	81.9	96.1	51	58	3	4	66	88	606	1592
Peru	61.1	81.9	25	65	8	25	65	185	704	1771
Venezuela	63.3	84.7	27	46	7	26	62	175	542	1645

* All literacy rates are for 1960 and 1980 except: first figure for Singapore is for 1957; for Indonesia, Colombia, Peru and Venezuela, for 1961; second figure for Korea and Jamaica is for 1970; for Hong Kong, 1971; for Colombia, Peru and Venezuela, 1981; and for Chile, 1983.
+ The first Psacharopoulos index for Chile is for 1970.

Notes: Enrollment data have been expressed as a percentage of the respective age cohorts. The Harbison–Myers index is derived from the secondary school enrollment rate plus five times the university enrollment rate: Frederick H. Harbison, Jan Maruhnic and Jane R. Resnick (1970), *Quantitative Analyses of Modernization and Development*. Princeton, NJ: Industrial Relations Section, Department of Economics, Princeton University, pp. 175–6. The Psacharopoulos index measures the per caput educational capital embodied in the labor force.

Sources: School enrollment data from World Bank, *World Development Report, 1989*. Literacy rates are from UNESCO, *Statistical Yearbook*, various issues. Data for Taiwan are from Council for Economic Planning and Development, Republic of China, *Taiwan Statistical Data Book, 1987*.

latter given five times the weight of the former. It does not require discussion beyond its components.

The Psacharopoulos index measures per caput educational capital embodied in the work force. This index is higher in the East Asian NICs (except for Singapore) than in the Latin American NICs. It is 2166 in Korea and is about the 1900 mark in Hong Kong and Taiwan. By contrast, the index is 1371 in Argentina and it does not reach 1000 in Mexico (data for Chile are not available for 1984 but the ratio was 1062 in 1970), falling behind Singapore where it is 1167.

Literacy rates were high in Jamaica at the beginning of the period and surpassed all the other countries under consideration by the end. Colombia, Venezuela and Peru also have higher literacy rates than the East Asian NECs, the exceptions being the Philippines and Thailand. It appears, then, that literacy rates are not related to growth performance in the NECs, although the more successful of these (Malaysia and Indonesia) made great strides in literacy.

Among the NECs, the Philippines leads in terms of enrollment ratio in secondary schools and in higher education. It is followed by Peru, Jamaica, Malaysia and Colombia in regard to the former and by Venezuela, Peru, Thailand and Colombia in regard to the latter. Finally, the Philippines leads in terms of the Psacharopoulos index, followed by Peru, Venezuela and Jamaica.

TRENDS IN INTERNATIONAL TRADE

We have seen that, in the 1963–87 period, the Pacific Area developing countries other than the Philippines showed a superior economic performance when compared with countries at similar levels of industrialization elsewhere in the developing world. These differences in performance are also apparent in the trends in exports and imports that are shown in Tables 1.11 and 1.12.

Between 1963 and 1988, the share of the Pacific Area developing countries in the total exports of the developing countries rose from 11.8 percent to 41.8 percent. The contrast with the Latin American regime is particularly noteworthy: the region had 30.7 percent of developing country exports in 1963, but its share fell to 16.9 percent by 1988.

The contrasting trends between the Pacific Area developing countries and Latin America are also apparent in imports. While the share of the former group of countries in total developing country imports increased from 14.3 percent in 1963 to 37.2 percent in 1988, a decline

Table 1.11 Country composition of world exports (percent)

	1963	1973	1981	1988
Developed Countries	64.7	76.2	63.8	71.1
United States	15.0	13.5	12.2	11.6
Western Europe	39.7	48.3	38.4	44.2
Japan	3.5	7.0	7.9	9.6
Canada, Australia, New Zealand	6.5	7.3	5.2	5.7
Developing Countries	22.8	22.6	31.0	24.9
Pacific countries (other than China)	2.7	4.9	7.1	10.4
East Asian NICs	1.6	3.1	4.5	8.1
Hong Kong	0.6	1.0	1.1	2.3
Korea	0.1	0.6	1.1	2.2
Singapore	0.7	0.7	1.1	1.4
Taiwan	0.2	0.8	1.2	2.2
East Asian NECs	1.2	1.8	2.5	2.3
Indonesia	0.4	0.6	1.2	0.7
Malaysia	NA	0.6	0.6	0.8
Philippines	0.5	0.4	0.3	0.3
Thailand	0.3	0.3	0.4	0.6
China	0.9	0.8	1.1	1.7
Other developing countries	19.2	16.9	22.8	12.8
Other Asia	3.0	0.6	1.0	1.2
Africa	4.6	4.2	4.0	2.7
Europe	0.7	0.6	0.8	1.1
Middle East	3.9	6.3	11.2	3.6
Latin America	7.0	5.2	5.8	4.2
*European Socialist Countries**	11.9	1.2	5.2	4.0

* 1973 European socialist country figures are only for Romania and Yugoslavia.

Notes: Taiwanese figures for 1981 and 1987 were added from the source cited above to world exports. The figures for the People's Republic of China were added to the world export figures for 1973. Regional aggregates may not sum to 100 percent due to inclusion in denominator of special categories and other countries not specified.

Sources: IMF, *Direction of Trade Statistics*, various issues. Taiwanese data for 1981 and 1987 from Board of Foreign Trade, Ministry of Economic Affairs, *Foreign Trade Development of the Republic of China, 1988*.

from 26.7 percent to 15.4 percent occurred in the share of the latter.

The shift in the import share of the Pacific Area developing countries was smaller than that in their export share because the $1.2 billion trade deficit of these countries in 1963 turned into a surplus of $23.9 billion by 1988 (see Table 1.13). Nonetheless, the countries in

Table 1.12 Country composition of world imports (percent)

	1963	1973	1981	1988
Developed Countries	63.0	76.7	65.2	71.1
United States	11.0	13.6	13.7	16.0
Western Europe	42.0	49.5	39.2	43.1
Japan	4.0	7.1	7.2	6.5
Canada, Australia, New Zealand	5.9	6.4	5.1	5.4
Developing Countries	22.4	21.8	31.5	24.7
Pacific countries (other than China)	3.2	5.2	7.2	9.2
East Asian NICs	2.2	3.5	5.0	7.3
Hong Kong	0.8	1.0	1.2	2.2
Korea	0.3	0.8	1.3	1.8
Singapore	0.8	1.0	1.4	1.5
Taiwan	0.2	0.7	1.1	1.7
East Asian NECs	1.1	1.7	2.2	1.9
Indonesia	0.3	0.5	0.7	0.5
Malaysia	NA	0.5	0.6	0.6
Philippines	0.4	0.3	0.4	0.3
Thailand	0.4	0.4	0.5	0.6
China	0.7	0.8	1.1	1.9
Other developing countries	18.5	15.8	23.2	13.6
Other Asia	3.6	1.5	1.6	1.7
Africa	4.9	3.7	4.5	2.5
Europe	1.4	1.7	4.2	1.7
Middle East	2.6	3.4	6.8	3.9
Latin America	6.0	5.4	6.1	3.8
European Socialist Countries*	12.1	1.5	3.3	4.2

* 1973 European socialist country figures are only for Romania and Yugoslavia.

Notes: Taiwanese figures for 1981 and 1987 were added from the source cited above to world exports. The figures for the People's Republic of China were added to the world export figures for 1973. Regional aggregates may not sum to 100 percent due to inclusion in denominator of special categories and other countries not specified.

Sources: IMF, *Direction of Trade Statistics*, various issues. Taiwanese data for 1981 and 1987 from Board of Foreign Trade, Ministry of Economic Affairs, *Foreign Trade Development of the Republic of China, 1988*.

question have become important markets for foreign suppliers.

The latter conclusion applies in a world context as well. Whereas the Pacific Area developing countries took only 3.2 percent of world imports in 1963, their share reached 9.2 percent in 1988. The increase is even more impressive if one considers the importance of intrare-

Table 1.13 World trade balances (million US$)

	1963	1973	1981	1988
World Total	−11 593	−11 919	−79 747	−85 600
Developed Countries	−4 553	−11 920	−78 800	−70 700
United States	4 898	−2 245	−39 612	−139 525
Western Europe	−8 443	−12 306	−46 310	−11 411
Japan	−1 290	−1 364	8 632	77 478
Canada, Australia, New Zealand	282	3 995	−1 510	2 758
Developing Countries	−2 006	1 708	−34 456	−19 519
Pacific countries (other than China)	−1 187	−1 846	−7 976	23 889
East Asian NICs	−1 190	−2 496	−13 025	15 372
Hong Kong	−424	−580	−2 952	−734
Korea	−474	−1 015	−4 884	9 745
Singapore	−263	−1 482	−6 601	−4 547
Taiwan	−29	581	1 412	10 908
East Asian NECs	3	650	5 049	8 517
Indonesia	89	481	10 540	5 887
Malaysia	NA	542	192	4 558
Philippines	47	96	−2 756	−1 628
Thailand	−133	−469	−2 927	−300
China	223	−224	−155	−7 689
Other developing countries	−1 042	3 778	−26 325	−35 719
Other Asia	−1 387	−5 138	−12 166	−15 524
Africa	−968	1 850	−12 994	580
Europe	−1 219	−6 077	−68 755	−18 459
Middle East	1 697	14 887	78 147	−10 124
Latin America	835	−1 744	−10 557	7 808
*European Socialist Countries**	−1 696	−1 707	33 509	−9 795

* 1973 European socialist country figures are only for Romania and Yugoslavia.

Notes: Taiwanese figures for 1981 and 1988 were added from the source cited above to total exports and imports. The figures for the People's Republic of China were added to the total figures for 1973.

Sources: IMF, *Direction of Trade Statistics*, various issues. Taiwanese data for 1981 and 1988 from Board of Foreign Trade, Ministry of Economic Affairs, *Foreign Trade Development of the Republic of China, 1989*.

gional trade in North America and Western Europe. Excluding trade between the United States and Canada, as well as intra-EEC trade, the Pacific Area developing countries had 11.1 percent of world imports in 1988. In that year, they imported two-thirds more than Japan while they were in approximate equality in 1963.

In 1988, the Pacific Area developing countries surpassed Japanese exports by one tenth. This resulted from the increase in their share in world exports from 2.7 percent in 1963 to 10.4 percent in 1988.

Within the Pacific total, the four NICs loom large, with a share of 8.1 percent in world exports and 7.3 percent in world imports in 1988. This compares with an export share of 1.6 percent and an import share of 2.2 percent in 1963.

Increases are shown in the East Asian NECs as well. During the period under consideration, these countries increased their export share from 1.2 percent to 2.3 percent and their import share from 1.0 to 1.9 percent.

The observed differences between export and import trends reflect differences in trade balances. In 1988, there was a combined trade surplus of $15.4 billion in the East Asian NICs (of which Taiwan had $10.9 billion) and $8.5 billion in the East Asian NECs (of which Indonesia had $5.9 billion and Malaysia $4.6 billion).

CONCLUSIONS

This chapter has reviewed economic developments in the Pacific Area developing countries, making comparisons with Latin American countries at similar levels of development. The results show that, with the exception of the Philippines, the Pacific Area developing countries experienced much larger increases in per caput incomes than their Latin American counterparts in the 1963–87 period. These differences find their origin in higher levels of investment efficiency as well as savings ratios.

The Pacific Area developing countries attained their superior growth performance in the framework of an open economy, with high and rising ratios of exports to the gross domestic product. Export expansion involved an increasing shift toward manufactured goods. Pacific Area exports were promoted by the system of incentives that entail no discrimination, or limited discrimination, against exports, the major exception being the Philippines. These countries also relied to a considerable extent on export promotion in response to external shocks and did not engage in excessive foreign borrowing, the Philippines again being an exception.

Another policy difference between East Asian and Latin American countries has been that the latter engaged in considerable interventions in the market system, such a labor legislation, price control and industrial licensing. Such interventions also have adverse effects on economic growth.

Available data indicate the continuation of differences in growth performance in 1988. According to the data, 1988 GNP growth rates were especially high in the East Asian NICs: Hong Kong, 7.4 percent; Korea, 11.3 percent; Singapore 11.0 percent; and Taiwan, 7.3 percent. These results compare with a decline of GNP of 2.7 percent in Argentina and 0.3 percent in Brazil, and an increase of 1.1 percent in Mexico among the Latin American NICs. Only Chile had a GNP growth rate of 7.4 percent.

The comparisons are more favorable for the Latin American NECs, except for Peru where GNP appears to have declined by 8.9 percent. The 1988 figures are 3.1 percent for Colombia, 3.0 percent for Jamaica and 4.2 percent for Venezuela. Nevertheless, even Colombia has been surpassed by all but one of the East Asian NECs. Thus GNP growth rates were estimated at 11.0 percent in Thailand, 7.4 percent in Malaysia, 6.6 percent in the Philippines and 4.7 percent in Indonesia.

The favorable external debt situation of the East Asian NICs also augurs well for their future economic growth. Korea's debt–export ratio declined to 0.6 in 1988 and it had a large trade surplus in 1989 when Taiwan and Singapore increased their surpluses. In turn, the external debt ratio reached 6.6 in Argentina, 4.9 in Mexico, 3.6 in Brazil and 2.8 in Chile in 1988.

Similar increases were observed in Jamaica and Peru whose debt–export ratio reached 6.1 and 5.0, respectively, in 1988. Smaller increases were experienced in Colombia, with a 1988 ratio of 3.4 while the ratio for that year was 3.4 in Venezuela. Among the East Asian NECs, the debt–export ratio was highest in the Philippines (4.2), followed by Indonesia (2.7), which increased its foreign debt considerably as oil prices fell; the corresponding figures were 1.3 for Thailand and 1.0 for Malaysia.

2 Hong Kong

INTRODUCTION

In an area of 1052 square kilometers, Hong Kong supports a population of 5.6 million. Its population declined from 1.6 million in 1935 to 600 000 in 1945 but increased rapidly afterwards as several waves of immigrants came to Hong Kong from China. Sovereignty over Hong Kong will be transferred from Britain to China on July 1, 1997.

Before the Second World War, Hong Kong depended entirely on entrepôt trade. Having been destroyed during the Japanese occupation, entrepôt trade re-emerged after the war. It was, however, limited by the civil war in China and the subsequent Communist takeover, receiving a further severe shock in mid-1951 when China entered the Korean war and the UN imposed an embargo on trade with China.

The uncertainties associated with entrepôt trade contributed to the development of new activities in Hong Kong in the manufacturing sector which was practically non-existent before the war. This was helped by the entrepreneurial and technical skills and the labor force brought by the new arrivals from China. Hong Kong also benefited from the existence of trade ties and the availability of an efficient network of transportation, communication and banking facilities: but Hong Kong became an international financial center only in the latter part of the 1970s.

The development of manufacturing activities occurred in a *laissez-faire* economy under free trade and free capital movements. The role of Hong Kong's government has been to provide political stability and economic conditions that have permitted market forces\to stimulate the growth of manufacturing production and trade.

Manufacturing activities were originally dominated by textiles and clothing, when the transplantation of firms from Shanghai and the availability of low-cost labor provided an advantage. Exports of plastic articles, toys, sporting goods, other miscellaneous manufactured products and of electrical products emerged at a later date.

GOVERNMENT POLICIES

The Hong Kong government owns no manufacturing establishments, it applies no tariffs or import restrictions, it does not subsidize exports, and it does not attempt to influence the activities of the manufacturing sector. Firms are set up freely and there are few regulations affecting their operations. Furthermore, there is no minimum wage legislation and, while trade unions are free to operate, their influence has been limited as only 7 percent of industrial workers are unionized.

There are no legal restrictions on hours of work for men; for women and young people aged 15–17 the statutory maxima are eight hours a day and 48 hours per week; the employment of children under 15 is illegal. The government also sets standards of safety and health.

Taxes are low. Income tax rates range from 5 to 25 percent, but the total tax paid cannot exceed the standard rate of 15 percent. Corporate income taxes are levied at a standard rate plus a 1.5 percent surcharge (i.e., a total of 16.5 percent). There are reduced depreciation allowances for new investment.

The government provides physical and social infrastructure. It has been involved in land reclamation, has enlarged the port, has built roads and highways, has constructed the mass transit railway, and has built the Hong Kong airport. The government is also responsible for water supply and sewage while other utilities are in private hands. Private interests also operate most transportation facilities.

The government has provided low-rent housing to about two-fifths of the population of Hong Kong. It also provides free primary education in government schools, which have four-fifths of all students. And while government schools account for only one-fourth of secondary education, the government subsidizes about nine-tenths of the students up to the age of 15 when compulsory education stops. Beyond that age the government provides for needy students only. This is also the case in higher education in the form of grants and, more importantly, interest-free loans.

Through its centers, the Family Health Service provides a fairly comprehensive health care program for women of child-bearing age and for all children up to 5 years old. Only a token charge is paid in government-owned and government-assisted hospitals but these are rather overcrowded.

As to the role of the state in economic life, the dominant view in the 1960s was well expressed by the then Financial Secretary, Sir John Cowperthwaite: 'In my own simple way I should have thought that a desirable industry was, almost by definition, one which could establish itself and thrive without special assistance in ordinary market conditions' (*Hong Kong Hansard*, 1968, p. 212).

Sir John's successor, Sir Philip Haddon-Cave, formulated the idea of 'positive non-interventionism'. He expressed the view

> that attempts to frustrate the operation of market forces will tend to damage the growth rate of the economy, particularly as it is so difficult to predict, let alone control, market forces that impinge on an open economy. But . . . the government must play an active role in the provision of those services and facilities essential in a civilized community. (*Hong Kong Hansard*, 1977–78, p. 813)

The Financial Secretary noted four areas where the state is called upon to play a role, including the control of monetary policy (which is largely ineffectual in practice); the regulation of the financial sector (also rather ineffectual); the provision of basic social services; and the establishment of industrial and economic advisory boards.

As to the latter, an advisory committee for diversification, established in 1977, noted that light engineering, electronics and precision machinery were industries appropriate for Hong Kong but did not propose that the government take measures to further the development of these industries. And while, at the recommendation of the advisory committee for diversification, an Industrial Development Board (IDB) was established, this has seen its task as concerning the commissioning of studies rather than proposing new policy initiatives.

A case in point is the electronics industry where several leading firms called for a levy on electronics exports to support a common research and development (R & D) facility and a report prepared for the IDB called for government intervention in the industry. Neither of these proposals has been endorsed by the IDB or accepted by the government.

At the same time, the government's long-term involvement in sponsoring technical education has been strengthened by the establishment of the Hong Kong Training Council. Also, it has established a new polytechnical institute and has sponsored R & D programs at the university level.

The establishment of small firms in the textiles and clothing industries was helped by the government leasing factory space. In the 1970s two industrial estates were established, providing low-cost leases to qualified industrial firms. But the leases have been taken up only slowly, in part because of the isolation of the sites and in part because of the stringent conditions for qualifications.

The government intervened in the financial sphere in response to the crisis of 1983, brought about by uncertainty concerning Hong Kong's future relationship with China. It established a fixed exchange rate and, through the Exchange Stabilization Fund, it took over one bank and aided a second.

These actions have not affected, however, the financial system of Hong Kong. This consists of licensed banks, licensed deposit-taking companies (mostly merchant banks) and registered deposit-taking companies (mostly finance companies), established freely by domestic as well as foreign nationals, subject to capital adequacy tests and prudential regulations. There is no central bank in Hong Kong.

International financial transactions are completely free, contributing to the emergence of Hong Kong as a financial center. Restrictions are not imposed on foreign direct investment in Hong Kong or on direct investment abroad by Hong Kong residents.

Note should finally be taken of Hong Kong's legal system that efficiently provides for property rights and contractual rights, which are at the foundation of the operation of the Hong Kong economy. This point was strongly made by John Griffith, the former Attorney General of Hong Kong:

> It is the predictability and continuity of the economic and financial environment taken together with the commercial and social stability given by strict adherence to the Rule of Law – so that arbitrary decisions or unconstitutional changes are not just unlikely but impossible – which have been essential elements in creating the climate for success . . . Certain it is that the Rule of Law has played an inestimable part in creating among outsiders the trust and confidence in Hong Kong upon which the economic miracle has been and is totally dependent. Without it, Hong Kong could not be what it is today. (Cited in David Lethbridge (ed.), *The Business Environment in Hong Kong*; Hong Kong, Oxford University Press, 1984, p. 235)

Table 2.1 Economic performance indicators: Hong Kong

Growth rates	1963–73	1973–81	1981–7	1963–87
GDP	8.9	9.1	7.2	8.5
Population	2.1	2.6	1.3	2.1
GDP per caput	6.7	6.3	5.8	6.3
Investment	4.1	12.0	2.1	6.1
Manufacturing production	.	.	.	.
Agricultural production	.	.	.	.
Exports	11.1	10.5	13.4	11.5
Imports	9.8	11.8	11.7	11.0

Source: World Bank.

ECONOMIC GROWTH

Starting from low income levels, rapid growth in Hong Kong led to a per caput income level in excess of that of other East Asian developing countries by 1963 while it remained behind most of the larger Latin American countries. The situation changed in subsequent years, with Hong Kong reaching per caput income levels of $8000 in 1988, far surpassing Latin American countries (see Table 1.1).

Per caput income growth averaged 6.3 percent in Hong Kong between 1963 and 1987, with some deceleration shown at the end of the period (see Table 2.1). Growth originated in the manufacturing sector and, increasingly, from services (see Table 2.2). Both manufacturing and services were oriented towards exports, with the exports of goods and services rising by over 11 percent a year between 1963 and 1987 (Table 2.1).

In the same period, the share of manufacturing in the GDP declined slightly, from 24.3 percent in 1963 to 21.8 percent in 1987. In turn, the share of services increased from 71.8 percent to 77.6 percent. The individual service categories are gas, electricity and water, 2.9 percent; construction, 4.5 percent; transportation, 8.4 percent; wholesale and retail trade, 21.8 percent; banking, 17.0 percent; and other services, 22.8 percent.

Economic growth was supported by a high rate of investment. Between 1973 and 1981 the share of investment in the GDP rose from 24 percent to 36 percent, although it declined afterwards as Hong Kong's planned reintegration with China raised questions about its economic future (see Table 2.3).

Table 2.2 Industrial composition and trade: Hong Kong (percent of GDP)

	1963	1973	1981	1987*
Industrial composition				
Agriculture	2.8	1.4	0.7	0.5
Mining and quarrying	1.1	0.4	0.2	0.1
Manufacturing	24.3	25.0	22.7	21.8
Gas, electricity and water	1.9	1.6	1.4	2.9
Construction	11.4	5.2	7.5	4.5
Transportation	13.1	6.6	7.5	8.4
Wholesale and retail trade	20.2	22.7	19.4	21.8
Banking, real estate	17.1	16.9	23.7	17.0
Ownership of dwellings	.	.	.	.
Public administration	.	.	.	.
Other services	8.2	20.2	16.5	22.8
Imputed bank service charge, duty	.	.	.	.
Trade				
Exports of goods and nonfactor services	78.6	89.0	94.0	115.8
Imports of goods and nonfactor services	89.7	86.4	99.8	111.0

* 1987 GDP at factor cost.
Source: World Bank.

Table 2.3 Savings and investment ratios: Hong Kong (percent of GDP)

	1973	1974	1975	1976	1977	1978	1979	1980
Private savings	.	.	.	.	.	.	.	.
Government budget balance	.	.	.	.	.	.	.	.
Domestic savings	26.4	26.1	25.3	33.6	30.3	26.4	31.1	31.4
Foreign savings	−2.5	−0.7	−1.0	−6.8	−2.3	3.6	2.9	4.6
Domestic investment	24.0	25.4	24.2	26.8	27.9	30.0	34.0	36.0

	1981	1982	1983	1984	1985	1986	1987
Private savings	.	.	.	.	.	.	.
Government budget balance	.	.	.	.	.	.	.
Domestic savings	30.4	28.2	25.1	28.9	27.3	27.9	30.7
Foreign savings	5.6	3.6	2.0	−4.2	−5.7	−4.6	−5.4
Domestic investment	36.0	31.8	27.1	24.7	21.7	23.3	25.3

Source: World Bank.

Investment was largely financed by domestic savings, except that foreign savings assumed importance in the late 1970s and early 1980s, when investment activity was at its peak. Hong Kong experienced an outflow of capital in the mid-1970s as well as in recent years during external political uncertainty. More detailed data are not available because of the lack of balance-of-payments statistics in Hong Kong.

Hong Kong traditionally had a merchandize trade deficit while it had a surplus in the service account (see Table 2.4). Approximate balance in the trade account was reached in 1986 following the establishment of a fixed exchange rate in the previous year which gave Hong Kong a competitive edge.

INTERNATIONAL TRADE

With the rapid expansion of domestic exports (i.e., the exports of domestically produced goods), the relative importance of entrepôt trade declined to a considerable extent in Hong Kong. By 1977, re-exports hardly exceeded one-fifth of total exports. The situation changed, however, in subsequent years as Hong Kong assumed increasing importance as a place of transshipment to China as well as in the marketing of Chinese exports. Thus, while domestic exports continued to rise at a rapid rate, re-exports increased considerably more over the last decade. As a result, re-exports came to reach 45 percent of total exports.

The rising share of re-exports was associated with substantial increases in the share of China in Hong Kong's trade. While China accounted for only 1.4 percent of Hong Kong's exports in 1963, its share reached 9.0 percent in 1981 and 27.0 percent in 1988 (see Table 2.5). In turn, the share of China in Hong Kong's imports rose from 20.1 percent in 1963 to 21.3 percent in 1981 and to 31.2 percent in 1988 (see Table 2.6).

The relatively small increase in China's share in Hong Kong's imports is explained by the declining importance of food imports, reflecting largely the low income elasticity of demand for food, which originates in great part in China. The share of these imports in Hong Kong's total imports fell from 16.9 percent in 1973 to 10.1 percent in 1981 and, again, to 5.3 percent in 1988; it was 23.1 percent in 1963 (Table 2.8).

The share of the United States increased in Hong Kong's exports from 20.3 percent in 1963 to 28.4 percent in 1973, declining to 24.8

Table 2.4 Hong Kong balance of payments: (millions of US$)

	1978	1979	1980	1981	1982	1983	1984	1985	1986	1987
Merchandise exports	11 499	15 155	19 720	21 737	20 985	21 951	28 317	30 039	35 439	48 474
Merchandise imports	13 451	17 137	22 413	24 680	23 554	24 009	28 567	29 567	35 365	48 463
Trade balance	−1 952	−1 982	−2 693	−2 943	−2 569	−2 058	−250	472	74	11
Other goods, services, and income: credit	3 147	3 850	4 454	4 858	5 042	5 083	5 609	5 885	6 879	8 636
Other goods, services, and income: debit	1 767	2 392	2 997	3 456	3 458	3 473	3 842	4 305	4 997	5 868
Other goods, services, and income: net	1 379	1 457	1 457	1 403	1 584	1 609	1 767	1 580	1 883	2 768
Unrequited transfers	NA	NA	NA	NA	NA	NA	NA	NA	NA	NA
Current account balance	−573	−525	−1 236	−1 540	−985	−449	1 517	2 052	1 957	2 779

Sources: Merchandise trade figures from UN, *Monthly Bulletin of Statistics*, various issues; other goods and services balance from DRI, LDC data base.

Table 2.5 Geographical composition of exports: Hong Kong (percent of total exports)

	1963	1973	1981	1988
Developed Countries	61.2	68.7	59.5	52.6
United States	20.3	28.4	27.8	24.8
Western Europe	29.1	23.9	21.9	18.0
Japan	6.1	9.8	4.7	5.9
Canada, Australia, New Zealand	5.7	6.6	5.2	4.0
Developing Countries	38.6	31.1	39.9	46.9
Pacific countries (other than China)	6.6	16.3	15.5	12.3
East Asian NICs	1.6	10.6	8.2	9.0
Hong Kong	–	–	–	–
Korea	0.4	1.5	1.3	2.6
Singapore	NA	5.0	4.1	2.8
Taiwan	1.2	4.2	2.8	3.6
East Asian NECs	5.1	5.7	7.4	3.2
Indonesia	1.7	2.8	3.8	0.8
Malaysia	NA	1.2	0.8	0.7
Philippines	1.1	0.7	1.7	0.9
Thailand	2.2	1.0	1.0	0.9
China	1.4	1.1	9.0	27.0
Other developing countries	30.6	13.7	15.3	7.6
Other Asia	19.3	5.8	2.9	2.6
Africa	6.1	2.9	4.0	1.7
Southern Europe	NA	0.2	0.4	0.3
Middle East	2.8	2.9	5.0	1.8
Latin America	2.4	1.8	3.0	1.2
European Socialist Countries	0.0	0.2	0.4	0.5

Note: Taiwanese figures derived as difference between total exports, the regional aggregates, special categories and other countries not included. Regional aggregates may not sum to 100 percent due to inclusion in world total of special categories and other countries not specified.

Sources: IMF, *Direction of Trade Statistics*, various issues. Taiwanese figures were derived as a residual.

percent in 1988. In turn, the share of its traditional markets in Western Europe fell from 29.1 percent in 1963 to 18.0 percent in 1988. Finally, after increasing from 6.1 percent in 1963 to 9.8 percent in 1973, Japan's share declined to 5.9 percent in 1988, confirming views expressed in Hong Kong about the difficulties encountered in entering Japanese markets.

All in all, the share of the developed countries in Hong Kong's

Table 2.6 Geographical composition of imports: Hong Kong (percent of total imports)

	1963	1973	1981	1988
Developed Countries	55.3	54.0	50.4	41.7
United States	10.6	13.2	10.5	8.3
Western Europe	23.9	16.6	14.2	12.9
Japan	16.7	20.7	23.2	18.6
Canada, Australia, New Zealand	4.1	3.5	2.5	1.9
Developing Countries	44.0	45.1	48.9	57.8
Pacific countries (other than China)	7.6	15.2	22.9	21.5
East Asian NICs	3.0	11.5	19.4	17.9
Hong Kong	–	–	–	–
Korea	0.7	2.1	4.0	5.3
Singapore	NA	3.4	7.7	3.7
Taiwan	2.3	6.0	7.8	8.9
East Asian NECs	4.6	3.7	3.4	3.7
Indonesia	0.8	0.6	0.5	0.8
Malaysia	NA	0.7	0.8	1.2
Philippines	0.2	0.5	0.8	0.5
Thailand	3.6	1.9	1.3	1.2
China	20.1	20.0	21.3	31.2
Other developing countries	16.4	9.9	4.8	5.0
Other Asia	9.7	4.2	2.0	2.0
Africa	2.9	2.0	1.0	0.8
Southern Europe	NA	0.2	0.1	0.1
Middle East	2.2	2.0	1.0	1.0
Latin America	1.6	1.5	0.6	1.1
European Socialist Countries	0.7	0.9	0.4	0.5

Note: Taiwanese figures derived as difference between total exports, the regional aggregates, special categories and other countries not included. Regional aggregates may not sum to 100 percent due to inclusion in world total of special categories and other countries not specified.

Sources: IMF, *Direction of Trade Statistics*, various issues. Taiwanese figures were derived as a residual.

exports increased from 61.2 percent in 1963 to 68.7 percent in 1973 but declined afterwards to 59.5 percent in 1981 and 52.6 percent in 1988. These changes were mirrored by changes in the share of the developing countries: this fell from 38.6 percent in 1963 to 31.1 percent in 1973, increasing afterwards to 39.9 percent in 1981 and 46.9 percent in 1988.

Among developing countries, the share of the East Asian NICs in

Hong Kong's exports rose from 1.6 percent in 1963 to 9.0 percent in 1988. For 1963 and 1988, the data are 0.4 percent and 2.6 percent for Korea, not available and 2.8 percent for Singapore, and 1.2 percent and 3.6 percent for Taiwan. The corresponding figures were 5.1 percent and 3.2 percent for the East Asian NECs, with Indonesia, the Philippines and Thailand all experiencing decreases; 1963 figures for Malaysia are not available.

The largest decline occurred in the export share of the other developing countries, from 30.6 percent in 1963 to 7.6 percent in 1988. All country groups contributed to this result, with other Asia dominating the outcome, having shares of 19.3 percent in 1963 and 2.6 percent in 1988. Much of this decline occurred in Vietnam.

On the import side, apart from China, the East Asian NECs were the principal gainers. Their share increased from 3.0 percent in 1963 to 11.5 percent in 1973 and 19.4 percent in 1981, declining afterwards to 17.9 percent in 1988. Large increases were shown for Korea as well as for Taiwan; data for Singapore in 1963 are again not available.

The share of the developed countries in Hong Kong's imports shows a continuous downward trend, from 55.3 percent in 1963 to 41.7 percent in 1988. Only Japan went against the trend, with an import share of 16.7 percent in 1963 and 18.6 percent in 1988. The corresponding figures were: the United States, 10.6 percent and 8.3 percent; Western Europe, 23.9 percent and 12.9 percent; and Canada, Australia and New Zealand, 4.1 percent and 1.9 percent.

In turn, the share of the East Asian NECs declined from 4.6 percent to 3.7 percent and that of the other developing countries from 16.4 percent to 5.0 percent in 1988. The largest change occurred in Other Asia, from 9.7 percent in 1963 to 2.0 percent in 1988.

Hong Kong's merchandise exports continue to be dominated by manufactured goods, accounting for 95.3 percent of the total (see Table 2.7). Within manufacturing, the principal categories are textiles, apparel and leather products, and engineering products. Taking a long-term view, the rise in engineering exports, from a share of 9.0 percent in 1963 to 39.7 percent in 1988, is very impressive. But despite the decline in the share of textiles, apparel and leather products from 47.7 percent in 1963 to 39.7 percent in 1988, this sector continues to loom large in Hong Kong's exports. Among the remaining product groups, other industries had a 6.1 percent share in 1988, compared with 9.7 percent in 1963.

Within the textiles, apparel and leather products category, considerable shifts occurred over time. There was a decline in the share of textile yarn and fabrics, from 15.2 percent in 1963 to 6.1 percent in

Table 2.7 Commodity composition exports: major product groups: Hong Kong (percent of total exports)

		1963	1973	1981	1988
FUELS	(SITC 3)	0.0	0.0	0.1	0.2
Nonfuel primary products		7.8	3.3	3.0	3.2
Food and live animals	(SITC 0)	3.8	1.5	1.3	0.7
Beverages and tobacco	(SITC 1)	1.6	0.2	0.2	0.9
Industrial Materials	(SITC 2+4+68)	2.5	1.6	1.5	1.5
Manufactures	(SITC 5+6+7+8−68)	91.7	96.5	96.5	95.3
Other	(SITC 9)	0.5	0.2	0.4	1.3
Total		100.0	100.0	100.0	100.0
Manufactures (industrial classification)		72.7	95.5	96.1	95.4
Textile, apparel, leather	(ISIC 32)	47.7	51.4	44.2	39.7
Wood product and furniture	(ISIC 33)	0.7	1.0	0.6	0.4
Paper and paper products	(ISIC 34)	0.7	1.0	1.4	2.7
Chemicals	(ISIC 35)	3.6	8.8	6.4	6.0
Nonmetallic mineral products	(ISIC 36)	0.4	0.3	0.4	0.7
Iron and steel	(ISIC 37)	0.8	0.3	0.1	0.1
Engineering products	(ISIC 38)	9.0	21.4	32.9	39.7
Other industries	(ISIC 39)	9.7	11.5	10.2	6.1

Source: UN, COMTRADE data base.

1987 and of footwear, from 2.2 percent to 0.6 percent. At the same time, wearing apparel increased its share for 27.5 percent in 1963 to 33.0 percent in 1987 as did other textile products from 2.0 percent to 2.4 percent. Finally, the share of leather and leather products remained 1 percent.

Yarn and textile fabrics are standardized products, and here Hong Kong encountered competition in the capital-intensive segments from developed countries and in the labour-intensive segments from low-wage developing countries. Also, domestic value added can be increased by exporting wearing apparel rather than textiles.

It is particularly noteworthy that Hong Kong was able to increase the share of wearing apparel in its rapidly growing exports. This result reflects transformation of the product composition of the industry from low-grade shirts, suits and underwear to high fashion apparel and leisure wear. The change in product composition, involving susbtantial increases in domestic value added, permitted Hong Kong to overcome the quantitative limitations imposed in the framework of the Multifiber Arrangement.

Engineering products have also undergone considerable transformation over time, from the assembly of transistor radios to the production of electronic goods. Hong Kong has become a leading producer of watches (electronic digital watches, LCD timepieces and electronic quartz analogs) and also supplies watch parts for the Swiss industry. Watches, together with photographic equipment, account for much of the rise in the export share of professional goods (from 0.7 percent in 1963 to 8.8 percent in 1987). Furthermore, with the shift to television exports, the share of radio and television products rose from 1.9 percent in 1963 to 9.6 percent in 1987. Other electrical machinery (mainly semiconductors and integrated circuits) and office and computing equipment represented about 5 percent of total exports in 1987.

A substantial transformation occurred in the 'other' industries category as well. While in earlier periods wigs and low-grade toys and sporting goods dominated the industry, Hong Kong has become the leading producer of toys that often incorporate considerable sophistication.

On the import side, the high income elasticity of demand for industrial goods and increased intra-industry specialization led to a rise in the share of manufactured products from 57.5 percent of imports in 1963 to 75.2 percent in 1988. Within the manufacturing sector, the share of engineering products nearly tripled during this period. The share of textiles, apparel and leather products increased also, reflecting increased imports for re-export from China, which are included in the import but not in the export data.

In turn, the share of fuels declined slightly from 3.5 percent in 1963 to 3.4 percent in 1988, while larger declines were experienced in the other primary product categories. Note was taken above of the decline in the share of food imports. Also, the share of industrial materials fell from 13.4 percent in 1963 to 12.7 percent in 1988 as the ratio of value added in production value increased over time.

PROSPECTS FOR THE FUTURE

Economic growth rates in Hong Kong averaged 8.9 percent in 1963–73, 9.1 percent in 1973–81, and 7.2 percent in 1981–7. Any projection entails a large measure of error, with Hong Kong's economic future being dependent to a considerable extent on developments in China.

Assuming that China will again adopt open economy policies after

Table 2.8 Commodity composition of imports: major product groups: Hong Kong (percent of total imports)

		1963	1973	1981	1988
Fuels	(SITC 3)	3.5	2.7	7.9	3.4
Nonfuel primary products		38.7	28.1	17.4	20.9
Food and live animals	(SITC 0)	23.1	16.9	10.1	5.3
Beverages and Tobacco	(SITC 1)	2.3	2.0	1.5	2.8
Industrial materials	(SITC 2+4+68)	13.4	9.1	5.8	12.7
Manufactures	(SITC 2+6+7+8−68)	57.5	69.0	74.2	75.2
Other	(SITC 9)	0.3	0.2	0.5	0.5
Total		100.0	100.0	100.0	100.0
Manufactures (industrial classification)		45.5	64.9	72.0	73.4
Textile, apparel, leather	(ISIC 32)	16.4	20.1	19.5	12.9
Wood product and furniture	(ISIC 33)	0.3	0.9	1.2	2.2
Paper and paper products	(ISIC 34)	0.7	1.9	2.0	3.0
Chemicals	(ISIC 35)	7.1	8.7	7.6	9.4
Nonmetallic mineral products	(ISIC 36)	1.9	1.6	2.0	3.6
Iron and steel	(ISIC 37)	2.8	2.2	2.9	2.1
Engineering products	(ISIC 38)	12.7	23.3	32.3	35.3
Other industries	(ISIC 39)	3.5	6.3	4.6	5.0

Source: UN, COMTRADE data base.

the ongoing adjustment is completed, Hong Kong could reach GDP growth rates of 7.5 percent a year in the 1987–2000 period. This assumes that, after a temporary bulge, emigration will return to the recent average of 40 000 per year. With continued immigration from China, population may rise 1 percent a year, resulting in increases in per caput income of 6.4 percent.

No policy changes have been assumed in making the growth projection. This reflects the view that the basically *laissez-faire* policies applied in Hong Kong will continue to be appropriate. There is no sign that the Chinese government would wish to change these policies, although the June 1989 events considerably increased uncertainty as to the future of Hong Kong.

Bibliography

Aikman, David, 1986. 'China's Periphery: Hong Kong and Taiwan', Chapter 5 in David Aikman, *Pacific Rim: Area of Change, Area of Opportunity*. Boston: Little, Brown.

Beazer, William F., 1978. *The Commercial Future of Hong Kong*. New York: Praeger.

Chai, Joseph, 1983. 'Industrial Co-operation between China and Hong Kong', in A. J. Youngson (ed.), *China and Hong Kong: The Economic Nexus*. Hong Kong: Oxford University Press.

Chou, K. R., 1969. 'Hong Kong's Changing Pattern of Trade and Economic Interdependence in Southeast Asia', in Theodore Morgan and Nyle Spoelstra (eds), *Economic Interdependence in Southeast Asia*. Madison, WI: University of Wisconsin Press.

Fong, Pang Eng, 1988. 'The Distinctive Features of Two City-States' Development: Hong Kong and Singapore', in Peter L. Berger and Hsin-Huang Michael Hsiao (eds), *In Search of an East Asian Development Model*. New Brunswick, NJ: Transaction Books.

Geiger, Theodore, assisted by Frances M. Geiger, 1973. *Tales of Two City-States: The Development Process of Hong Kong and Singapore*. Washington, DC: National Planning Association.

Haggard, Stephen and Tun-jen Cheng, 1987. 'Hong Kong', Chapter V in Stephen Haggard and Tun-jen Cheng, *Newly Industrializing Asia in Transition: Policy Reform and American Response*. Policy Papers in International Affairs, no. 17. Berkeley, CA: University of California Press.

Hopkins, Keith (ed.), 1971. *Hong Kong: The Industrial Colony*. Hong Kong: Oxford University Press.

Hsia, Ronald and Laurence Chau, 1978. *Industrialisation, Employment, and Income Distribution*. London: Croom Helm.

King, Ambrose Y. C. and Peter J. L. Man, 1979. 'Small Factory in Economic Development: The Case of Hong Kong', in T. B. Lin et al. (eds), *Hong Kong: Social and Political Studies in Development*. New York: M. E. Sharpe.

Lethbridge, David (ed.), 1984. *The Business Enviroment in Hong Kong*. Hong Kong: Oxford University Press.

Lin, Tzong Biau and Ying Ping Ho, 1981. 'Export-Oriented Growth and Industrial Diversification in Hong Kong', in Wontack Hong and Lawrence B. Krause (eds), *Trade and Growth of the Advanced Developing Countries of the Pacific Basin*. Seoul: Korea Development Institute.

Lin, Tzong Biau and Victor Mok, 1985. 'Trade, Foreign Investment, and Development in Hong Kong', in Walter Galenson (ed.), *Foreign Trade and Investment: Economic Growth in the Newly Industrializing Asian Countries*. Madison, WI: University of Wisconsin Press.

Rabushka, Alvin, 1973. *The Changing Face of Hong Kong*. Washington, DC: American Enterprise Institute for Public Policy Research.

Rabushka, Alvin, 1979. *Hong Kong: A Study in Economic Freedom*. Chicago: University of Chicago Press.

Riedel, James, 1974. *The Industrialization of Hong Kong*. Tubingen: J. C. B. Mohr.

Scott, Robert H., K. A. Wong and Y. K. Ho (eds), 1986. *Hong Kong's Financial Institutions and Markets*. Hong Kong: Oxford University Press.

Szczepanik, Edward, 1958. *The Economic Growth of Hong Kong*. London: Oxford University Press.

Wong, A. W. F., 1980. 'Non-purposive Adaptation and Administrative Change in Hong Kong', in Chi-keung Leung *et al.* (eds), *Hong Kong: Dilemmas of Growth*. Canberra: Australian National University, Center for Asian Studies.

Woronoff, Jon, 1986. 'Hong Kong, Capitalist Paradise', Chapter 5 in Jon Woronoff, *Asia's Miracle Economies*. New York: M.E. Sharpe.

Youngson, A. J., 1987. *Hong Kong: Economic Growth and Policy*. Hong Kong: Oxford University Press.

3 Korea

INTRODUCTION

Occupying an area of 98 000 square kilometers, Korea (the Republic of Korea, or South Korea) has a population of 42.1 million. It has few mineral resources and its mountainous terrain does not favor agriculture which, nevertheless, was the mainstay of its economy until independence from Japan in 1945.

After having been part of the Japanese empire between 1910 and 1945, Korea was divided into two parts after the Second World War. The North came under Soviet influence while the South was governed by the American military until 1948, when an independent Korean government was established on its territory.

The Korean war began in June 1950 when the North invaded the South, extending its occupation to its entire area except for the Pusan perimeter. Subsequently, the fighting stabilized around the present dividing line between the North and the South. But much of the South's territory was devastated at the time the war ended in July 1953, with material losses reportedly equalling Korea's annual GDP.

Economic growth was slow in the 1953–60 period. Apart from reconstruction, the policies applied were oriented towards import substitution behind high protection, while exports were discouraged by overvalued exchange rates. At the same time, balance-of-payments deficits were financed by large inflows of US military and economic aid.

In 1960 income levels in North Korea, which retained much of Korea's industrial establishments after partition, were 50 percent higher than in the South. In the 1970s, however, the South surpassed the North in terms of per caput incomes, and it may now have double the incomes in the North. The transformation of the Korean economy can be indicated by a few figures.

In 1960, the exports of goods and services did not exceed 3 percent of GDP. Imports were 13 percent of GDP, so that capital inflow (mostly US aid) equalled 10 percent of GDP. Notwithstanding the large inflow of foreign capital, the share of investment in Korea's GDP was only 11 percent, because domestic savings were negligible.

In 1987, the exports of goods and services amounted to 45 percent of GDP while imports were 38 percent of GDP, resulting in a net outflow of capital of 7 percent. In the same year, 30 percent of GDP was invested.

These changes resulted from rapid economic growth engendered by export expansion under an outward-oriented development strategy. This strategy was established in the mid-1960s, following abortive attempts at exchange rate unification and liberalization in the early 1960s.

GOVERNMENT POLICIES

After the end of the Korean war, the government resumed the policy of import substitution behind high protection that was begun once the Second World War had ended. At the same time, exports were discouraged by the overvaluation of the exchange rate as rapid domestic inflation was not fully offset by the depreciation of the won, the Korean currency. As a result the real exchange rate, calculated by adjusting the official exchange rate for changes in wholesale prices at home and abroad, fell to half of its 1948–50 value by January 1960.

Devaluations undertaken over the following year led to a depreciation of the official exchange rate from 50 won to the dollar in January 1960 to 130 won to the dollar in February 1961. At the same time, exchange rates were unified, import controls were liberalized, and subsidies were provided to exports.

The measures reflected the liberalization philosophy of the civilian government established in April 1960. However, under the military government installed in May 1961, the real exchange rate appreciated again as rapid inflation was not compensated for by further devaluations. The resulting deterioration of the balance of payments, in turn, led to the adoption of increased import restrictions and to the re-establishment of the multiple exchange rate system.

Far-reaching reforms were undertaken after the election in August 1964 of the government of Park Chung Hee, who retained power until his assassination 15 years later. The reforms involved the devaluation of the official exchange rate from 130 to 247 won to the dollar, the unification of exchange rates, import liberalization, and increased incentives to exports, representing the adoption of an outward-oriented development strategy.

In 1967 the 'positive' list of admissible imports was replaced by a 'negative' list of imports whose importation required government authorization. This meant, in practice, further reducing the scope of import restrictions.

Exporters were given the right to import their inputs duty-free and without restrictions; they were also given generous wastage allowances for the importation of raw materials. In 1965, these incentives were extended to indirect exports (the production of domestic inputs for exports) and increased credit preferences were also provided to exporters. In the following year, tariff exemptions were granted to the importers of machinery and equipment used to produce direct and indirect exports, and accelerated depreciation was introduced. Furthermore, inputs used in export production were free from indirect taxes and exporters received a 50 percent reduction in their income tax.

The export regime established after 1964 provided a free trade status to exporters, with some additional incentives. As a result of these changes, on the average, exports received similar incentives as import substitution, thereby eliminating the anti-export bias of the system of incentives which is characteristic of countries following inward-oriented policies. Exporters also benefited from the stability of the incentive system.

Apart from price incentives, the government-sponsored Korea Trade Promotion Association (KOTRA) was founded in 1964 to promote Korean exports and to carry out market research abroad. The government also sent special trade missions to foreign countries and authorized the Korean Traders' Association to collect 1 percent of the value of imports for use as an export promotion fund.

The government established export targets for individual firms. The importance of these targets should not be overstated, however. The duty-free entry of imported inputs and the provision of export incentives did not depend on the fulfillment of export targets, although successful Korean exporters reportedly received advantageous treatment in pending tax cases. Thus, export targets had a largely psychological value as did the honors bestowed on large exporters.

The adoption of an outward-oriented development strategy was accompanied by the reform of the financial system. Real interest rates had been negative, but with the rate of inflation exceeding nominal interest rates by a substantial margin, they turned strongly positive as deposit as well as loan rates were substantially raised. This led to considerable increases in financial savings and while not all of this represented new savings as some of it came from the curb market, total savings also increased.

As will be discussed subsequently, the measures applied led to rapid increases of exports and GDP. The world economic environment deteriorated, however, in 1973–4, with the quadrupling of oil prices and the world recession. The initial reactions to these changes were to modify Korea's outward-oriented development strategy.

The Discussion Paper on the Developmental Strategy for the Fourth Five-Year Plan, 1977–81, prepared by the Korea Development Institute, argued that 'it is only judicious to reduce Korea's vulnerability to the trade effects of foreign countercyclical policies and to the growing imperfections of a world market for basic commodities' (1975, p. 24). In accordance with the proposed change in strategy, the *Guidelines for the Fourth Five-Year Economic Development Plan*, prepared by the Korea Economic Planning Bureau, envisaged 'the increase of import substitution and conservation of resources in order to reduce the growth rate of imports to the level of the GNP growth rate' (1975, p. 15).

In an advisory report prepared for the government of Korea, the author suggested, however, that it would be inappropriate to change a long-term developmental strategy on the basis of essentially short-term considerations. At the end, the proponents of outward orientation won and the continuation of this policy was decided upon in the course of preparing the final version of the Fourth Five-Year Plan.

The measures taken involved liberalizing import restrictions and lowering tariffs. While wastage allowances to exporters were reduced and the income tax benefits of exporters were eliminated, the subsidy equivalent of preferential export credits was increased and new medium-term and long-term export credit facilities were established. Correspondingly, on the average, exports and import substitution continued to receive similar incentives.

Policy changes occurred, however, in subsequent years. These changes favored capital-intensive industries producing intermediate goods and heavy machinery over traditional export industries. Capital-intensive industries producing intermediate products, such as ferrous and nonferrous metals, petrochemicals, chemicals and heavy machinery (such as electrical power generation and heavy construction and engineering equipment) were given priority in the allocation of domestic credit and in access to foreign credit. Furthermore, the cost of credit to these industries was reduced through preferential interest rates. Fiscal incentives in the form of exemption from corporate income taxes and accelerated depreciation provisions further lowered the cost of capital to the industries in question.

The application of these measures affected the pattern of investment. In the first three years of the Fourth Five-Year Plan (1977–81) the amount of investment in basic metals was 130 percent and that in chemicals and other intermediate products 121 percent of the investment planned for the entire period, compared with an overall average of 80 percent. By contrast, only 50 percent of planned investment was undertaken in the textile industry and 42 percent in other light industries. Machinery, electronics, and shipbuilding occupied a middle position, the corresponding figures being 101 percent, with larger than planned increases in heavy machinery.

The reduced availability of funds for traditional export industries was aggravated by the increasing overvaluation of the exchange rate. Despite domestic inflation rates in excess of world market rates, the exchange rate was maintained at 485 won to the dollar from 1975 onward. As a result, between 1975 and 1979 the real exchange rate appreciated by 12 percent.

These policy changes could not fail to have adverse effects on exports. Export growth rates declined after 1976 and the volume of exports fell in absolute terms in 1979. This contrasts with the experience of Korea's major competitors as export growth rates increased in 1979 in Hong Kong and Singapore and export volume rose by 7 percent in Taiwan.

At the same time, the growth of fixed investment accelerated in Korea, financed in large part from foreign borrowing which added to Korea's external debt. The feverish construction activity, in turn, created pressures for wage increases, contributing to the acceleration of inflation.

The high import intensity of fixed investment and of industries producing intermediate goods and heavy machinery, together with the deterioration of the competitiveness of Korean industry, contributed to rapid increases in imports, with average annual increases of 21 percent in volume between 1977 and 1979 compared with 14 percent in the 1970–7 period. The acceleration of import growth was even greater when excluding the import content of exports (from 11 percent in 1970–7 to 25 percent in 1977–9).

Policy changes were instituted following the assassination of President Park. The won was devalued by 20 percent in January 1980 and, following smaller adjustments in the rest of the year, the exchange rate reached 656 won to the dollar by the end of 1980. The depreciation of the exchange rate contributed to increases in exports but Korea again fell behind the other three East Asian NICs. GDP also declined, by 5 percent, although the 22 percent fall in agricultural production contributed significantly to this result.

The adverse effects of the policies applied led to a reconsideration of the policy framework. The *Preliminary Outline of the Fifth Five-Year Economic and Social Development Plan of the Republic of Korea* (1982–6), issued in June 1981, called for a return to a fully-fledged outward-oriented development strategy. It stated that 'the basic strategy Korea will follow . . . will be to promote competition at home and liberalize its external economic policies' (p. 10). The document added that 'there is no escape from the conclusion that during the Fifth Five-Year Plan period export expansion should continue to be the major engine of growth for Korea' (p. 13). The preliminary plan further indicated the general orientation of policies to serve these objectives:

In order to expand exports during the First Five-Year Plan period, the government will make every effort to strengthen the competitiveness of Korea's export industries. (p. 16)

In order to sustain long-term growth of exports and the economy as a whole, import liberalization is essential. There is a limit to which a country can improve its industrial structure without import liberalization. Furthermore, a country cannot possibly hope to improve its price competitiveness while its cost of living rises due to import restriction. (p. 17)

The single most important change in government industrial policy during the Fifth Five-Year Plan period will be the reduction of the government's role in promoting so-called strategic industries. Investment choices will be left to the initiative of the private sector and the government will provide only the general framework in which such choices will be made by private entrepreneurs in cooperation with their bankers and financiers. Stated differently, during the 1980s the government industrial policy will aim at reducing the preferential treatment for selected industries and expose domestic producers to foreign competition in order to enhance their international competitiveness. (pp. 22–3)

During the Fifth Five-Year Plan period the government will make special efforts to make greater use of the market mechanism and private intiative for continued social and economic progress. (p. 30)

In addition, special efforts will be made to maintain the real interest rate on bank loans and deposits at a positive level and gradually reduce the scope of policy preference loans. (p. 31)

Making a greater use of the market mechanism also implies equalizing in terms of competition and policy incentives for all industries . . . During the Fifth Five-Year Plan period the government plans to gradually phase out specific incentives and provide instead generalized uniform incentives for investment in all industries. (p. 31)

The preliminary outline for the Fifth Five-Year Plan indicated the determination of the government to reverse tendencies toward greater inward orientation and government intervention. This was based on the perception that outward orientation is not only the best guarantee for long-term economic growth, but also helps overcome the effects of external shocks. The rationale was explained in the preliminary plan:

It is true that the above assessment of the world economic environment expected to prevail in the 1980's does not spell an optimistic outlook for a trade-oriented economy such as Korea's. But one should be careful not to draw from such an assessment a policy conclusion that the country should in any way compromise its outward-looking development strategy. If anything, the only way for Korea to meet effectively the challenges posed by external uncertainties is to pursue a development strategy that is even more outward-looking than in the past. The validity of this view has been underlined by Korea's own experience in dealing with the severe impact of two rounds of oil price increases during the 1970's and also the experiences of such other countries as Japan. Both Korea's and other countries' experiences clearly show that an open, trade-oriented economy can alleviate the initial impact of higher oil prices first by increasing exports and then by shifting the burden of higher oil prices through subsequent improvement in terms of trade. (pp. 12–13)

In accordance with the plan objectives, the increases in protection undertaken in conjunction with promotion of capital-intensive industries in the second half of the 1970s were reversed during the early 1980s. According to figures published by the Ministry of Commerce and Industry, the share of liberalized import items rose from 68.6 percent in 1980 to 74.7 percent in 1982, increasing further to 87.7 percent in 1985. And while the degree of import liberalization is somewhat less in terms of import value, the same tendency is observed in this respect, too.

The Sixth Five-Year Plan (1987–91) continued the process of import liberalization. By 1986, 91.5 percent of items were liberalized; this increased to 93.5 percent by 1987, and 95.4 percent by 1988. However, special laws, such as the Science and Technology Development Law, gave ministries the authority to establish and enforce local control requirements and to deny import licenses. Examples include computers, sophisticated medical equipment and machine tools.

In turn, tariff rates were reduced in the early 1980s and again in the framework of the Tariff Reform Act of 1984. As a result, the simple average of tariff rates declined from 31.7 percent in 1982 to 23.7 percent in 1983 and 21.8 percent in 1984. Tariffs were reduced further in subsequent years, averaging 19.3 percent in 1987, 18.1 percent in 1988 and 12.7 percent in 1989.

Within the overall average, the tendency has been to reduce tariffs on all major categories of products. Compared with average tariffs of 20 percent on raw materials, 25 percent on intermediate and capital goods and 30 percent on final goods, tariffs were set at 5–10 percent, 20 percent and 20–30 percent in 1988. At the same time, within each category greater uniformity was attained.

Agriculture is an exception to this general tendency toward trade liberalization. While in the 1960s industry and agriculture received similar incentives, subsequently agriculture came to be favored. Agriculture increasingly received higher than world market prices while sheltering it from foreign competition.

Korean agricultural protection is dominated by the use of quotas. Recent calculations by the United States Department of Agriculture found that producer subsidy equivalents (the ratio of the domestic producer price inclusive of subsidies to the border price expressed in domestic currency) for 1984 were rice, 3.05; wheat, 1.10; coarse grains, 2.35; sugar, 4.20; dairy products, 2.00; beef and veal, 3.25; and pork and poultry, 1.30 (see D. P. Vincent, 1988: 'Domestic Effects of Agricultural Protection in Asian Countries with Special Reference to Korea', paper prepared for the Global Agriculture Trade Study organized by the Centre for International Economics, Carribean, Australia).

Reversing earlier moves towards financial liberalization, the financial sector was strictly regulated in the second half of the 1970s. Real interest rates became negative; directed credit and extensive preferences were introduced in favor of capital-intensive industries; and the government exercised tight control over the operation of the banks.

A number of financial liberalization measures were taken during the 1980s. The monetary authorities eased restrictions on the establishment of nonbanking financial institutions, released control over the asset management of these institutions and deregulated their interest rates. As a result, nonbank financial institutions assumed increasing importance in Korea and the ratio of the broadly defined money supply to GDP rose to a considerable extent.

The government denationalized commercial banks and reduced its control on their operations. Two new commercial banks were established in joint ventures with foreign interests, and the local branches of foreign banks were given greater freedom in their operations. Credit ceilings for individual banks were abolished and an indirect credit control system through reserve changes was introduced while simultaneously reducing reserve requirements. Commercial banks were permitted to enter into new areas, including the issue of negotiable certificates of deposit, sales of public bonds with repurchase agreements and of discounted commercial bills, and trust banking. At the same time, outside the banking sector, markets for corporate bonds and commercial paper assumed importance.

In addition, the scope of directed credit was reduced, credit preferences to capital-intensive industries eliminated and the share of large conglomerates in bank credit frozen. The government furthermore imposed an obligation on the commercial banks to provide at least 35 percent of their loans to small and medium sized firms.

The government aimed to increase competition in the nonfinancial sector as well. In 1981, it established the Office of Fair Trade to guard against restrictive trade practices. But the unused capacity resulting from excessive investments in capital-intensive industries in the late 1970s induced the government to undertake restructuring operations. It merged major heavy equipment producers, initiated a rationalization plan in the shipbuilding industry, and organized mergers while reducing capacity in the fertilizer industry.

At the same time, the promotional laws established during the 1970s in favor of capital-intensive industries were abolished and the industry-specific approach was replaced by a functional approach. It is of particular importance that the new industrial policy apparatus lacks a mechanism for 'picking winners' (who often turn out to be losers).

Among functional areas, the promotion of technology has been given pride of place. Several institutions have been established to train scientists and engineers and to conduct research. They include the Korea Advanced Institute of Science and Technology, the Korea Institute of Electronics Technology and the Korea Electrotechnology and Telecommunications Research Institute.

Under the Fifth Five-Year Plan, spending on research and development increased from 0.9 percent of GDP in 1980 to 2.0 percent in 1986; the Sixth Plan set out to raise this ratio to 2.5 percent by 1990, equal to the Organization for Economic Cooperation and Development average. At the same time, the share of the private sector in R & D spending increased to a considerable extent. While the public sector was dominant in R & D in earlier years, by 1985 three-quarters of such spending was undertaken by the private sector. This reflects the effect of the tax incentives for R & D provided under the Technology Development Promotion Act of 1973 that was strengthened in 1981, as well as the establishment of the National Project for Research and Development in 1982 which funds joint private–public R & D projects in the fields of engineering and electronics.

It may be concluded that, after increasing intervention in the second half of the 1970s, Korea has liberalized its economy in the 1980s. Although Korea is far from having a *laissez-faire* economy, it pursues an outward-oriented development strategy that provides similar incentives, on the average, to exports and to import substitution. This strategy has been supported by the government taking a favorable attitude towards exports, while in inward-oriented economies exports often suffer from restrictive regulations and red tape.

An important factor contributing to Korea's ability to exploit the advantages of an outward-oriented development strategy has been education. While the 1944 Census showed that 90 percent of the population had no formal education, and only 300 Korean students were enrolled at the single university at that time, rapid progress occurred after the Second World War. Following the introduction of compulsory public education immediately after the war, there was considerable expansion in secondary and higher education.

As shown in *World Development Report, 1989* by the World Bank, by 1965 there were 35 percent of children of the relevant age group enrolled in secondary schools, and this proportion reached 95 percent by 1986. The corresponding rates were 6 percent in 1965 and 33 percent in 1986 for higher education. These figures are considerably higher than in countries at similar levels of development and the secondary school rates, although not the higher education rates, are on the same level as in industrial economies.

Another distinguishing characteristic of Korean industry has been the importance of conglomerates, the *chaebol*. The largest fifty-five firms account for more than one-third of industrial output, a figure that is considerably higher than in Japan or in other East Asian NICs. Also, eleven out of twenty-eight developing country firms in the Fortune 500 category of foreign firms are Korean.

Industrial concentration was helpful to Korea in providing economies of scale in production and in foreign sales as well as name recognition abroad. But the comparatively small number of the large conglomerates made it easier for the government to impose its will on firms in the second half of the 1970s. In addition, some of the conglomerates may be overly large and suffer losses in efficiency and in flexibility. Conglomerates are also highly leveraged, and that creates considerable risks.

The large conglomerates are domestic firms. Apart from the entrepreneurial spirit of the Koreans, this reflects the earlier policy of strictly limiting foreign direct investment, following the Japanese example. This policy has changed as high-technology industries need foreign knowledge. In fact, from its inception, the electronics industry has had an important share of foreign capital, including wholly foreign-owned firms, although these have to export at least 50 percent of their output.

Furthermore, the December 1983 revision of the Foreign Capital Inducement Law greatly eased the conditions of establishment by foreign firms. The most important changes were the shift from a positive to a negative list and the introduction of an automatic approval system.

Whereas previously foreign direct investment was allowed only in specifically listed areas, it is now allowed in all areas unless restricted by law. Also, as long as the foreign equity share is less than 50 percent the investment is automatically approved, while investments with a foreign share of 50 percent or higher are subject to review. The revised foreign investment law further removed restrictions on the regulation of capital and earnings.

Table 3.1 Economic performance indicators: Korea

Growth rates	1963–73	1973–81	1981–7	1963–87
GDP	9.3	7.8	8.9	8.7
Population	2.4	1.6	1.4	1.9
GDP per caput	6.8	6.1	7.4	6.7
Investment	14.4	11.2	10.2	12.3
Manufacturing production	19.8	13.0	11.5	15.4
Agricultural production	4.1	2.3	2.4	3.1
Exports	33.6	14.3	13.8	21.8
Imports	18.8	12.2	9.9	14.3

Source: World Bank.

ECONOMIC GROWTH

The policies applied led to rapid economic growth in Korea. Per caput incomes increased fivefold between 1963 and 1988, reaching $2849 per head in 1988 (see Table 1.1). As a result, Korea now ranks among the higher-middle-income developing countries according to the terminology used by the World Bank.

Korea's GDP increased at average annual rates of 9.3 percent in 1963–73, 8.2 percent in 1973–81, and 8.9 percent in 1981–7 (Table 3.1). This means that the problems associated with capital-intensive industries did not have a lasting effect on economic expansion in Korea.

Economic growth was concentrated in the manufacturing sector, which saw its share in the GDP rise from 14.7 percent in 1963 to 25.1 percent in 1973 and, again, to 29.2 percent in 1981 and to 30.3 percent in 1987 (see Table 3.2). And while manufacturing growth rates declined from 19.8 percent in 1963–73 to 13.0 percent in 1973–81 and 11.5 percent in 1981–7, the torrid pace of earlier years could not be maintained.

Agricultural growth averaged 3.1 percent over the entire 1963–87 period, with a slower increase shown for 1973–81 that includes the disastrous harvest year of 1980. As a result of these changes, agriculture's share in GDP declined from 43.4 percent in 1963 to 11.4 percent in 1987.

In turn, the share of the service sector in the GDP increased from 40.2 percent in 1963 to 57.1 percent in 1987. Gas, electricity and water; construction; transportation; banking; and public administra-

Table 3.2 Industrial composition and trade: Korea (percent of GDP)

	1963	1973	1981	1987
Industrial composition				
Agriculture	43.4	24.5	15.8	11.4
Mining and quarrying	1.7	1.1	1.6	1.2
Manufacturing	14.7	25.1	29.2	30.3
Gas, electricity and water	1.0	1.4	2.1	3.2
Construction	2.9	4.4	7.3	8.2
Transportation	4.0	6.8	8.3	8.2
Wholesale and retail trade	14.3	17.8	13.1	13.2
Banking, real estate	6.1	7.2	9.5	10.8
Ownership of dwellings	.	.	.	.
Public administration	5.5	6.3	7.5	7.2
Other services	6.4	4.9	5.0	5.6
Imputed bank service charge, duty	.	0.5	0.6	0.6
Trade				
Exports of goods and nonfactor services	4.8	29.7	36.6	44.9
Imports of goods and nonfactor services	15.9	32.6	41.9	36.4

Source: World Bank.

tion all experienced increases in their GDP shares, with declines occurring in wholesale and retail trade and in the 'other services' category.

Economic growth was promoted by the rapid expansion of exports. Whereas the exports of goods and services amounted to only 4.8 percent of GDP in 1963, this share reached 29.7 percent in 1973, 36.6 percent in 1981 and 45 percent in 1987. The share of the imports of goods and services also increased but at a lower rate from 15.9 percent in 1963 to 36.4 percent in 1987. Correspondingly, the large import surplus of 1963 gave place to an export surplus in 1987, when the outflow of savings equalled 7.2 percent of GDP (see Table 3.3).

The outflow of savings was not at the expense of domestic investment. In fact, the share of investment in GDP has been maintained at 29–30 percent in recent years, exceeding the ratios of 25–27 percent in the mid-1970s (except for 31.3 percent in 1974). Increasing investment shares and the shift from positive to negative foreign savings meant a considerable increase in domestic savings. Thus, while the share of domestic savings in GDP reached 25 percent only in 1976, it was above 30 percent in 1984 and 1985 and it approached 37 percent in 1987.

The shift from positive to negative foreign savings is reflected in

Table 3.3 Savings and investment ratios: Korea (percent of GDP)

	1973	1974	1975	1976	1977	1978	1979	1980
Private savings	22.2	22.7	20.4	25.2	29.0	29.5	29.8	25.5
Government budget balance	-0.5	-2.2	-2.0	-1.4	-1.8	-1.2	-1.7	-2.2
Domestic savings	21.7	20.5	18.5	23.9	27.2	28.4	28.1	23.3
Foreign savings	2.9	10.8	8.5	1.2	-0.2	3.0	7.2	7.8
Domestic investment	24.6	31.3	27.0	25.1	27.0	31.4	35.3	31.1

	1981	1982	1983	1984	1985	1986	1987
Private savings	27.1	27.8	28.7	31.7	32.0	35.0	36.2
Government budget balance	-3.4	-3.1	-1.1	-1.2	-1.2	-0.1	0.5
Domestic savings	23.7	24.7	27.7	30.5	30.7	34.9	36.7
Foreign savings	5.4	2.5	1.3	0.3	-0.5	-5.8	-7.2
Domestic investment	29.1	27.2	28.9	30.8	30.2	29.2	29.5

Source: World Bank.

the turnaround of Korea's current account balance (see Table 3.4). This turnaround was associated with the shift from a negative to a positive merchandise trade balance while the negative service balance declined relatively little.

In the capital account, an outflow is shown for both long-term and short-term capital as well as in errors and omissions that may also reflect the outflow of short-term capital. At the same time, Korea continued to accumulate reserves. On the other side of the ledger, foreign direct investment in Korea accelerated, owing to the revision of the Foreign Capital Inducement Law, but it remained small in absolute terms.

INTERNATIONAL TRADE

The United States is Korea's principal export market. While its share declined between 1973 and 1981, it increased again afterwards, reaching a peak of 35.4 percent in 1988 (see Table 3.5). This result reflects the fact that Korea increased its share in the rising US imports from 2.0 percent in 1981 to 4.2 percent in 1988.

In turn, Japan's share increased from 28.6 percent in 1963 to 38.5 percent in 1973 but declined afterwards, equalling 19.8 percent in 1988. In that year, exports to Japan exceeded exports to Western Europe only by one-fourth. Yet in 1963 and 1973 exports to Japan were more than three times greater than exports to Western Europe. These results indicate the efforts made by Korea to increase its European sales as well as the difficulties encountered in selling to Japan, which have been eased only recently.

Exports to developing countries show a roller-coaster ride. Their share in total exports fell from 33.9 percent in 1967 to 14.2 percent in 1973, to increase again to 33.0 percent in 1981, subsequently declining to 23.1 percent in 1988.

Within the developing country total, the share of exports to the Pacific Area developing countries declined to a considerable extent after 1963 and subsequent increases did not suffice to reach their earlier share. A similar decline occurred in exports to other developing countries, but the earlier share was surpassed in 1981 as Korea benefited from the increased import capacity of Middle Eastern countries following the rise of oil prices, with a partial reversal in subsequent years as oil prices fell again.

Korea does not report trade with China and the European socialist

Table 3.4 Balance of payments: Korea (million US$)

	1978	1979	1980	1981	1982	1983	1984	1985	1986	1987
Merchandise exports	12 711	14 705	17 214	20 671	20 879	23 204	26 335	26 442	33 913	46 244
Merchandise imports	-14 491	-19 100	-21 598	-24 299	-23 473	-24 967	-27 371	-26 461	-29 707	-38 585
Trade balance	-1 780	-4 395	-4 384	-3 628	-2 594	-1 763	-1 036	-19	4 206	7 659
Other goods, services, and income: credit	4 450	4 825	5 363	6 598	7 477	7 179	7 317	6 664	8 052	10 011
Other goods, services, and income: debit	-4 226	-5 020	-6 749	-8 117	-8 032	-7 614	-8 194	-8 110	-8 680	-9 034
Other goods, services, and income: net	224	-195	-1 386	-1 519	-555	-435	-877	-1 446	-628	977
Unrequited transfers	471	439	449	501	499	592	541	578	1 039	1 218
Current account balance	-1 085	-4 151	-5 321	-4 646	-2 650	-1 606	-1 372	-887	4 617	9 854
Direct investment	61	16	-7	60	-76	-57	73	200	325	418
Long-term capital	2 050	3 055	1 994	3 577	1 873	1 848	2 939	2 095	-2 896	-8 890
Short-term capital	18	2 282	3 983	1 090	2 159	524	-189	-333	-1 422	-462
Capital account balance	2 129	5 353	5 970	4 727	3 956	2 315	2 823	1 962	-3 993	-8 934
Errors and omissions	-313	328	-338	-410	-1 301	-945	-891	-883	-547	1 184
Overall balances	731	874	311	-329	5	-236	560	192	77	2 104
Net use of reserves	-710	-896	-350	244	-74	171	-527	-158	-165	-2 263

Note: The overall balance is the sum of the current account and capital account balances and errors and omissions. Net use of reserves was derived by adding the following items to overall balance: counterpart to the monetization and demonetization of gold, counterpart to SDR allocation, and counterpart to valuation changes.

Source: IMF, *International Financial Statistics*, various issues.

Table 3.5 Geographical composition of exports: Korea (percent of total exports)

	1963	1973	1981	1988
Developed Countries	65.7	85.8	62.5	75.1
United States	28.1	31.6	26.7	35.4
Western Europe	8.7	10.8	15.5	15.5
Japan	28.6	38.5	16.5	19.8
Canada, Australia, New Zealand	0.3	4.8	3.8	4.4
Developing Countries	33.9	14.2	33.0	23.1
Pacific Countries (other than China)	17.3	7.8	11.8	12.5
East Asian NICs	12.4	5.9	8.1	9.7
Hong Kong	10.5	3.6	5.4	5.9
Korea	–	–	–	–
Singapore	0.8	0.9	1.4	2.2
Taiwan	1.1	1.3	1.2	1.6
East Asian NECs	4.8	2.0	3.7	2.8
Indonesia	NA	1.0	1.7	0.7
Malaysia	NA	0.2	0.8	0.7
Philippines	3.0	0.2	0.6	0.6
Thailand	1.8	0.6	0.6	0.9
China	NA	NA	0.0	0.0
Other Developing Countries	16.7	6.4	21.2	10.6
Other Asia	16.6	1.3	2.8	2.0
Africa	0.1	1.0	2.7	1.3
Southern Europe	NA	1.0	0.6	0.6
Middle East	NA	1.4	11.5	4.2
Latin America	NA	1.7	3.7	2.5
European Socialist Countries	NA	NA	0.0	0.0

Note: Taiwanese figures for 1981 and 1988 derived as difference between total exports, the regional aggregates, special categories, and other countries not included. Regional aggregates may not sum to 100 percent due to inclusion in denominator of special categories, and other countries not specified.

Sources: IMF, *Direction of Trade Statistics*, various issues.

countries. Trade with these countries partly takes the indirect route and partly appears in the unspecified geographical category. It is the existence of this category which explains why the sum of the export share of developed and developing countries in Table 3.5 is less than 100 percent.

Table 3.6 shows the geographical composition of Korea's imports. In this case, the US share shows a continuing decline, from 51.0

Table 3.6 Geographical composition of imports: Korea (percent of total imports)

	1963	1973	1981	1988
Developed Countries	90.1	81.3	62.5	75.4
United States	51.0	28.4	23.1	24.8
Western Europe	7.3	7.7	9.1	13.6
Japan	29.2	40.8	24.4	30.8
Canada, Australia, New Zealand	2.6	4.4	5.8	6.2
Developing Countries	9.7	18.7	33.5	18.8
Pacific countries (other than China)	7.5	10.2	8.4	8.6
East Asian NICs	4.3	2.2	2.8	3.5
Hong Kong	1.1	0.7	0.8	1.1
Korea	–	–	–	–
Singapore	0.5	0.2	0.6	0.8
Taiwan	2.7	1.3	1.4	1.5
East Asian NECs	3.2	8.1	5.6	5.2
Indonesia	0.3	3.6	1.5	1.8
Malaysia	0.4	3.1	2.5	2.6
Philippines	2.2	0.9	1.0	0.4
Thailand	0.3	0.4	0.7	0.5
China	NA	NA	0.0	0.0
Other developing countries	2.2	8.4	25.1	10.2
Other Asia	1.7	0.8	0.7	1.3
Africa	0.1	0.5	0.5	0.5
Southern Europe	NA	0.6	0.3	0.2
Middle East	NA	6.2	20.9	5.4
Latin America	0.4	0.3	2.8	2.8
European Socialist Countries	NA	NA	0.0	0.0

Note: Taiwanese figures for 1981 and 1987 derived as difference between total imports, the regional aggregates, special categories, and other countries not included. Regional aggregates may not sum to 100 percent due to inclusion in denominator of special categories and other countries not specified.

Sources: IMF, *Direction of Trade Statistics*, various issues.

percent in 1963 to 24.8 percent in 1988. This contrasts with the rise in the share of Western Europe: from 7.3 percent in 1963 to 13.6 percent in 1988. The share of imports from Japan in 1988 (30.8 percent) exceeded the 1963 share, although the peak figure of 40.8 percent in 1973 was not reached again.

The import share of the developing countries again showed a roller-coaster ride, with 9.7 percent in 1963, 18.7 percent in 1973,

Table 3.7 Commodity composition of exports: major product groups: Korea (percent of total exports)

		1963	1973	1981	1988
Fuels	(SITC 3)	3.0	1.1	0.7	1.5
Nonfuel primary products		51.8	14.7	8.7	6.1
Food and live animals	(SITC 0)	19.0	7.6	6.2	4.3
Beverages and tobacco	(SITC 1)	0.3	0.7	0.6	0.2
Industrial materials	(SITC 2+4+68)	32.5	6.3	1.9	1.6
Manufactures	(SITC 5+6+7+8–68)	45.1	84.0	90.0	92.4
Other	(SITC 9)	0.2	0.2	0.5	0.0
Total		100.0	100.0	100.0	100.0
Manufactures (industrial classification)		45.0	84.0	90.0	92.3
Textile, apparel, leather	(ISIC 32)	14.5	39.9	35.8	31.9
Wood product and furniture	(ISIC 33)	7.5	10.0	2.3	0.8
Paper and paper products	(ISIC 34)	0.3	1.5	0.8	1.2
Chemicals	(ISIC 35)	2.4	4.7	6.8	6.8
Nonmetallic mineral products	(ISIC 36)	0.8	1.4	2.8	1.4
Iron and steel	(ISIC 37)	13.5	6.1	9.3	5.1
Engineering products	(ISIC 38)	5.2	15.7	29.3	42.1
Other industries	(ISIC 39)	0.8	4.5	2.9	3.1

Source: UN, COMTRADE data base.

33.5 percent in 1981, and 18.8 percent in 1988. Much of this change occurred in the group of other developing countries, reflecting in part changes in oil prices and in part efforts made in Korea to economize with oil.

In turn, the share of imports from the East Asian NICs was about 4 percent in both 1963 and 1987, with lower figures in between. Finally, the share of imports from the East Asian NECs declined from the peak reached in 1973 as the price of raw materials fell.

The commodity composition of Korea's exports underwent considerable changes over time, with the share of nonfuel primary products declining from 51.8 percent in 1963 to 6.1 percent in 1988, and that of manufactured goods rising from 45.1 percent to 92.4 percent (see Table 3.7). The share of Korea's fuel exports (coal in earlier years and petroleum products in later years) fell from 3.0 to 1.5 percent during this period.

In 1963, crude minerals (mainly tungsten ores and concentrates) and fish and fish preparations (including seaweed) dominated Korea's primary exports, followed by animals and animal products, the other agricultural products category, and natural fibers. By 1987, only fish and fish preparations had any importance.

Significantly, 1963 was the year before the Korean policy reforms that led to the rapid expansion of manufactured exports. Apart from textiles, apparel and leather products, iron and steel was an important item at the time, owing to the excess of domestic supplies. Within the textiles, apparel and leather products category, yarn and fabrics were of importance.

Textiles, apparel and leather products came to account for 39.9 percent of Korean exports in 1973, followed by engineering products (15.7 percent) and wood products and furniture (10.0 percent). At the same time, clothing surpassed textiles while other textile products assumed importance. In turn, plywood and veneer, produced from logs imported mostly from Indonesia and the Philippines, became one of Korea's major exports; radios and television sets came to dominate the exports of engineering products.

The importance of the exports of textiles, apparel and leather products declined in subsequent years. This product category supplied 31.9 percent of exports in 1988, and it was surpassed by engineering products (42.1 percent). In the same year, chemicals accounted for 6.8 percent of exports and iron and steel for 5.1 percent.

Except for rising footwear exports, little change has occurred in the composition of the textiles, apparel and leather products category in recent years. In turn, radios and television sets came to account for 16.3 percent of total exports, followed by motor vehicles (7.5 percent) and other machinery (3.7 percent). The latter two items are of particular interest, indicating the diversification of Korean exports.

Within the chemicals category, relatively simple commodities, such as plastic products (1.6 percent) and rubber products (1.6 percent), provided 40 percent of the total in 1987, followed by a variety of miscellaneous chemicals. In turn, exports of iron and steel depend in part on domestic capacity coming on stream and in part on formal or informal restrictions imposed on Korean steel by foreign countries. Finally, with rising wages, the profitability of plywood and veneer declined greatly in Korea.

On the import side, the share of manufactured goods rose from 50.6 percent in 1963 to 64.7 percent in 1988 (see Table 3.8), while that of nonfuel primary products fell from 43.1 percent to 20.8 percent. The increase in the share of fuels (from 6.1 percent in 1963 to 14.3 percent in 1988) is largely explained by the rise in petroleum prices.

Table 3.8 Commodity composition of imports: major product groups: Korea (percent of total imports)

		1963	1973	1981	1988
Fuels	(SITC 3)	6.1	7.4	29.8	14.3
Nonfuel primary products		43.1	37.0	26.8	20.8
Food and live animals	(SITC 0)	21.5	13.4	10.5	6.2
Beverages and tobacco	(SITC 1)	0.1	0.1	0.3	0.0
Industrial materials	(SITC 2+4+68)	21.5	23.4	16.1	14.6
Manufactures	(SITC 5+6+7+8−68)	50.6	55.6	43.3	64.7
Other	(SITC 9)	0.2	0.0	0.1	0.2
Total		100.0	100.0	100.0	100.0
Manufactures (industrial classification)		50.3	55.2	42.6	64.7
Textile, apparel, leather	(ISIC 32)	5.3	7.7	3.1	5.3
Wood product and furniture	(ISIC 33)	0.0	0.1	0.1	0.4
Paper and paper products	(ISIC 34)	0.6	0.5	0.4	2.0
Chemicals	(ISIC 35)	14.6	8.6	8.5	12.5
Nonmetallic mineral products	(ISIC 36)	1.3	0.5	0.6	1.1
Iron and steel	(ISIC 37)	5.9	7.5	4.1	4.6
Engineering products	(ISIC 38)	22.3	29.8	25.3	38.4
Other industries	(ISIC 39)	0.1	0.6	0.5	0.5

Source: UN, COMTRADE data base.

Within manufacturing the increase was concentrated in engineering products, whose import shares rose from 22.3 percent in 1963 to 38.4 percent in 1988. This increase reflected in part the rise of domestic investment in Korea's GDP and in part the importance of imported inputs for Korea's own exports of engineering products.

In turn, the decline in the share of imports in nonfuel primary products occurred largely in food and live animals, whose share in total imports fell from 21.5 percent in 1963 to 6.2 percent in 1988. These changes indicate the combined effects of the low income elasticity of demand for food, the rise in Korean food production, and the fall in food prices.

PROSPECTS FOR THE FUTURE

Economic growth rates averaged 8.7 percent in Korea during the 1963–87 period, with an 8.9 percent growth rate experienced in 1981–7. Somewhat slower growth can be expected over the

1987–2000 period; we project a GDP growth rate of 8.0 percent.

There would be hardly any slowdown in per caput terms, however, as population is expected to increase 1.2 percent a year in 1987–2000, compared with 1.8 percent in 1963–87. The resulting per caput rates are 6.7 percent in 1963–87 and 6.6 percent in 1987–2000.

Continued rapid economic growth in Korea would necessitate the application of appropriate policies. Exchange rate policy should first be mentioned. The depreciation of the Korean won between 1985 and 1987 was largely offset by an appreciation in the following two years. But, in view of Korea's continued current account surplus, some further appreciation would be desirable.

One may welcome Korea's intention to reduce average tariffs to 7.9 percent by 1993. In that year, tariffs on manufactured goods would average 6.2 percent, which is comparable to tariff averages in the United States (6.1 percent) and the EC (6.7 percent).

It would also be desirable to complete the process of import liberalization. Korea should eliminate all import restrictions, except in cases when health and security considerations favor such restrictions. Lowering import protection would permit Korea to forgo the use of export incentives which are employed to minimize the anti-export bias of the incentive system. This, then, would represent a further step towards a free trade situation.

Korea also needs to liberalize its financial system. This would involve greater interest rate flexibility, the elimination of directed credits and the increased presence of foreign banks. Also, capital markets should be promoted by easing existing restrictions and providing more flexibility for pension funds and insurance companies to buy equities.

Finally, Korea needs to invest in the physical and social infrastructure to raise living standards and to reduce regional inequalities. Mortgages and consumer credit should also be liberalized to provide for investment in housing and the purchase of consumer durables.

Bibliography

Aikman, David, 1986. 'Korea: No Calm in the Morning', Chapter 2 in David Aikman, *Pacific Rim: Area of Change, Area of Opportunity*. Boston: Little, Brown.

Amsden, Alice H., 1988. 'Growth and Stabilization in Korea, 1962–1984', in Lance Taylor (ed.), *Stabilization in Developing Countries: A Structuralist Approach*. Oxford: Clarendon Press.

Balassa, Bela, 1975. 'Korea's Development Strategy for the Fourth Five-Year Plan Period (1977–81)', an Advisory Report prepared for the Government of Korea. Published as Essay 8 in Bela Balassa, *Policy Reform in Developing Countries*, pp. 139–64. Oxford: Pergamon Press, 1977.

Balassa, Bela, 1985. 'The Role of Foreign Trade in the Economic Development of Korea', in Walter Galenson (ed.), *Foreign Trade and Investment: Economic Growth in the Newly Industrializing Asian Countries*. Madison, WI: University of Wisconsin Press.

Brown, Gilbert T., 1973. *Korean Pricing Policies and Economic Development in the 1960s*. Baltimore, MD: The Johns Hopkins University Press.

Casse, Thorkil, 1985. *The Non-Conventional Approach to Stability: The Case of South Korea. An Analysis of Macro-Economic Policy, 1978–84*. Copenhagen: Centre for Development Research, 1985.

Cheng, Tun-jen, 1987. 'Sequencing and Implementing Development Strategies: Korea and Taiwan', in Gary Gereffi and Don Wyman (eds), *Pathways of Development in Latin America: A Comparative and Historical Inquiry* (Forthcoming).

Cho, Yoon Je, 1986. 'The Effects of Financial Liberalization on the Development of the Financial Market and the Allocation of Credit to Corporate Sectors: The Korean Case'. Discussion Paper, Report No. DRD166, Development Research Department, Economics and Research Staff, World Bank.

Chung, Joseph S., 1986. 'Korea', in Frances W. Rushing and Carol Ganz Brown (eds), *National Policies for Developing High Technology Industries: International Comparisons*. Boulder, CO: Westview Press.

Chung, Joseph S., 1988. 'The Politics of Industrialization in Korea and Taiwan', in Helen Hughes (ed.), *Explaining the Success of East Asia's Industrialization*.

Cole, David C. and Princeton N. Lyman, 1971. *Korean Development: The Interplay of Politics and Economics*. Cambridge, MA: Harvard University Press.

Dee, Philippa S., 1986. *Financial Markets and Economic Development: The Economics and Politics of Korean Financial Reform*. Tubingen: J. C. B. Mohr.

Dornbusch, Rudiger and Yung Chul Park, 1987. 'Korean Growth Policy', *Brookings Papers on Economic Activity*, 2.

Frank, Charles R., Jr, Kwang Suk Kim and Larry Westphal, 1975. *Foreign*

Trade Regimes and Economic Development: South Korea. New York: National Bureau of Economic Research.

Haggard, Stephen and Tun-jen Cheng, 1987. 'Korea', Chapter II in Stephen Haggard and Tun-jen Cheng, *Newly Industrializing Asia in Transition: Policy Reform and American Response.* Policy Papers in International Affairs, number 17. Berkeley CA: University of California.

Hamilton, Carl, 1986. 'An Assessment of Voluntary Restraints on Hong Kong Exports to Europe and the USA', *Economica*, vol. 53, no. 211.

Hamilton, Clive, 1986. 'A General Equilibrium Model of Structural Change and Economic Growth, with Application to South Korea', *Journal of Development Economics*, vol. 23, no. 1.

Hasan, Parvez, 1976. *Korea: Problems and Issues in a Rapidly Growing Economy.* A World Bank Country Economic Report. Baltimore, MD: The Johns Hopkins University Press.

Hasan, Parvez and D. C. Rao, 1979. *Korea: Policy Issues for Long-Term Development.* A World Bank Country Economic Report. Baltimore, MD: The Johns Hopkins University Press.

Hong, Wontack, 1979. *Trade, Employment, and Employment Growth in Korea.* Seoul, Korea: Korea Development Institute.

Hong, Wontack, 1981. 'Trade, Growth and Income Distribution: The Korean Experience', in Wontack Hong and Lawrence B. Krause (eds), *Trade and Growth of the Advanced Developing Countries in the Pacific Basin.* Seoul, Korea: Korea Development Institute.

Hong, Wontack, 1986. 'Financing Export-Oriented Growth on Korea', in Augustine H. H. Tan and Basant Kapur (eds), *Pacific Growth and Financial Interdependence.* North Sydney, Australia: Allen & Unwin Australia Pty.

Hong, Wontack, and Lawrence B. Krause (eds), 1981. *Trade and Growth of the Advanced Developing Countries in the Pacific Basin.* Seoul, Korea: Korea Development Institute.

Hong, Wontack, and Anne O. Krueger (eds), 1975. *Trade and Development in Korea.* Seoul, Korea: Korea Development Institute.

Jones, Leroy P., 1975. *Public Enterprise and Economic Development: The Korean Case.* Seoul, Korea: Korea Development Institute.

Jung, Woo S. and Gyu Lee, 1986. 'The Effectiveness of Export Promotion Policies: The Case of Korea', *Weltwirtschaftliches Archiv* (*Review of World Economics*), vol. 122, no. 2.

Kihwan, Kim, 1985. *The Korean Economy: Past Performance, Current Reforms, and Future Prospects*. Seoul, Korea: Korea Development Institute.

Kim, Chuk Kyo (ed.), 1977. *Planning Model and Macroeconomic Policy Issues. Essays on the Korean Economy*, vol. I. Seoul, Korea: Korea Development Institute.

Kim, Kwang Suk and Park Joon-kyung, 1985. *Sources of Economic Growth in Korea: 1963–1982*. Seoul, Korea: Korea Development Institute.

Kim, Kwang Suk and Michael Roemer, 1979. *Growth and Structural Transformation. Studies in the Modernization of the Republic of Korea: 1945–1975*. Cambridge, MA: Harvard University Press.

Kim, Kyong-Dong, 1988. 'The Distinctive Features of South Korea's Development', in Peter L. Berger and Hsin-Huang Michael Hsiao (eds), *In Search of an East Asian Development Model*. New Brunswick, NJ: Transaction Books.

Kohsaka, A., 1987. 'Financial Liberalization in Asian NICs: A Comparative Study of Korea and Taiwan in the 1980s', *The Developing Economies*, vol. XXV, no. 4.

Koo, Bohn Young, 1985. 'The Role of Direct Foreign Investment in Korea's Recent Economic Growth', in Walter Galenson (ed.), *Foreign Trade and Investment: Economic Growth in the Newly Industrializing Asian Countries*. Madison, WI: University of Wisconsin Press.

Korea Development Institute, 1975. *Discussion Paper on the Development Strategy for the Fourth Five-Year Plan 1977–81*. Seoul, Korea.

Korea Economic Planning Board, 1975. *Economic Guidelines for the Fourth Five-Year Plan*. Seoul, Korea.

Korea Economic Planning Board, 1981. *Preliminary Outline of the Fifth Five-Year Economic and Social Development Plan of the Republic of Korea*. Seoul, Korea.

'Korea: Transition to Maturity', 1988. *World Development*, Special Issue (January).

Korea, Government of the Republic of, 1986. *The Sixth Five-Year Economic and Social Development Plan: 1987–1991*. Seoul, Korea.

Krueger, Anne O., 1979. *The Developmental Role of the Foreign Sector and Aid. Studies in the Modernization of the Republic of Korea: 1945–1975*. Cambridge, MA: Harvard University Press.

Kuznets, Paul W., 1977. *Economic Growth and Structure in the Republic of Korea*. New Haven, CT: Yale University Press.

Kwack, Sung Y., 1987. 'External Influences on the Korean Economy and Their Policy Implications', in M. Dutta (ed.), *Asia–Pacific Economies: Promises and Challenges*. Greenwich, CT: JAI Press.

Kwon, Jene K., 1986. 'Capital Utilization, Economies of Scale and Technical Change in the Growth of Total Factor Productivity: An Explanation of South Korean Manufacturing Growth', *Journal of Development Economics*, vol. 24, no. 1.

Lau, Lawrence J. and Lawrence R. Klein (eds), 1986. *Models of Development: A Comparative Study of Economic Growth in South Korea and Taiwan*. San Francisco, CA: Institute for Contemporary Studies.

Lee, Eddy (ed.), 1981. *Export-Led Industrialization and Development*. Geneva: International Labor Office.

Leipziger, D. M. et al., 1987. *Korea. Managing the Industrial Transition*. A World Bank Country Study. Washington, DC: World Bank.

Lim, Youngil, 1981. *Government Policy and Private Enterprise: Korean Experience with Industrialization*. Berkeley, CA: Institute on East Asian Studies, University of California.

Mason, Edward S., Mahn je Kim et al., 1980. *The Economic and Social Modernization of the Republic of Korea. Studies in the Modernization of the Republic of Korea: 1945–1975*. Cambridge, MA: Harvard University Press.

Nam, Chong Hyun, 1981. 'Trade, Industrial Policies, and the Structure of Protection in Korea', in Wontack Hong and Lawrence B. Krause (eds), *Trade and Growth of the Advanced Developing Countries in the Pacific Basin*. Seoul, Korea: Korea Development Institute.

Park, Yung Chul, 1981. 'Export Growth and the Balance of Payments in Korea, 1960–78', in Wontack Hong and Lawrence B. Krause (eds), *Trade and Growth of the Advanced Developing Countries in the Pacific Basin*. Seoul, Korea: Korea Development Institute.

Park, Yung Chul, 1981. 'Export-Led Development: The Korean Experience, 1960–78', in Eddy Lee (ed.), *Export-Led Industrialization and Development*. Geneva: International Labor Office.

Park, Yung Chul, 1985. 'Foreign Debt, Balance of Payments, and Growth Prospects: The Case of Korea, 1965–1988'. Studies on International Monetary and Financial Issues for the Developing Countries. Report to the Group of Twenty-four.

Seabury, Paul, 1981. 'South Korea and Taiwan: Prospering but Threatened', Chapter 7 in Paul Seabury, *America's Stake in the Pacific*. Washington, DC: Ethics and Public Policy Center.

Smith, Michael, Jane McLoughlin, Peter Large and Rod Chapman, 1985. *Asia's New Industrial World*. New York: Methuen.

Verbruggen, Harmen, 1985. 'The Case of Korea', in Harmen Verbruggen *Gains from Export-Oriented Industrialization in Developing Countries with Special Reference to South-East Asia*. Amsterdam, Netherlands: Free University Press.

Virmani, Arvind, 1985. 'Government Policy and the Development of Financial Markets: The Case of Korea'. World Bank Staff Working Papers, no. 747. Washington, DC: World Bank.

Westphal, Larry E. and Kwang Suk Rin, 1982. 'Korea', Chapter 8 in Bela Balassa (ed.), *Development Strategies in Semi-Industrial Economies*. Baltimore, MD: The Johns Hopkins University Press.

World Bank, 1987. *Korea: Managing the Industrial Transition*, volumes I–II. Washington, DC: World Bank.

Woronoff, Jon, 1986. 'Korea, Man-Made Miracle', Chapter 3 in Jon Woronoff, *Asia's Miracle Economies*. New York: M. E. Sharpe.

Young, Soogil, 1985. 'A Global Perspective of the Korean Economy'. Working Paper 8506. Seoul, Korea: Korea Development Institute.

Yusuf, Shahid and R. Kyle Peters, 1985. 'Capital Accumulation and Economic Growth: The Korean Paradigm'. World Bank Staff Working Papers, no. 712. Washington, DC: World Bank.

4 Singapore

INTRODUCTION

In an area of 618 square kilometers Singapore has a population of 2.6 million. Seventy-six percent of the population is Chinese, 15 percent Malay and 7 percent comes from the Indian subcontinent while the rest is mostly of European origin.

Formerly a crown colony of Britain, Singapore became independent in 1959. In 1963, it joined the Federation of Malaysia but its participation lasted for only two years. Conflicts in a variety of areas contributed to the separation of Singapore from the Federation, pitting the Chinese against the Malays, the city against rural areas, and the bourgeoisie against feudal society. Also, Singapore had much higher per caput incomes and it competed with Malaysia for foreign capital.

Important changes in Singapore's economic structure occurred from 1959 onward. Before independence the economy was dominated by entrepôt trade and by the servicing of British military installations, which accounted for 17 percent of GDP. By contrast, the share of manufacturing was 9 percent.

In South-east Asia, entrepôt trade was carried out mostly with Indonesia and Malaysia, both of which aimed at increasing reliance on direct trading. In turn, Britain began withdrawing its military bases and personnel around 1960 and accelerated the withdrawal in 1968.

These changes necessitated expansion in other sectors of the economy. Manufacturing was given the pride of place, followed by international banking. Within two decades, the share of manufacturing in GDP reached 29 percent. Similar increases occurred in the financial sector.

Initially, Singapore followed many other developing countries in promoting import substitution behind protection. This phase soon came to an end, however, as it was understood that the small size of the domestic market could not lead to high living standards under protection. Thus the choice was made for exports, leading to a spectacular expansion of the exports of manufactured products.

In contradistinction to the other East Asian NICs, foreign direct investment played a very important role in Singapore's industrial development. Rather than limiting foreign direct investment, the government of Singapore encouraged it by financial incentives. At the same time, domestic capital continued to concentrate largely on trading activities, followed by finance. As a result, 71 percent of manufacturing output in Singapore is currently produced in fully- or majority-owned foreign enterprises.

The expansion of manufacturing industry and international finance contributed to rapid economic expansion in Singapore. By 1987, Singapore surpassed Spain and New Zealand in terms of per caput incomes.

GOVERNMENT POLICIES

Singapore was established in 1819 by Sir Thomas Stamford Raffles as a trading and military post. It developed into an important center of entrepôt trade, importing minerals and lumber and, later, rubber and palm oil from Malaysia and Indonesia for re-export (following grading, processing and repackaging) to Europe and the United States. In turn, it imported manufactured goods from the industrial countries for re-export to Malaya and Indonesia. Also, banking, insurance, shipping and communications developed in Singapore to service its entrepôt trade.

Until the Second World War, Singapore's economic destiny depended largely on entrepôt trade. In times of decline, some of the Chinese population returned to China and Indians to India. After the war, however, return to China became impossible. At the same time, Singapore's population increased at a rapid rate, due in part to a high birth rate and in part to migration, mostly from Malaya.

As entrepôt trade and the related service sectors did not provide sufficient employment opportunities, unemployment rose to a considerable extent. By 1958, 13.5 percent of the working age population was unemployed.

With Malaya and Indonesia attempting to increase direct trading, increases in employment in entrepôt trade did not appear promising for the future. Correspondingly, new avenues of economic expansion had to be found to provide employment and to ensure increases in living standards.

The solution chosen was industrialization. This meant transforming Singapore's small manufacturing sector which had provided employment for only 29 000 people in 1959. Manufacturing had been concentrated in the processing of primary commodities for export and the production of food, beverages, clothing and some other consumer goods for the small domestic market.

Industrialization was the central issue in the 1959 electoral manifesto of the People's Action Party (PAP), which has held power ever since. The manifesto listed four advantages and four weaknesses for industrialization in Singapore. The advantages were said to be hardworking, resourceful and enterprising people; a favorable geographical position and good sea communications; a large amount of capital accumulated by local enterprise and public authorities; and markets available in the region. The weaknesses were listed as free-port status, which was considered to be disadvantageous to industrialization; lack of free access to the market of Malaya; relatively small numbers of managers, technicians and skilled workers; and the predilection of entrepreneurs for trading rather than for manufacturing.

To bring about industrialization, the manifesto emphasized the desirability of establishing a common market with Malaya, upgrading the technological level of industry, encouraging foreign business, and protecting selected industries by tariffs and quotas. Upon coming to power, the PAP-dominated parliament enacted the Pioneer Industries Ordinance, the Industrial Expansion Ordinance and the Control of Manufacturing Ordinance, followed by the establishment of the Economic Development Board (EDB) to promote industrial development.

The Pioneer Industries Ordinance of 1959 was intended to promote the creation of new enterprises that were given relief from the prevailing 40 percent profits tax for a period of five years. Losses and depreciation allowances during the exemption period could be carried over and be set against profits in subsequent years.

The Industrial Expansion Ordinance of 1959 granted tax relief to existing enterprises that were increasing the production of approved products. Tax relief was provided for a period of five years on a sliding scale, depending on the amount of new capital invested. It ranged from 11 to 15 percent of profits.

The Control of Manufacturing Ordinance of 1959 tried to prevent excessive competition in domestic markets. This was to be done by limiting the number of firms that manufactured certain products designated by the Ministry of Finance.

In 1961, the government established the EDB. The EDB provided factory sites to investors for rental or purchase within industrial estates established for this purpose, of which Jurong Industrial Estates was the largest. EDB also extended medium- and long-term loans as well as equity financing to industrial enterprises, gave technical assistance to industry, and set up industrial training schemes.

Technical assistance included feasibility and market studies, industrial research, the setting of standards and some help with product development and industrial design. EDB also provided technical and managerial training, established training schemes in collaboration with industry, created vocational training schools and founded the Singapore Polytechnical Institute.

At the same time, government departments were instructed to buy from domestic producers whenever their prices did not exceed the prices of comparable imports by more than 10 percent. Protective tariffs were introduced for soap, detergents and paints, and quotas were imposed on the imports of flashlights, radio batteries, monosodium glutamate and wheat flour.

Protection was increased to a considerable extent during the years Singapore participated in the Federation of Malaysia. While protective tariffs were not imposed, 230 commodities were subjected to import quotas. This reflected the intention of orienting sales towards the Malaysian market while protecting domestic industries.

The ending of the 'Malaysian dream' was followed by a retrenchment behind Singapore's borders and the pursuit of a policy of import substitution within the confines of the local market. It also meant increasingly replacing import quotas by tariffs. In August 1953, the number of products subject to import licensing was reduced from 230 to 88. At the same time, protective duties were imposed on 183 commodities. The number of dutiable items increased to 198 in 1966 and to 229 in 1967. In turn, the number of products subject to import quotas was reduced to 72 in 1967.

It was soon understood that import substitution in Singapore's small domestic market held little promise. Correspondingly, the number of products subject to import quotas was reduced to 26 in 1968 and to three in 1973. In turn, after increases in 1968 and 1969, the number of items subject to tariffs was reduced again, reaching 91 in 1973.

Protection rates were never high in Singapore, however. Thus in 1967 the average rate of nominal protection (indicating the joint effects of tariff and quota protection) on domestic sales was 5 percent and the average rate of effective protection 9 percent. And, in the same year, export subsidies were introduced that provided incentives to export industries similar to those granted to import-substituting industries, on the average.

Export incentives were granted under the Economic Expansion Incentives Act of 1967 which reduced the company tax rates on profits earned from exports by approved manufacturing enterprises from 40 percent to 4 percent for a period of 15 years. The same act lowered the tax on royalties, licenses, technical assistance fees, and contributions to R & D costs payable to overseas enterprises to 20 percent.

Exporters were also given easier access to duty-free imports. Furthermore, tax allowances were provided for the development of markets abroad. Approved enterprises were allowed to make double deductions from taxable income for marketing expenditures aimed at increasing exports.

The resulting export expansion contributed to rapid increases in employment. As a result, by 1973 the unemployment rate declined to 4.5 percent, representing largely frictional unemployment. With the easing of unemployment, the policy changed from the attraction of labor-intensive industries to that of high-technology industries. Also, the educational system was reformed and technical training schemes were instituted.

The Technical Education Department was established in 1968. Subsequently, education curricula and structures were revised to increase emphasis on technical education in high schools. In addition, courses were established at the university to train an increasing number of students in engineering, accounting and business administration.

In 1972, the government established three training schemes. Under the Joint Industry–Government Training Scheme, the government contributes 50 percent to the cost of training provided by multinational corporations and local firms; under the Overseas Training Scheme, firms are supported in sending trainees to industrial countries; under the Industrial Training Grant Scheme, firms with approved in-house training facilities are given subsidies.

Additional measures were taken to promote exports. In October 1974, the government provided for the financing of export bills at 0.25 percent below the prime interest rate and for the financing of the purchase of capital equipment designed to increase exports. In November 1975, the Export Credit Insurance Corporation was established, with 50 percent government participation, to insure exports against defaults on commercial or political grounds.

In August 1975, an Amendment to the Economic Expansion Incentives Act was introduced to support the expansion of high-technology industries. On introducing this amendment, Hon Sui Sen, the Minister of Finance, noted:

> Industries such as machine tools, diesel engines, precision instruments, aircraft components, specialized electrical equipment and industrial machinery involve much heavier capital investment and require more sophisticated manufacturing skills which are only acquired after long periods of training. Such industries have long gestation periods and take a much longer time to become profitable. (*Parliamentary Debates*, 1975, vol. 34, pp. 1228–9)

Correspondingly, the period of pioneer status was extended from five to ten years.

In 1978 the government launched a program, termed a 'Second Industrial Revolution', to increase the relative importance of high-technology industries. This purpose was to be served by the expansion of educational and training facilities, by incentives for investment in R & D, and by the policy of raising wages.

The National University of Singapore rapidly increased its enrollment in engineering. The Nanyang Technology Institute opened in 1982 to train engineers for industry. Enrollment also increased rapidly in the Singapore Polytechnic, Ngee Ann Polytechnic and the Vocational Industrial Training Board, all of which train technicians and skilled workers for industry.

In addition to the formal post-secondary institutions, several practically-oriented training schemes were set up to impart general skills. EDB established four Joint Industry Training Centers, three of them operated jointly with multinational corporations, the fourth with the Japanese government. In cooperation with foreign countries, EDB also set up three institutes of technology, the German–Singapore Institute of Production Technology, the Japanese–Singapore Institute of Software Technology and the French–Singapore Institute of Electrotechnology, to provide specialized training in particular areas.

The government also set up schemes to upgrade industrial skills. In 1978, it established a Skills Development Fund through a 4 percent levy on the earnings of low-wage labor, with the funds raised used to provide grants to firms for upgrading the skills of their work force in the framework of training programs. Also, in 1982 the Basic Education for Skills Training program was established to improve the literacy, numeracy and English-language skills of workers with little formal schooling.

A list of priority industries was drawn up by EDB to favor projects which are technologically sophisticated in awarding pioneer status. The list includes computer, instrumentation and industrial controls, telecommunication equipment, advanced electronic components, solar cells, optical fibers, precision machine tools, photographic and optical instruments, medical instruments and devices, office equipment, industrial machinery, robotics, oilfield equipment, aircraft components, automotive components, ship machinery, mining equipment, specialty industrial chemicals, pharmaceuticals and engineering plastics.

Firms that do not qualify for pioneer status can obtain an investment allowance in the form of a tax credit up to 50 percent of new fixed investment in plant and machinery under the 1978 amendment to the Industrial Expansion Act. And the 1980 amendment provided incentives for R & D. Plant and machinery for R & D can be written off over three years and the purchase of computers in one year. Also, double deduction of R & D spending is permitted for tax purposes, and payments for manufacturing licenses can be capitalized and written off over three years.

The most radical policy introduced by the Singapore government to promote high-technology industries was the imposition of a high wage strategy. The assumption was that, if labor costs rose, manufacturers would be forced to move upstream from low value products. Labor costs, in fact, rose by an average of 10 percent a year in 1979 and 1980, and by 28 percent in 1981, including increases in wages and in compulsory contributions to government-managed funds.

This policy ignored the fact that Singapore's economy depended on a number of cost-sensitive industries and it did not have the high skill and technical labor rapidly to establish high-technology industries. Furthermore, while the other East Asian NICs were upgrading their economies they did not have to bear the burden of rapidly rising wages.

The result was that Singapore lost export market shares and experienced a considerable decline in economic growth rates. Eventually, the policy had to be reversed and labor costs reduced so as to re-establish Singapore's competitive position.

In July 1985 the National Wage Council, a tripartite body of the government, the employers and the trade unions, recommended wage increases between 3 and 7 percent, the lowest since 1972. The payroll tax (2 percent of the wage bill) was suspended and the skill development tax (4 percent of the wage bill) halved in the 1985 budget. Finally, the employers' contribution to the Central Provident Fund was reduced from 25 percent to 10 percent, effective from April 1, 1986.

The Central Provident Fund is an institution peculiar to Singapore. It was established with workers' and employers' contributions of 25 percent each of the wage bill. The workers received the accumulated amount upon retirement at age 55; they have also been able to make withdrawals for house purchases and, in recent years, medical costs.

The funds entrusted to the Central Provident Fund importantly added to the pool of savings in Singapore, thereby contributing to the high rate of investment. At the same time, labor costs were raised until the reduction of the employers' contribution led to a partial reversal.

Investment has also been promoted by public institutions. In 1968, the Development Bank of Singapore was established with a 49 percent government participation in order to finance industrial development. In the same year, the Jurong Town Corporation was formed to develop and manage industrial estates. In 1981, the Government of Singapore Investment Corporation was set up, drawing on the country's foreign exchange reserves, to upgrade the technological base of the economy.

There has also been considerable government investment in Singapore. In 1984, the public sector accounted for 33.4 percent of gross capital formation, far exceeding the 17.6 percent figure for Korea although falling behind the 42.7 percent ratio in Taiwan. In addition, Singapore has the peculiar characteristic of the public sector generating 69.0 percent of gross national savings, compared with 28.8 percent in Korea and 17.7 percent in Taiwan. (The data cited here originate in Lawrence B. Krause, 'The Government as Entrepreneur', in Lawrence B. Krause, Ai Tee Koh and Yuan (Tsao) Lee (eds), *The Singapore Economy Reconsidered*; Singapore: Institute of Southeast Asian Studies, 1987, pp. 107–27.)

Public savings originate in the government budget, the statutory boards and public enterprises. The number of public enterprises grew to a considerable extent over time, increasing from 180 in 1974 to 450 in 1983. These enterprises employ 5 percent of the labor force in Singapore.

Among statutory boards, the Housing and Development Board

manages four-fifths of dwelling units in Singapore; public utilities are handled by Public Utilities Board; and the Mass Rapid Transit Corporation provides local transportation facilities. Public enterprises also dominate air and sea transportation. Furthermore, manufacturing public enterprises employed 8.5 percent of the workers, produced 7.4 percent of output, provided 10.2 percent of value added and accounted for 5.1 percent of exports in 1986. Public enterprises receive no special privileges and are run along business lines. In recent years, plans have been made for the privatization of some of the enterprises.

Foreign direct investment has played a very important part in the industrial development of Singapore. Following the advice of a UN mission, the promotion of foreign direct investment was initially undertaken to increase employment. With unemployment of 46 000 in 1958 and expected increases in the working age population of 53 000 over a five-year period, the 1961–3 Development Plan concluded that eliminating unemployment necessitated attracting foreign direct investment.

A strong endorsement of foreign investment was made by the prime minister, Lee Kuan Yew, in a speech delivered at the 26th World Congress of the International Chamber of Commerce in Florida in October 1978:

> My ministers and economic advisors did not take long to convince me that the rate of development necessary if we were to generate jobs to mop up unemployment running at 10 percent of the workforce in 1960, could never be achieved at the pace at which Chinese and Indian Singaporean enterprise was slowly moving from traditional retail and entrepôt trade into the new manufacturing or servicing industries. They saw far greater potential in the expanding subsidiaries of American, European and Japanese corporations . . . We have never suffered from any inhibitions on borrowing capital, know-how, managers, engineers and marketing capabilities. Far from limiting the entry of foreign managers, engineers and bankers, we encouraged them to come . . . Had we tried to go into industry on our own, working from first principles, we would never have made it.

The major policy instrument designed to attract foreign direct investment has been tax incentives. Income tax concessions to encourage foreign investment were contained in the Pioneer Industries

Ordinance of 1963, with further extension in the Industrial Expansion Act of 1967 and its 1978 and 1980 amendments. The establishment of industrial estates and the provision of industrial finance further increased incentives to foreign direct investment.

Perhaps more importantly, there are no disincentives for foreign direct investment. There are no excluded sectors and no permission is needed to establish in Singapore. There are no requirements for joint ownership or for local content. Last but not least, there is free repatriation of profits, dividends and capital.

These policies have contributed to the increasing importance of foreign capital in Singapore's economy. According to official statistics, the share of resident foreign companies and resident foreigners in the GDP rose from 15.7 percent in 1966–73 to 23.6 percent in 1973–9 and to 28.1 percent in 1979–84.

Foreign investment is concentrated in manufacturing. The data of the Industrial Census show that in 1984 foreign companies, including wholly foreign-owned firms and firms with more than 50 percent foreign equity, produced 71 percent of output, provided 63 percent of value added and supplied 82 percent of manufacturing exports.

Foreign direct investment also extends to banking. In fact, according to data provided by the Monetary Authority of Singapore which acts as a central bank, the number of foreign commercial banks increased from 26 in 1970 to 108 in 1983, while the number of local commercial banks increased only from 11 to 13. In the same period, the number of representative offices of foreign banks rose from 8 to 59 and that of merchant banks, dominated by foreign banks, from 2 to 50.

Of the 108 foreign commercial banks, 24 are full license banks, 14 have a restricted license (which means they cannot set up local branches and accept deposits lower than 250 000 Singapore dollars), and 70 operate only in the offshore market. Merchant banks generally operate in the offshore market.

The offshore market increased rapidly in Singapore, surpassing that of Hong Kong. The expansion has been aided by governmental measures, including the abolition of exchange controls, the elimination of the withholding tax on interest earned, the concessionary 10 percent tax on loan interest and offshore income, the reduction of the *ad valorem* tax on offshore loan agreements from 0.5 percent to a flat rate of $500, and a five-year tax exemption on syndicated loans.

Initially, the Singapore government followed the policy of separating the domestic banking system from the offshore market. Singapore

Table 4.1 Economic performance indicators: Singapore

Growth rates	1963–73	1973–81	1981–7	1963–87
GDP	10.3	7.8	5.3	8.2
Population	2.0	1.4	1.1	1.6
GDP per caput	8.1	6.4	4.1	6.5
Investment	15.6	8.7	3.4	10.1
Manufacturing production	15.8	8.3	3.8	10.2
Agricultural production	4.3	0.8	−5.1	0.7
Exports	.	.	.	.
Imports	.	.	.	.

Source: World Bank.

residents were not allowed to deposit funds in the offshore market or to borrow from it to finance domestic operations. Gradually, however, the demarcation between the domestic banking system and the offshore markets has been reduced. Today, Singapore residents are permitted to deposit funds in the offshore market and can borrow from it.

The local stock market is relatively small. Growth of the stock market has been discouraged by large government stockholdings in major firms and by the practice of taxing brokers' profits. By contrast, the futures exchange, SIMEX, has been very successful. SIMEX recently launched the first oil futures contract trading in Asia and its trading volume exceeds that of the London futures exchange.

ECONOMIC GROWTH

The policies applied contributed to rapid economic growth in Singapore. Per caput incomes increased by a factor of 6.65 between 1963 and 1988, reaching $7623 a year (Table 1.1). As a result, Singapore surpassed Spain and New Zealand in terms of per caput incomes.

However, a slowdown occurred in economic growth over time. While the GDP grew at an average annual rate of 10.3 percent in 1963–73 and 7.8 percent in 1973–81, the growth rate was 5.3 percent in 1981–7 (see Table 4.1). In the latter period, the high-wage experiment contributed to the outcome, with GDP declining by 1.6 percent in 1985 and rising only by 1.8 percent in 1986. In turn, the rate of economic growth was 8.8 percent in 1987.

Economic growth was concentrated in the manufacturing and in

Table 4.2 Industrial composition and trade: Singapore (percent of GDP)

	1963	1973	1981	1987
Industrial composition				
Agriculture	3.0	2.1	1.2	0.5
Mining and quarrying	0.3	0.3	0.4	0.2
Manufacturing	12.6	23.7	28.5	28.6
Gas, electricity and water	2.0	2.1	1.6	2.3
Construction	4.9	7.1	7.4	6.7
Transportation	11.5	10.7	13.8	13.8
Wholesale and retail trade	32.3	25.9	19.9	17.6
Banking, real estate	14.5	17.3	22.5	28.7
Ownership of dwellings	.	.	.	.
Public administration	.	.	.	.
Other services	16.7	10.7	9.3	11.3
Imputed bank service charge, duty	2.0	0.1	−4.6	−9.7
Trade				
Exports of goods and nonfactor services	151.4	116.6	.	.
Imports of goods and nonfactor services	166.7	126.7	.	.

Source: World Bank.

the financial sector. The share of manufacturing in the GDP rose from 12.6 percent in 1963 to 23.7 percent in 1973, to 28.5 percent in 1981, and to 28.6 percent in 1987 (see Table 4.2).

The financial sector experienced continuous growth, with its GDP share rising from 14.5 percent in 1963 to 17.3 percent in 1973, to 22.5 percent in 1981 and to 28.7 percent in 1987. These figures indicate the rising importance of the financial sector in Singapore.

Increases were also experienced in the GDP shares of construction and transportation. In turn, the largest decline occurred in the shares of wholesale and retail trade, reflecting in great part the decreasing importance of entrepôt trade. The relevant figures are: 1963, 32.3 percent; 1973, 25.9 percent; 1981, 19.9 percent; and 1987, 17.6 percent. The share of the other services category, including housing and public administration, declined also.

Singapore experienced a high rate of investment throughout the period. In the years 1973–81, the share of domestic investment in the GDP fluctuated between a starting-point of 38.7 percent and the final figure of 46.7 percent. Its share increased towards the end of this subperiod and rose further afterwards, reaching a peak of 48.3

Table 4.3 Savings and investment ratios: Singapore (percent of GDP)

	1973	1974	1975	1976	1977	1978	1979	1980
Private savings	28.8	27.5	28.4	31.8	31.8	32.5	33.7	35.9
Government budget balance	−0.1	1.6	0.9	0.2	1.0	0.8	2.3	2.1
Domestic savings	28.7	29.0	29.3	32.0	32.9	33.3	36.0	38.0
Foreign savings	10.0	16.2	10.5	8.0	2.6	4.9	7.0	8.9
Domestic investment	38.7	45.2	39.8	40.1	35.4	38.3	42.9	46.9

	1981	1982	1983	1984	1985	1986	1987
Private savings	40.4	39.6	43.8	41.4	38.2	.	.
Government budget balance	0.7	3.4	1.8	4.1	2.1	.	.
Domestic savings	41.1	43.0	45.6	45.5	40.3	38.8	40.1
Foreign savings	5.6	4.4	1.8	2.8	2.4	−0.5	−0.4
Domestic investment	46.7	47.3	47.4	48.3	42.8	38.3	39.7

Source: World Bank.

percent in 1984. It subsequently declined, however, to 39.7 percent in 1987 (see Table 4.3).

In earlier years, a substantial part of domestic investment was financed by foreign savings whose GDP share attained a peak of 16.2 percent in 1974. It declined in an uneven fashion afterwards, reaching −0.4 percent in 1987. Correspondingly, the share of domestic savings in GDP rose over time, although decreasing from the peak reached in 1983.

Time series data are not available for the entire public sector that generated a substantial part of domestic savings as noted above. The government budget balance shows a generally rising trend, although it too declined from the 1984 peak. The peak was reached in 1983 in the GDP share of private savings that is defined to include the public sector other than the government.

While there being no foreign savings represents an equilibrium in the current account balance, Singapore traditionally had a large deficit in merchandise trade and a large surplus in services. This surplus reflects the important role played by entrepôt trade and international banking in Singapore.

As discussed previously, Singapore experienced a large inflow of foreign direct investment throughout the period under consideration (see Table 4.4). The inflow reached a peak in 1981 and declined afterwards. The inflow of long-term and short-term capital has given

Table 4.4 Balance of payments: Singapore (million US$)

	1978	1979	1980	1981	1982	1983	1984	1985	1986	1987
Merchandise exports	9 587	13 400	18 200	19 662	19 435	20 429	22 662	21 533	21 336	27 277
Merchandise imports	-12 090	-16 450	-22 400	-25 785	-26 196	-26 252	-26 734	-24 362	-23 402	-29 817
Trade balance	-2 503	-3 050	-4 200	-6 123	-6 761	-5 823	-4 072	-2 829	-2 066	-2 540
Other goods, services, and income: credit	4 191	5 248	7 039	9 705	10 951	10 600	9 184	8 197	8 370	9 971
Other goods, services, and income: debit	-2 101	-2 899	-4 294	-4 898	-5 281	-5 173	-5 275	-5 159	-5 572	-6 692
Other goods, services, and income: net	2 090	2 349	2 745	4 807	5 670	5 427	3 909	3 038	2 798	3 279
Unrequited transfers	-39	-35	-107	-153	-205	-215	-223	-213	-191	-200
Current account balance	-452	-736	-1 562	-1 469	-1 296	-611	-386	-4	541	539
Direct investment	186	669	1 138	1 675	1 298	1 085	1 210	809	479	982
Long-term capital	112	148	325	36	536	-301	-436	209	-139	-260
Short-term capital	714	181	119	456	475	1 680	807	-319	-1 648	-397
Capital account balance	1 012	998	1 582	2 167	2 309	2 464	1 581	699	-1 308	325
Errors and omissions	104	254	643	212	165	-793	328	642	1 304	230
Overall balance	664	516	663	910	1 178	1 060	1 523	1 337	537	1 094
Net use of reserves	-1 445	-516	-748	-982	-931	-784	-1 152	-2 431	-92	-2 288

Note: The overall balance is the sum of the current and capital account balances and errors and omissions. Net use of reserves was derived by adding the following items to overall balance: counterpart to the monetization and demonetization of gold, counterpart to SDR allocation, and counterpart to valuation changes.

Source: IMF, *International Financial Statistics*, various issues.

place to an outflow in recent years. This is in part offset by the positive errors and omissions figure that likely reflects an inflow of foreign capital.

INTERNATIONAL TRADE

Singapore does not report trade with Indonesia. Excluding trade with Indonesia, exports to developing countries nearly matched exports to developed countries in 1988 (see Table 4.5). The former were more important than the latter in 1963 and 1981 and slightly less important in 1973.

Among the developed countries, in earlier years Western Europe – in particular the United Kingdom – was Singapore's most important trading partner. Its share declined to a considerable extent, however, from the peak of 18.5 percent reached in 1973. It was 11.2 percent in 1981 and 14.2 percent in 1988.

By contrast, the export share of the United States increased from 6.7 percent in 1963 to 23.8 percent in 1988. Japan's share increased also, from 3.9 percent to 8.6 percent during this period, although declining from the peak of 10.1 percent reached in 1981. Finally, the combined share of Canada, Australia and New Zealand fluctuated between 4 and 6 percent during the period under consideration.

In 1963, Malaysia was by far the most important market for Singapore, with a share of 35.3 percent. This share decreased over time as the importance of entrepôt trade declined; it was 13.6 percent in 1988. In turn, the export shares of the Philippines and Thailand rose, although remaining relatively small in absolute terms. Similar considerations apply to China. Other Asian countries, especially those on the Indian subcontinent, are also important markets for Singapore, with their share varying between 6 and 11 percent. In turn, the share of the Middle East rose to a considerable extent between 1973 and 1981 but declined afterwards.

Among the East Asian NICs, Hong Kong is by far the most important market, followed by Taiwan and Korea. Apart from the partial reversal in Hong Kong after 1981, the shares of all three countries increased over time.

Japan has a much larger share of Singapore's imports than of its exports. (see Table 4.6). It surpassed the United States and Western Europe in 1973 and reached 22 percent in 1988. In turn, the shares of the United States and Western Europe are below 16 percent.

Table 4.5 Geographical composition of exports: Singapore (percent of total exports)

	1963	1973	1981	1988
Developed Countries	31.4	49.1	40.7	50.6
United States	6.7	17.0	13.2	23.8
Western Europe	16.3	18.5	11.2	14.2
Japan	3.9	8.0	10.1	8.6
Canada, Australia, New Zealand	4.5	5.5	6.2	4.0
Developing Countries	62.1	47.6	57.8	48.7
Pacific countries (other than China)	49.0	28.6	32.6	31.4
East Asian NICs	3.1	7.4	11.5	11.0
Hong Kong	2.6	5.5	8.8	6.2
Korea	0.2	0.9	1.4	2.0
Singapore	–	–	–	–
Taiwan	0.2	1.1	1.4	2.8
East Asian NECs	45.9	21.2	21.1	20.3
Indonesia	7.5	NA	NA	NA
Malaysia	35.3	18.1	15.6	13.6
Philippines	0.4	0.9	1.3	1.3
Thailand	2.8	2.2	4.2	5.5
China	0.5	1.4	0.9	3.0
Other developing countries	12.7	17.5	24.3	14.3
Other Asia	6.1	7.9	10.3	7.2
Africa	2.0	3.4	4.0	2.0
Southern Europe	0.7	1.6	0.7	0.8
Middle East	1.9	2.4	6.8	2.8
Latin America	2.1	2.1	2.5	1.5
European Socialist Countries	6.6	3.3	1.5	0.7

Note: Taiwanese figures for 1981 and 1987 derived as difference between total exports, the regional aggregates, special categories, and other countries not included. Regional aggregates may not sum to 100 percent due to inclusion in denominator of special categories, and other countries not specified.

Sources: IMF, *Direction of Trade Statistics*, various issues.

With 20.6 percent, Malaysia was again the most important source of Singapore's imports in 1963; its share was 14.7 percent in 1988. It was followed by Thailand (2.7 percent) and the Philippines (0.6 percent) among the East Asian NECs. In 1988, China accounted for 3.8 percent of Singapore's imports.

The increased importance of the Middle East as a source of Singapore's imports after the 1973 reflected the rise in petroleum prices. In turn, the fall in these prices cut the share of the Middle East

Table 4.6 Geographical composition of imports: Singapore (percent of total imports)

	1963	1973	1981	1988
Developed Countries	38.1	54.2	46.2	54.4
United States	5.3	15.1	12.6	15.6
Western Europe	19.0	16.5	11.8	14.0
Japan	9.5	18.3	18.8	22.0
Canada, Australia, New Zealand	4.3	4.3	2.9	2.9
Developing Countries	61.1	45.1	53.4	45.0
Pacific countries (other than China)	42.2	25.3	19.6	28.1
East Asian NICs	4.0	6.2	5.1	10.2
Hong Kong	2.9	2.8	1.9	2.8
Korea	0.1	0.6	1.1	2.9
Singapore	–	–	–	–
Taiwan	1.1	2.7	2.1	4.5
East Asian NECs	38.2	19.1	14.5	18.0
Indonesia	14.5	NA	NA	NA
Malaysia	20.6	16.3	12.4	14.7
Philippines	0.2	0.3	0.4	0.6
Thailand	2.9	2.5	1.7	2.7
China	4.9	4.6	2.8	3.8
Other developing countries	14.0	15.2	31.0	13.0
Other Asia	5.7	2.6	2.5	1.8
Africa	1.0	1.3	1.0	0.6
Southern Europe	0.0	0.1	0.0	0.3
Middle East	6.5	10.7	26.9	9.3
Latin America	0.8	0.5	0.6	1.1
European Socialist Countries	0.8	0.7	0.4	0.6

Note: Taiwanese figures for 1981 and 1987 derived as difference between total imports, the regional aggregates, special categories, and other countries not included. Regional aggregates may not sum to 100 percent due to inclusion in denominator of special categories, and other countries not specified.

Sources: IMF, *Direction of Trade Statistics*, various issues.

to a considerable extent. Finally, the import share of Other Asia declined greatly after 1963.

The share of domestic exports increased significantly over time as the relative importance of entrepôt trade declined. Thus, while domestic exports accounted for only 14.4 percent of total exports in 1960–7, their share reached 46.6 percent in 1968–73, 60.6 percent in 1976–82 and 64.8 percent in 1988.

The declining importance of entrepôt trade was in part responsible

Table 4.7 Commodity composition of exports: major product groups: Singapore (percent of total exports)

		1963	1973	1981	1988
Fuels	(SITC 3)	16.7	19.8	27.3	12.5
Nonfuel primary products		52.0	33.8	16.8	13.3
Food and live animals	(SITC 0)	16.4	6.9	4.8	4.6
Beverages and tobacco	(SITC 1)	1.5	0.4	0.4	0.7
Industrial materials	(SITC 2+4+68)	34.1	26.5	11.6	7.9
Manufactures	(SITC 5+6+7+8−68)	27.8	44.3	48.2	68.7
Other	(SITC 9)	3.3	2.1	7.7	5.5
Total		100.0	100.0	100.0	100.0
Manufactures (industrial classification)		26.7	43.0	43.0	70.2
Textile, apparel, leather	(ISIC 32)	5.9	7.8	4.0	5.2
Wood product and furniture	(ISIC 33)	0.3	2.6	1.2	1.9
Paper and paper products	(ISIC 34)	1.3	1.0	0.7	1.4
Chemicals	(ISIC 35)	3.8	4.2	4.4	7.6
Nonmetallic mineral products	(ISIC 36)	1.2	0.4	0.6	0.4
Iron and steel	(ISIC 37)	1.6	1.1	1.4	0.9
Engineering products	(ISIC 38)	11.9	25.2	29.8	51.7
Other industries	(ISIC 39)	0.8	0.7	0.9	1.0

Source: UN, COMTRADE data base.

for the fall in the share of nonfuel primary products in Singapore's exports from 52.0 percent in 1963 to 13.3 percent in 1988 (see Table 4.7). In turn, increases in the share of fuels from 16.7 percent in 1963 to 27.3 percent in 1981, and the subsequent decline to 12.5 percent in 1988, are explained by changes in oil prices.

The share of manufactured goods in Singapore's exports rose from 27.8 percent in 1963 to 68.7 percent in 1988. This increase was largely due to the rise observed in the share of engineering products (from 11.9 percent to 51.7 percent). The share of chemicals also increased (from 3.8 percent to 7.6 percent) while the shares of the textiles, apparel and leather products declined from 5.9 percent to 5.2 percent. None of the other manufacturing product categories had a share exceeding 2 percent.

Thus the data indicate a considerable upgrading of Singapore's exports. Further interest attaches to changes within individual commodity categories. Among engineering products, radios and television sets place first with a share of 18.8 percent in 1987, followed by office and computer equipment (11.7 percent), other nonelectrical

Table 4.8 Commodity composition of imports: major product groups: Singapore (percent of total imports)

		1963	1973	1981	1988
Fuels	(SITC 3)	13.7	12.9	33.7	17.1
Nonfuel primary products		45.6	25.1	12.9	11.2
Food and live animals	(SITC 0)	19.8	10.0	5.6	4.3
Beverages and tobacco	(SITC 1)	1.8	0.9	0.5	1.4
Industrial materials	(SITC 2+4+68)	24.0	14.2	6.8	5.6
Manufactures	(SITC 5+6+7+8−68)	38.6	60.7	52.3	70.4
Other	(SITC 9)	2.1	1.3	1.1	1.3
Total		100.0	100.0	100.0	100.0
Manufactures (industrial classification)		38.0	59.8	51.6	69.7
Textile, apparel, leather	(ISIC 32)	9.4	9.4	4.4	3.9
Wood product and furniture	(ISIC 33)	0.4	0.7	0.5	1.3
Paper and paper products	(ISIC 34)	1.8	1.9	1.1	2.9
Chemicals	(ISIC 35)	5.7	6.3	5.8	6.4
Nonmetallic mineral products	(ISIC 36)	1.2	1.7	1.4	4.2
Iron and steel	(ISIC 37)	2.5	4.7	4.1	2.2
Engineering products	(ISIC 38)	15.8	33.5	33.1	47.6
Other industries	(ISIC 39)	1.3	1.6	1.1	1.0

Source: UN, COMTRADE data base.

machinery (5.4 percent) and other electrical machinery (4.9 percent). In the case of chemicals, increases were concentrated in basic chemicals, synthetic resins, drugs and medicine, and plastic products.

An upgrading is also evident in the textiles, apparel and leather products category. This represented a shift from textile yarn and fabrics, whose share in total exports declined from 4.0 percent in 1963 to 1.8 percent in 1987, to wearing apparel, whose share increased from 1.0 percent to 3.4 percent during the same period. The share of other textile products and of leather and leather products remained at 0.5 percent and 0.2 percent, respectively, while footwear experienced a decline from 0.2 to 0.1 percent.

Overall changes on the import side mirrored the changes that occurred on the export side. The share of fuels increased until 1981 and declined afterwards; that of nonfuel primary products fell more or less continuously; and the share of manufactured good rose (see Table 4.8).

Within the manufacturing categories, increases were again concentrated in engineering products. Some increases also occurred in chemicals. In turn, textiles, apparel and leather products, paper and paper products, and other industries experienced decreases in their import shares until 1981 that were only partially offset by increases that occurred between 1981 and 1986.

PROSPECTS FOR THE FUTURE

Economic growth in Singapore has been projected at 7.0 percent a year from the 1987–2000 period. This is below the 8.2 percent growth rate of the 1963–87 period but substantially above the growth rate of 5.3 percent for 1981–7. Population is projected to rise by 0.9 percent a year, giving rise to a 6.0 percent growth of per caput income.

Singapore has practically a free trade system and it welcomes foreign direct investment. At the same time, it would be desirable to give a greater role to private business and to avoid the establishment of additional state enterprises in the manufacturing sector. Furthermore, technical education should be upgraded.

Singapore would also need to appreciate its currency. Without such appreciation, the current account surplus would grow and inflation threaten its economy. With appreciation, it would be possible to rely to a greater extent on domestic demand for economic growth.

Bibliography

Agell, Jonas, 1983. 'Subsidy to Capital through Tax Incentives in the ASEAN Countries: An Application of the Cost of Capital Approach under Inflationary Situations', *Singapore Economic Review*, vol. 23, no. 2.

Buchanan, Ian, 1972. *Singapore in Southeast Asia: An Economic and Political Appraisal*. London: G. Bell & Sons.

Chen, Peter S. J. (ed.), 1983. *Singapore Development Policies and Trends*. Selangor, Malaysia: Oxford University Press.

Chew, David C. E., 1970. 'Labour Problems in the Economic and Social Development of Singapore'. Paper prepared for Southeast Asian Workshop on Active Labour Policy Development. Geneva: International Institute for Labor Studies.

Economist Intelligence Unit, 1986. *Country Profile: Singapore 1986–87*. London: The Economist.

Economist Intelligence Unit, 1988. *China, Japan and the Asian NICs, Hong Kong and Macau, Singapore, South Korea, Taiwan: Economic Structure and Analysis*. London: The Economist.

Fong, Pang Eng, 1988. 'The Distinctive Features of Two City-States' Development: Hong Kong and Singapore', in Peter L. Berger and Hsin-Huang Michael Hsiao (eds), *In Search of an East Asian Development Model*. New Brunswick, NJ: Transaction Books.

Gayle, Dennis John, 1986. *The Small Developing State: Comparing Political Economies in Costa Rica, Singapore, and Jamaica*. Brookfield, VT: Gower.

Geiger, Theodore, assisted by Frances M. Geiger, 1973. *Tales of Two City-States: The Development Progress of Hong Kong and Singapore*. Washington, DC: National Planning Association.

Haggard, Stephen and Tun-jen Cheng, 1987. 'Singapore', Chapter IV in Haggard, Stephen and Tun-jen Cheng, *Newly Industrializing Asia in Transition: Policy Reform and American Response*. Policy Papers in International Affairs, no. 17. Berkeley, CA: University of California.

Hughes, Helen and You Poh Seng (eds), 1969. *Foreign Investment and Industrialization in Singapore*. Canberra: Australian National University Press.

Krause, Lawrence B., Ai Tee Koh and Yuan Lee, 1987. *The Singapore Economy Reconsidered*. Singapore: Institute of Southeast Asian Studies.

Lee, Sheng-Yi, 1986. *The Monetary and Banking Development of Singapore and Malaysia*. Singapore: Singapore University Press.

Lee, Soo Ann, 1973. *Industrialization in Singapore*. Camberwell, Vic.: Longman Australia.

Lee, Soo Ann, 1977. *Singapore Goes Transnational*. Singapore: Eastern Universities Press.

Lian, Koh Kheng *et al.*, 1982. *Credit and Security in Singapore: The Legal Problems of Development Finance*. New York: Crane, Russak & Co.

Lim, Chong-Yah, 1984. *Economic Restructuring in Singapore*. Kuala Lumpur: Federal Publications.

Lim, Joo-Jock *et al.*, 1977. 'Foreign Investment in Singapore: Some Broader Economic and Socio-Political Ramifications'. Field Report Series, no. 13. Singapore: Institute of Southeast Asian Studies.

Lim, Linda and Pang Eng Fong, 1986. *Trade, Employment and Industrialization in Singapore*. Geneva: International Labor Office.

Mirza, Hafiz, 1986. *Multinationals and the Growth of the Singapore Economy*. New York: St Martin's Press.

Otani, Ichiro and Cyrus Sassanpour, 1988. 'Financial, Exchange Rate, and Wage Policies in Singapore, 1979–86'. IMF Working Paper. Washington, DC: IMF.

People's Action Party, 1958. *The Tasks Ahead*. Singapore.

Price Waterhouse Center for Transnational Taxation, 1984. *Doing Business in Singapore*. New York: Price Waterhouse.

Rodan, Garry, 1985. *Singapore's Second Industrial Revolution: State Intervention and Foreign Investment*. ASEAN–Australia Economic Papers, No. 18. Kuala Lumpur and Canberra: ASEAN–Australia Joint Research Project.

Swee, Goh Keng, 1972. *The Economic of Modernization and other Essays*. Singapore: Asia Pacific Press.

Tan, Augustine H. H. and Ow Chin Hock, 1982. 'Singapore', in Bela Balassa and Associates, *Development Strategies in Semi-Industrial Economies*. Baltimore, MD: The Johns Hopkins University Press.

Verbruggen, Harmen, 1985. 'The Case of Singapore', in Harmen Verbruggen, *Gains from Export-Oriented Industrialization in Developing Countries with Special Reference to South-East Asia*. Amsterdam, Netherlands: Free University Press.

Wilson, Dick, 1972. *The Future Role of Singapore*. London: Oxford University Press.

Wong, Kum Poh, 1981. 'The Financing of Trade and Development in the ADCs: The Experience of Singapore', in Hontack Wong and Lawrence B. Krause (eds), *Trade and Growth of the Advanced Developing Countries in the Pacific Basin*. Seoul: Korea Development Institute.

Woronoff, Jon, 1986. 'Singapore, Capitalist Haven', Chapter 5 in Jon Woronoff, *Asia's Miracle Economies*. New York: M. E. Sharpe.

Yeh, Stephen H. K. (ed.), 1975. *Public Housing in Singapore: A Multi-Disciplinary Study*. Singapore: Singapore University Press.

Yoshihara, Kunio, 1976. *Foreign Investment and Domestic Response: A Study of Singapore's Industrialization*. Singapore: Eastern Universities Press.

You, Poh Seng and Lim Cheng Yah (eds), 1984. *Singapore: Twenty-Five Years of Development*. Singapore: Nan Yang Xing Zhou Lianhe Zaobao.

Yue, Chia Siow, 1985. 'The Role of Foreign Trade and Investment in the Development of Singapore', in Walter Galenson (ed.), *Foreign Trade and Investment: Economic Growth in the Newly Industrializing Asian Countries*. Madison, WI: University of Wisconsin Press.

5 Taiwan

INTRODUCTION

In an area of 36 000 square kilometers, Taiwan (the Republic of China) has a population of 19.5 million. Taiwan has few mineral resources and, while it has fertile agricultural land, the ratio of population to arable land is high.

Following several centuries of Chinese rule during which the Chinese settled on the island, Taiwan was ceded to Japan in 1895 in the treaty ending the Sino–Japanese war. Under Japanese rule, Taiwan was to supply agricultural foodstuffs and raw materials (in particular, rice and sugar) to Japan. Subsequently, during the war with China and the Second World War, emphasis was put on industrial development to support the Japanese war effort.

Taiwan was returned to China after the Second World War. Following the defeat of his armies on the mainland, Chiang Kai-shek withdrew to Taiwan in December 1948. In the next decade, Taiwan benefited from substantial American foreign aid which supported its import-substitution program. As this policy ran into difficulties due to the limitations of its domestic market, Taiwan adopted an outward-oriented development strategy in the early 1960s. This involved providing export incentives and liberalizing imports, so as to remove discrimination in the system of incentives against exports.

The policies applied led to rapid increases in exports. While the exports of goods and services amounted to less than 18 percent of the GDP in 1963, they surpassed 60 percent in 1987. Imports of goods and services increased to a lesser extent, from 19 percent in 1963 to 41 percent in 1987, reflecting Taiwan's rising current account surplus.

Export expansion importantly contributed to Taiwan's economic growth. Between 1963 and 1988, per caput incomes increased by $4\frac{1}{2}$ times in Taiwan. Growth has been accompanied by equity. Taiwan had one of the most equitable income distribution among developing countries following the land reform of the late 1940s and early 1950s, and the equality of income distribution has increased further after the adoption of an outward-oriented development strategy.

GOVERNMENT POLICIES

Following the loss of markets in Japan after the Second World War, Taiwan suffered severe foreign exchange shortages and rapid inflation. Measures to reconstruct the economy began to be introduced in 1949; they included land reform, currency reform and the application of inward-oriented trade policies.

The first step in land reform was the distribution to tenant farmers of land formerly owned by the Japanese. This was followed by the compulsory sale of land by landlords to the state, which resold it to tenant farmers.

Since tenant farmers managed the farms even before the land reform, the reform program did not modify the size of farm managerial units. At the same time, it favorably affected incentives, leading to the introduction of multiple cropping and the rapid growth of land productivity.

The increased incomes of the former tenants also contributed to the educational expansion of subsequent years. At the same time, rising agricultural incomes created increased demand for manufactured products.

The currency reform introduced in June 1949 had several features. The new currency, named the New Taiwan (NT) dollar, was equal to 40 000 units of the old currency; the exchange rate was set at NT$5 to US$1; and the maximum amount of the currency issue was limited to NT$200 million. Because of government budget deficits and the easy credit granted to public enterprises, however, this limit was soon breached and the resulting inflation induced the government to devalue the exchange rate repeatedly. Also, the single exchange was replaced by a multiple exchange rate system.

Exports of sugar and rice received a relatively unfavorable exchange rate. For imports, exchange rates depended on the type of the commodity and the source of foreign exchange. A lower exchange rate was applied to imports financed from US aid as well as to raw materials and capital equipment.

The multiple exchange rate system and tariff and nontariff protection increased the profitability of import substitution and contributed to the doubling of manufacturing production between 1950 and 1958. However, the system of foreign exchange allocation discriminated among products without an economic rationale, induced entrepreneurs to compete for licenses rather than to lower production costs, and encouraged corruption.

At the same time, the preferential allocation of foreign exchange for imported raw materials and capital equipment created incentives to increase capacity even when existing capacity was not utilized fully. Domestic market limitations and the lack of incentives to export further contributed to low rates of capacity utilization. An industrial survey of 1959 in fact shows that many plants producing simple manufactures were operating at low levels of capacity. The industries in question included rubber and canvas shoes (23.3 percent), electric fans (38.1 percent), soap (39.1 percent), insulated wire (40.0 percent), plywood (46.7 percent), synthetic fabrics (49.7 percent) and woolen yarn (52.6 percent).

Domestic market limitations also constrained the possibilities for further import substitution. The expansion of manufacturing industries, and economic growth in general, slowed down as a result. In response to this situation, policy reforms were adopted involving increased outward orientation.

In 1958 the exchange rate was substantially devalued and the multiple exchange rate system was replaced by a dual rate; the basic official exchange rate and the exchange certificate rate. Exports were paid for with transferable exchange certificates that could be used for importation.

The exchange certificate rate stabilized at NT$60 to US$1 in 1959. The basic official exchange rate and the exchange certificate rate were merged at this level in late 1961. The unified and stable exchange rate provided favorable terms to exporters.

Exporters further benefited from a variety of export promotion measures. They included the rebate of customs duties (including the defense surtax and harbor charges) on imported raw materials and intermediate products and the rebate of commodity taxes on imported and domestically produced materials and intermediate products. This meant eliminating the disadvantages exporters suffered as a result of taxes and duties on inputs into export production. Exporters could also deduct 2 percent of total export earnings from taxable income, with a 10 percent deduction for those firms that exported more than 50 percent of their output.

Low-cost loans were provided to exporters. Interest rates of 6 percent a year were charged on loans repayable in foreign currencies and 11.7 percent on loans repayable in domestic currencies. These rates were substantially lower than the 19.8 percent interest rate on secured loans and 22.3 percent on nonsecured loans provided to private sector enterprises for general business purposes. This favorable margin was preserved throughout the 1960s.

Under government auspices, manufacturers' associations were formed to subsidize exports from levies on domestic sales. Such associations operated in cotton spinning, woolen yarn and fabrics, iron and steel, rubber products, paper and paper products and monosodium glutamate.

At the same time, export promotion facilities were established by semigovernmental agencies that provided export inspection, managerial, technical and consultation services, and market research. The China External Trade Development Council was set up to promote exports and to contribute to the cost of participation in trade missions and trade fairs.

The government established duty-free export processing zones, first in Kaohsiung and subsequently at two other sites. The purpose of these zones was to encourage processing and assembly operations in the garment, plastic products and electronics industries by minimizing red tape. But the importance of the export processing zones should not be overstated as in 1975, after ten years of operation, they accounted for only 8.5 percent of exports. This indicates the relative efficiency of the export incentives system in Taiwan.

On the import side, tariffs and other import charges were repeatedly raised during the period of import substitution. The 1955 revision of the tariff code increased duties on finished goods as well as on intermediate products. Also, in November 1958 the harbor charge on imports was raised from 2 to 3 percent. But the defense surtax of 20 percent, imposed in July 1958, was offset by the removal of a tax of equal magnitude on foreign exchange settlements.

In 1959 tariffs were lowered on a wide variety of finished goods and intermediate products, although duties were raised on automobiles and agricultural machinery. Tariffs on automobiles were reduced, however, in the framework of the 1965 revision that brought tariff reductions on a substantial number of finished goods and intermediate products. Further reductions were made in subsequent years.

The effects of these tariff reductions are apparent in the decrease in the ratio of customs revenues to c.i.f. import value. This ratio was 30 percent in 1957–8; it declined to 22 percent in 1958–9, 17 percent in 1959–60, fluctuated between 16 and 17 percent during the 1960s, and fell again to 10 percent in 1974–5 and below 8 percent in 1986. Further declines occurred in 1987 and 1988, when additional tariff reductions were undertaken.

The number of items under import control changed little until

1962. In subsequent years, however, more items were removed from the controlled list than added to it and, in 1970, 1056 items were removed without a single addition. By 1976, the number of controlled items was reduced to 531, accounting for 2.7 percent of imports; this compares with 780 items in 1970. Furthermore, import prohibitions were practically eliminated in 1972; there were 208 prohibited items in 1970.

At the same time, the treatment of controlled items was considerably liberalized. Under the regulations introduced in 1960, domestic manufacturers of a particular product could request the application of import restrictions only if the imported raw materials amounted to less than 70 percent of the product price and this price did not exceed the cost of imports by more than 25 percent. Import costs were defined to include the tariff, the defense surtax, harbor charge, the interest costs of the importer and the foreign exchange settlement fee, in addition to the c.i.f. import price.

Import controls procedures were liberalized further in the 1960s. In 1961 the interest costs of importers and the foreign exchange settlement fee were excluded from the calculation of import costs, a time limit of three years was set for import restrictions, and the permissible excess cost of domestic products was reduced to 15 percent. This ratio was reduced further, to 10 percent, in January 1968.

The described changes in incentives practically eliminated the bias against manufactured exports that was due to the existence of tariff and nontariff barriers and to the practical lack of export incentives in the 1950s. This meant that, on the average, sales of manufactured goods in domestic and in foreign markets received similar incentives. At the same time, to a limited extent, manufactured goods continued to be favored against primary products.

The preference for manufactured goods, observed in the 1960s, subsequently gave place to preference for agriculture as the domestic prices of some staples, such as rice and sugar, came to exceed world market prices. This was the result of a policy that was intended to avoid a deterioration in the relative income position of farmers as increases in manufacturing productivity exceeded that in agriculture.

In the 1950s, the government provided a three-year tax holiday for investment law approved enterprises. In September 1960 these benefits were increased to a considerable extent and were extended to a large number of sectors in the framework of the Investment Encouragement Law. The main provisions of this law were as follows:

1 five-year tax holiday;
2 reduction of the rate of the business income tax from 32.5 percent to 18 percent;
3 tax exemption for reinvested profits;
4 exemption or reduction in the stamp tax;
5 tax exemption on foreign currency debt.

Investment incentives were increased further in June 1965, when the Investment Encouragement Law was revised. The business income tax was further reduced and provisions were made for the payment by installments of import duties on plant and equipment. Also, the authorities were enabled to use public land or, if necessary, procure private land for the development of industrial parks. In fact 49 industrial parks were developed, including the three export processing zones referred to above.

The industrial parks have played an important role in the continued growth of small and medium-sized firms in Taiwan. The parks have provided infrastructural facilities, enabled investors to rent rather than buy land and buildings, and made available loans to the would-be entrepreneur.

Between 1966 and 1976 the number of manufacturing firms increased by 150 percent in Taiwan, while the average size of the individual enterprises (measured by the number of employees) increased by only 28 percent. This compares with Korea, where the number of firms increased by 10 percent while the number of employees per firm rose by 176 percent in the same period. As a result, the average Taiwan manufacturing enterprise in 1976 was only half as big as in Korea, with an average of 34.6 employees in Taiwan as compared to 68.8 in Korea.

The disparity is even greater if one looks at the size of the largest firms. In 1981, the $10 billion gross receipts of Hyundai, Korea's largest conglomerate, were three times as large as the $3.5 billion gross receipts of Taiwan's ten largest private firms combined. The next three largest Korean firms (Samsung, Daewoo and Lucky) each had an annual gross turnover of at least $5 billion. (The data come from Tibor Scitovsky, 'Economic Development in Taiwan and South Korea, 1965–81', in Laurence J. Lau (ed.), *Models of Development. A Comparative Study of Economic Growth in South Korea and Taiwan*; San Francisco: Institute for Contemporary Studies, 1986, pp. 146, 156.)

These comparisons pertain to the private sector. After the Second

World War, Taiwan had a public enterprise sector that accounted for 55.9 percent of manufacturing output in 1953. In the following two decades the share of the public sector substantially declined, not because of denationalizations but because of the rapid growth of the private sector. Thus the share of the public sector in Taiwan's manufacturing output fell to 44.6 percent in 1963, 26.7 percent in 1968 and 13.1 percent in 1972. The share increased, however, to 15.4 percent in 1979 in conjunction with the establishment of new public firms in heavy industries in the framework of investments in ten major development projects under the Seventh Plan (1976–81).

Investments in heavy industry included the integrated steel mill, the Kaohsiung shipyard, and petrochemical installations. While at one time it was thought that these would be joint public–private sector projects, in the end they became public investments.

Most of the major development projects were oriented towards infrastructure, however. They included the North–South Expressway, the new Taipei international airport, harbor development, the East Coast railway and rural electrification. These projects, in turn, contributed to the development of private industry.

Private enterprise became the center of development in the next plan, when the machinery, electronics and information industries were designated as strategic industries, and the share of the public sector declined again to 13.9 percent in 1982. More generally, the emphasis was put on encouraging the development of high-skill industries oriented toward the adoption of new technologies.

A variety of incentives were provided to the strategic industries. They included giving firms the right to delay the start of the five-year income tax holiday by four years, the right to retain earnings up to 200 percent of paid-in capital, and low interest loans. The government also encouraged the establishment of venture capital firms to promote high-technology industries.

Furthermore, the Hsinchu science-based industrial park was created around two national universities, technology research institutes and research laboratories. Firms setting up in the park receive additional incentives, including a five-year consecutive tax holiday within the first nine years of operation, exemptions from business taxes and import duties, tax credit to stockholders, and low rentals of land and buildings.

The Hsinchu science-based park began operations in September 1981 and has attracted, among others, firms producing computer components, telecommunications equipment, laser equipment and carbon fiber. It has also attracted highly educated Taiwanese working in the United States whose return is an important objective of the government.

The high-technology orientation is also reflected in the increasing number of foreign direct investment and technical cooperation projects with foreign interests. It has further led to the rise of the share of R & D expenditures in GNP from 0.3 percent in 1978 to 0.7 percent in 1982 and 0.9 percent in 1986.

Technological policy developed largely outside the framework of the national plans that have been prepared in Taiwan with considerable regularity, ranging from the First Plan (1953–6) to the Ninth Plan (1986–9). These plans are neither compulsory nor indicative in the French sense. They do not provide industrial targets and, while macroeconomic projections are included, they are often widely off the mark. It has been reported, for example, that in 1964 exports were 80 percent higher than predicted in 1961. Also, in 1967 national income was 10 percent higher than estimated in 1964; exports were 30 percent higher and imports 60 percent higher (see I. M. D. Little, 'An Economic Reconnaissance', in Walter Galenson (ed.), *Economic Growth and Structural Change in Taiwan*; Ithaca, NY, and London: Cornell University Press, 1978, p. 487).

The first two plans were prepared by the Economic Stabilization Board as a condition of receiving US aid; they were oriented towards import substitution. With the shift towards outward orientation, the Board was disbanded and planning was decentralized. Some recentralization occurred in conjunction with the Fourth and Fifth Plans, which were prepared by the Council of International Economic Cooperation and Development, but the Council had a coordinating rather than a directing function. For the Sixth Plan, there was again a move towards decentralization and the newly-established Economic Planning Council had responsibility mainly for macroeconomic forecasts. With this plan the emphasis was shifted to the discussion of policies, where the sectoral ministries play an important role.

It would appear, then, that the success of the Taiwanese economy cannot be attributed to planning. At one time, it was suggested that foreign aid played such a role (Neil H. Jacoby, *U.S. Aid to Taiwan. The Study of Foreign Aid, Self-Help, and Development*; New York: McGraw Hill 1966).

In fact, during the 1950s foreign aid accounted for 5–7 percent of the GNP. Aid financed a substantial proportion of imports, ranging up to 60 percent in some years. It was suggested that without foreign aid imports would have to be cut to an extent which would cripple the economy. An alternative view is that aid largely financed defense expenditures, which amounted to about 10 percent of the GNP.

Whatever the effects of foreign aid during the 1950s, its importance declined much during the 1960s, falling to 2 percent of GNP in 1964 and below 1 percent in 1967; thus in Taiwan's high growth period foreign aid played a negligible role. Rather, it was the policies applied that were responsible for rapid economic growth. In this connection, the preceding analysis should be extended to include educational policy and financial policy.

In 1940, Taiwan had a literacy rate of 21 percent. Illiteracy was eradicated after the Second World War, when the primary school enrollment ratio (expressed as a percent of the relevant age cohort) reached 100 percent and the secondary school enrollment rate 88 percent, slightly exceeding the 87 percent average for the industrial countries.

Taiwan's educational effort greatly contributed to industrial development in providing the skills necessary for its manufacturing industries. Taiwan remained behind, however, in higher education where the enrollment ratio hardly reaches 20 percent, compared with a 37 percent average in the industrial countries.

Another important factor contributing to economic growth was the reform of the financial sector in the early 1960s. The reform involved setting high interest rates, with a view to evening out the demand for, and the supply of, funds. This policy had favorable effects on savings as well as on allocation of savings among alternative investments.

To begin with, Taiwan's economy experienced financial deepening as the ratio of the broadly-defined money supply, M2, to the GDP increased from 28.5 in 1961–5 to 37.8 percent in 1966–70, to 49.8 percent in 1971–5, to 58.6 percent in 1976–80 and to 72.0 percent in 1981–6. This increase, in part, represented a shift from investment in physical assets, such as gold and real estate, and from the informal money market towards financial instruments. It also represented an increase in savings ratios as the proportion of net private national savings to national income rose from 9.7 percent in 1961–5 to 12.3 percent in 1966–70, to 17.0 percent in 1971–5, declining to 16.3 percent in 1976–80, and rising again to 18.0 percent in 1981–6.

Apart from providing savings for new investment, the financial reforms assured the rationing of funds by interest rates. This has made investment allocation more efficient, replacing credit rationing by the banks and by the government. Credit rationing tends to favor established firms and import-substitution activities where there is less risk, although the rate of return may be lower. Also, the negative real interest rates of the earlier period encouraged self-investment at low returns.

High interest rates, in turn, have ensured the choice of investments that have high returns. They have also contributed to the choice of labor-intensive industries and production methods that have conformed to Taiwan's comparative advantage and have led to a more equitable distribution of income.

Nevertheless, the modernization of Taiwan's financial sector has been a slow process. There is little venture capital in Taiwan and there is a tendency to lend on the basis of physical collateral. This situation in turn may be explained by the structure of the Taiwanese financial system.

The financial system consists largely of the Central Bank, the commercial banks, the postal savings system and the credit cooperatives. Of lesser importance are the credit departments of the farmer associations, the medium-term business banks, investment and trust companies, and life insurance companies.

The commercial banks account for three-fourths of the assets of the financial system, excluding Central Bank. Apart from two private banks, a joint-venture bank and local branches of foreign banks (which are limited to a small proportion of financial assets), the commercial banks are owned by the government, having taken them over from the Japanese after the end of the Second World War.

The commercial banks tend to be overly conservative. Improvements are expected, however, following the adoption of the new banking law in July 1989. This will allow more competition from privately-owned banks by granting the first banking licenses in 20 years. Interest rate controls will be eliminated and the treatment of foreign banks will be liberalized. Foreign banks will be able to accept long-term deposits and make long-term loans. Furthermore, foreign banks that have been in Taiwan for at least five years, most of which are limited to one branch, will be able to open more branches. Finally, foreign banks will be allowed to apply for underwriting licenses for securities.

The government has developed an open money market, where commercial paper and bankers' acceptances are the main instruments used. This has, in turn, increased the opportunities for business

Table 5.1 Economic performance indicators: Taiwan

Growth rates	1963–73	1973–81	1981–7	1963–87
GDP	11.1	8.0	7.6	9.2
Population	2.8	2.0	1.4	2.2
GDP per caput	8.1	5.9	6.1	6.8
Investment	17.4	9.6	1.7	10.7
Manufacturing production	18.6	9.3	9.1	13.1
Agricultural production	3.8	1.4	1.3	2.4
Exports	25.5	10.4	13.9	17.4
Imports	21.4	9.4	10.1	14.4

Source: World Bank.

finance, at least in the short term. Also, the government has liberalized interest rates.

In recent years, private financing has been adversely affected by Central Bank borrowing for the purpose of sterilizing the inflow of funds as Taiwan has run increasing balance of payment surpluses. In order to do this, the Central Bank has been paying above-market interest rates that tend to crowd out private sector borrowers. In fact, new borrowing by the Central Bank has grown from nil in 1985 to NT$600 billion a year, while the one-year increment in the banking systems loans to the private sector declined from NT$200 billion to NT$100 billion.

ECONOMIC GROWTH

In 1963, Taiwan's per caput income was lower than Brazil's and it was less than one-third that of Argentina and Chile. By 1988, however, Taiwan surpassed all these countries by a considerable margin (see Table 1.1). Per caput income growth averaged 6.8 percent in the 1963–87 period and, while some deceleration is shown over time, per caput incomes rose at an average annual rate of 6.1 percent a year between 1981 and 1987 (see Table 5.1).

The impetus to economic growth was provided by exports which increased 17.4 percent a year between 1963 and 1987, compared with the average annual rate of increase of GDP of 9.2 percent. As a result, the share of exports of goods and nonfactor services reached 60.7 percent of the GDP in 1987, compared with 17.8 percent in 1963 (see Table 5.2). Imports rose to a lesser extent (14.4 percent a year)

Table 5.2 Industrial composition and trade: Taiwan (percent of GDP)

	1963	1973	1981	1987
Industrial composition				
Agriculture	23.4	12.2	7.4	5.3
Mining and quarrying	2.1	1.1	0.9	0.5
Manufacturing	24.9	42.4	40.2	43.5
Gas, electricity and water	4.0	4.1	5.8	4.2
Construction	1.9	2.0	3.4	3.8
Transportation	16.9	12.6	13.8	14.2
Wholesale and retail trade	5.0	5.9	6.0	6.0
Banking, real estate	1.7	2.5	4.5	2.9
Ownership of dwellings	6.9	5.5	5.6	5.5
Public administration	10.5	9.0	9.9	8.9
Other services	4.0	4.7	5.9	6.8
Imputed bank service charge, duty	−1.4	−1.9	−3.4	−1.7
Trade				
Exports of goods and nonfactor services	17.8	46.8	52.2	60.7
Imports of goods and nonfactor services	18.9	41.5	50.1	41.5

Source: World Bank.

as Taiwan accumulated large trade surpluses, with an import share of 41.5 percent in 1987, compared to 18.9 percent in 1963.

Economic growth was concentrated in manufacturing which experienced a growth rate of 13.1 percent between 1963 and 1987. And while growth slowed down over time, the share of manufacturing in the GDP continued to rise in the 1980s. This share was 25.0 percent in 1963; it reached 43.5 percent in 1987 (see Table 5.2). In turn, the share of agriculture in the GDP declined from 23.4 percent in 1963 to 5.3 percent in 1987. A similar trend has been observed in regard to mining.

The GDP share of the service sectors increased from 49.5 percent in 1963 to 50.7 percent in 1987. The increase was concentrated in construction, wholesale and retail trade, banking, and other services. By contrast, the share of transportation, the ownership of dwellings and public administration declined while little change was experienced in gas, electricity and water.

Domestic investment increased very rapidly in the early part of the period (17.4 percent a year between 1963 and 1973) and matched the growth of GDP between 1973 and 1981. However, investments

Table 5.3 Savings and investment ratios: Taiwan (percent of GDP)

	1973	1974	1975	1976	1977	1978	1979	1980
Private savings	.	28.4	25.9	31.7	32.5	34.1	32.7	33.6
Government budget balance	.	3.3	1.4	1.3	0.8	1.0	1.7	−0.6
Domestic savings	34.6	31.7	27.3	33.0	33.3	35.1	34.5	33.1
Foreign savings	−5.3	7.8	3.3	−2.2	−4.9	−6.5	−1.1	1.2
Domestic investment	29.3	39.5	30.6	30.8	28.4	28.5	33.3	34.3

	1981	1982	1983	1984	1985	1986	1987
Private savings	32.6	31.4	33.1	32.9	32.3	37.9	38.5
Government budget balance	−0.3	−1.0	−1.1	0.1	0.0	−0.8	0.3
Domestic savings	32.4	30.4	32.0	33.0	32.3	37.1	38.8
Foreign savings	−2.1	−5.3	−9.0	−11.6	−14.5	−20.8	−19.2
Domestic investment	30.3	25.2	23.0	21.5	17.9	16.2	19.6

Source: World Bank.

increased little after 1981. Correspondingly, having equalled around 30 percent of GDP in much of the earlier period, the share of investments in GDP decreased to 25 percent in 1982 and it did not reach 20 percent in 1987 (see Table 5.3).

With the major exception of the unusually high investment year of 1974, investment was financed by domestic savings. In fact, a large surplus developed from the early 1980s. It reached 9.0 percent of GDP in 1983, 11.6 percent in 1984, 14.5 percent in 1985 and 19.2 percent in 1987. Savings originate in the private sector, with small positive public savings observed in the second half of the 1970s, and small negative public savings in the early 1980s (see Table 5.3).

The maintenance of high domestic savings in the face of falling domestic investment led to a massive outflow of savings. This is reflected in the growing trade surplus (see Table 5.4). While the surplus varied between nil and $2 billion in the late 1970s, it reached $6.3 billion in 1983, $9.2 billion in 1984, $11.2 billion in 1985 and $20.8 billion in 1987. In turn, the service deficit showed a more-or-less continuous increase from $0.5 billion in 1978 to $2.1 billion in 1984, followed by a decline to $1.7 billion in 1985 and $0.4 billion in 1986 and an increase to $1.9 billion in 1987.

The resulting current account surplus was largely matched by the accumulation of reserves, with Taiwan having the largest reserves

Table 5.4 Balance of payments: Taiwan (million US$)

	1978	1979	1980	1981	1982	1983	1984	1985	1986	1987
Merchandise exports	12 602	15 829	19 575	22 408	21 776	25 028	30 185	30 466	39 492	53 224
Merchandise imports	−10 413	−14 509	−19 498	−20 583	−18 130	−18 760	−20 952	−19 296	−22 635	−32 442
Trade balance	2 189	1 320	77	1 825	3 646	6 268	9 233	11 170	16 857	20 782
Other goods, services, and income: credit	1 824	2 585	3 052	3 672	3 915	3 804	4 550	4 955	6 744	8 413
Other goods, services, and income: debit	−2 346	−3 502	−3 947	−4 886	−5 178	−5 617	−6 637	−6 681	−7 087	−10 350
Other goods, services, and income: net	−522	−917	−895	−1 214	−1 263	−1 813	−2 087	−1 726	−343	−1 937
Unrequited transfers	−28	−222	−95	−92	−135	−43	−170	−249	−297	−673
Current account balance	1 639	181	−913	519	2 248	4 412	6 976	9 195	16 217	18 172
Direct investment	110	122	124	91	71	130	131	260	261	11
Long-term capital	243	361	1 087	795	1 197	913	−870	−1 037	−1 669	−2 389
Short-term capital	84	−421	−254	109	−529	−397	−89	284	1 421	3 933
Capital account balance	437	62	957	995	739	646	−828	−493	13	1 555
Errors and omissions	−125	−205	−363	−326	−498	−352	−408	494	168	−397
Overall balance	1 951	38	−319	1 188	2 489	4 706	5 740	9 196	16 398	19 330
Net use of reserves	−1 951	−96	127	−1 299	−2 589	−4 862	−5 859	−9 352	−16 620	−20 322

Note: The overall balance is the sum of the current and capital account balances and errors and omissions. Net use of reserves was derived by adding the following items to overall balance: counterpart to the monetization and demonetization of gold, counterpart to SDR allocation, and counterpart to valuation changes.

Source: Council for Economic Planning and Development, Republic of China, *Taiwan Statistical Data Book*, 1987 and 1988.

worldwide after Japan and Germany, accounting for more than two years of imports. In turn, Taiwan experienced an inflow of short-term capital and an outflow of long-term capital.

INTERNATIONAL TRADE

The United States is by far Taiwan's principal export market. Its share in Taiwanese exports rose from 16.5 percent in 1963 to 38.6 percent in 1973, with a decline to 36.1 percent in 1981 followed by an increase to 44.2 percent in 1987 (see Table 5.5). In the latter part of the period, Taiwan raised its share in the US market from 3.2 percent to 6.2 percent.

By contrast, Japan's share in Taiwan's exports declined from 32.1 percent in 1963 to 18.9 percent in 1973 and 11.0 percent in 1981, rising slightly to 13.0 percent in 1987. The rest of the developed countries increased their share in Taiwan's exports, Western Europe from 8.3 percent in 1963 to 14.7 percent in 1987, and Canada, Australia and New Zealand from 2.8 percent in 1963 to 5.4 percent in 1987. For developed countries, taken together, the corresponding figures were 1963, 59.7 percent; 1973, 76.9 percent; 1981, 65.8 percent; and 1987, 77.3 percent. The remaining exports were destined for developing countries.

Among the developing countries, the share of the Pacific Area developing countries declined more-or-less continuously during the period under consideration, from 24.7 percent in 1963 to 14.4 percent in 1987. Decreases were of similar magnitude in proportional terms for the East Asian NICs (from 17.0 percent to 11.4 percent) and the East Asian NECs (from 7.7 percent to 3.0 percent). Taiwan did not trade directly with China.

Among the East Asian NICs, the largest decreases were experienced in Korea, whose share in Taiwan's exports fell from 4.8 percent in 1963 to 1.2 percent in 1987; but declines were also observed in the shares of Hong Kong (from 8.9 to 7.7 percent) and Singapore (from 3.3 percent to 2.5 percent).

Among the East Asian NECs, the decline in export market shares was concentrated in Thailand and Malaysia, followed by the Philippines. In 1963, Taiwan did not report exports to Indonesia whose share in its total exports reached 0.8 percent in 1987.

The decline in the share of the other developing countries was concentrated in Other Asia, where Vietnam had taken an important

Table 5.5 Geographical composition of exports: Taiwan (percent of total exports)

	1963	1973	1981	1987
Developed Countries	59.7	76.9	65.8	77.3
United States	16.5	38.6	36.1	44.2
Western Europe	8.3	12.9	12.7	14.7
Japan	32.1	18.9	11.0	13.0
Canada, Australia, New Zealand	2.8	6.5	6.1	5.4
Developing Countries	40.0	23.0	32.8	21.9
Pacific countries (other than China)	24.7	16.4	17.1	14.4
East Asian NICs	17.0	10.9	12.3	11.4
Hong Kong	8.9	6.7	8.4	7.7
Korea	4.8	1.2	1.2	1.2
Singapore	3.3	2.9	2.7	2.5
Taiwan	–	–	–	–
East Asian NECs	7.7	5.5	4.8	3.0
Indonesia	0.0	2.7	1.9	0.8
Malaysia	2.3	0.7	0.8	0.5
Philippines	2.0	0.7	1.2	0.9
Thailand	3.4	1.5	0.9	0.8
China	0.0	0.0	0.0	0.0
Other developing countries	15.2	6.6	15.7	7.6
Other Asia	11.3	0.9	0.9	0.8
Africa	1.1	2.0	4.9	2.0
Southern Europe	0.0	0.3	NA	NA
Middle East	2.1	2.0	5.5	2.7
Latin America	0.7	1.4	4.4	2.0
European Socialist Countries	0.0	0.0	0.0	0.0

Notes: The category for Canada, Australia and New Zealand is composed of Canada and Oceania for the years 1981 and 1988. Figures may not sum to 100 percent due to inclusion of a residual category in the denominator. All trade with Europe for 1981 and 1987 is classified under Western Europe.

Sources: IMF, *Direction of Trade Statistics*, various issues. Figures for 1981 and 1988 are from Board of Foreign Trade, Ministry of Economic Affairs, *Foreign Trade and Development of the Republic of China, 1988.*

part of Taiwan's exports in 1963. In turn, Africa, the Middle East and Latin America increased their export market shares to a considerable extent between 1963 and 1981; while this was followed by a decline between 1981 and 1987, the 1987 share of these regions much exceeded their 1963 share, although remaining small in absolute terms.

The overall changes were quite different on the import side com-

Table 5.6 Geographical composition of imports: Taiwan
(percent of total imports)

	1963	1973	1981	1987
Developed Countries	83.3	79.2	64.1	76.7
United States	42.9	25.3	22.5	22.1
Western Europe	6.8	12.2	9.3	15.1
Japan	30.5	37.9	28.0	34.3
Canada, Australia, New Zealand	3.0	3.8	4.4	5.2
Developing Countries	16.7	20.8	35.5	22.8
Pacific countries (other than China)	6.8	11.8	9.3	10.0
East Asian NICs	1.4	4.5	3.8	5.1
Hong Kong	1.0	2.7	1.5	2.0
Korea	0.2	1.1	1.4	1.5
Singapore	0.2	0.7	0.9	1.5
Taiwan	–	–	–	–
East Asian NECs	5.4	7.3	5.5	4.9
Indonesia	0.0	2.7	2.2	1.6
Malaysia	1.6	1.6	2.1	2.1
Philippines	3.2	1.5	0.6	0.6
Thailand	0.6	1.5	0.6	0.6
China	0.0	0.0	0.0	0.0
Other developing countries	9.9	9.0	26.2	12.8
Other Asia	0.7	0.7	0.4	1.1
Africa	1.2	1.4	3.4	2.1
Southern Europe	0.0	0.3	NA	NA
Middle East	6.8	3.4	20.0	7.4
Latin America	1.3	3.1	2.4	2.2
European Socialist Countries	0.0	0.0	0.0	0.0

Notes: The category for Canada, Australia and New Zealand is composed of Canada and Oceania for the years 1981 and 1987. Figures may not sum to 100 percent due to inclusion of a residual category in the denominator. All trade with Europe for 1981 and 1987 is classified under Western Europe.

Sources: IMF, *Direction of Trade Statistics*, various issues. Figures for 1981 and 1987 are from Board of Foreign Trade, Ministry of Economic Affairs, *Foreign Trade and Development of the Republic of China, 1988*.

pared with the export side. The developed country share declined from 83.3 percent in 1963 to 79.2 percent in 1973 and 64.1 percent in 1981, followed by an increase to 76.7 percent in 1987, with the developing countries experiencing the mirror image of these changes (see Table 5.6).

Within the developed country group, the share of the United

States fell from 42.9 percent in 1963 to 25.3 percent in 1973, declining further to 22.5 percent in 1981 and 22.1 percent in 1987.

Japan dominates among suppliers of Taiwan's imports. After increasing from 30.5 percent in 1963 to 37.9 percent in 1973, its share declined to 28.0 percent in 1981 but rose again to 34.3 percent in 1987. Increases were experienced also in the shares of Western Europe (from 6.8 percent in 1963 to 15.1 percent in 1987) and Canada, Australia and New Zealand (from 3.0 percent in 1963 to 5.2 percent in 1987).

The share of the Pacific Area developing countries in Taiwan's imports increased from 6.8 percent to 11.8 percent between 1963 and 1973 but declined again slightly afterwards. Larger than average increases were experienced in the East Asian NICs, whose share rose from 1.4 percent in 1963 to 4.5 percent in 1973 and to 5.1 percent in 1987.

In contrast with its declining export share, the import share of Korea increased from 0.2 percent in 1963 to 1.1 percent in 1973 and 1.5 percent in 1987. Increases of similar magnitude were experienced in Singapore, while Hong Kong's share rose to a lesser extent from a higher base level.

The share of the East Asian NECs in Taiwan's imports increased from 5.4 percent in 1963 to 7.3 percent in 1973, declining afterwards to 5.5 percent in 1981 and to 4.9 percent in 1987. For the entire period, a larger decrease was experienced in the Philippines, no change in Thailand and an increase in Malaysia; imports from Indonesia were not reported in 1963.

Finally, the import share of the other developing countries fell from 9.9 percent in 1963 to 9.0 in 1973, increased to 26.2 percent in 1981 and declined to 12.8 percent in 1987. The largest fluctuations were observed in the Middle East, reflecting mainly variations in oil prices; their import share fell from 6.8 percent in 1963 to 3.4 percent in 1973, increased to 20.0 percent in 1981 and fell again to 7.4 percent in 1987. In turn, Africa and Latin America experienced initial increases, followed by declines.

In 1963, Taiwan's exports were dominated by nonfuel primary products, accounting for 61.0 percent of the total (see Table 5.7) and consisting largely of food and live animals (54.7 percent). In that year, sugar, bananas and rice were Taiwan's principal primary exports, followed by canned pineapple, canned mushrooms and canned asparagus.

The share of nonfuel primary products declined greatly in sub-

Table 5.7 Commodity composition of exports: major product groups: Taiwan (percent of total exports)

		1963	1973	1981	1988
Fuels	(SITC 3)	0.9	0.3	1.9	0.6
Nonfuel primary products		61.0	16.0	9.2	7.4
Food and live animals	(SITC 0)	54.7	13.3	7.1	4.9
Beverages and tobacco	(SITC 1)	0.3	0.1	0.1	0.1
Industrial materials	(SITC 2+4+68)	6.0	2.5	2.0	2.4
Manufactures	(SITC 5+6+7+8–68)	38.0	83.6	88.7	91.8
Other	(SITC 9)	0.0	0.1	0.1	0.2
Total		100.0	100.0	100.0	100.0
Manufactures (industrial classification)		18.4	83.4	88.4	91.2
Textile, apparel, leather	(ISIC 32)	9.3	31.5	28.3	22.7
Wood product and furniture	(ISIC 33)	0.0	8.8	5.2	3.7
Paper and paper products	(ISIC 34)	0.0	1.0	1.0	1.1
Chemicals	(ISIC 35)	2.0	8.7	9.7	10.3
Nonmetallic mineral products	(ISIC 36)	4.1	1.3	2.2	2.4
Iron and steel	(ISIC 37)	1.9	1.3	2.0	1.6
Engineering products	(ISIC 38)	1.1	26.2	33.1	43.7
Other industries	(ISIC 39)	0.0	4.5	6.9	6.2

Source: UN, COMTRADE data base.

sequent years, to 16.0 percent in 1973, 9.2 percent in 1981, and 7.4 percent in 1988. An increasing share of the total consists of processed food.

In turn, the share of manufactured goods in Taiwan's exports rose from 38.0 percent in 1963 to 83.6 percent in 1973, 88.7 percent in 1981 and 91.8 percent in 1988. Within this total, engineering products and, to a lesser extent, chemicals gained ground at the expense of textiles, apparel and leather products, and wood products and furniture.

In 1963, textiles, apparel and leather products accounted for the bulk of Taiwan's manufactured exports (9.3 percent of total exports), followed by nometallic metal products (4.1 percent). Within the first category textiles predominated while the group of other nonmetallic products loomed large in the second category.

The share of textiles, apparel and leather products in total exports reached 31.5 percent in 1973; it declined afterwards to 28.3 percent in 1981 and 22.7 percent in 1988. Within this category, wearing apparel assumed importance, with textiles placing second, footwear third and other textile products fourth.

The export share of wood products, consisting largely of plywood, reached 8.8 percent in 1973 but fell to 5.2 percent in 1981 and 3.7 percent in 1988. The share of nonmetallic minerals was 1.3 percent, 2.2 percent and 2.4 percent for the same years. In turn, the shares of paper and paper products and iron and steel fluctuated around 1 percent and between 1.5 and 2.0 percent, respectively.

The share of chemicals in total exports rose throughout the period, from 2.0 percent in 1963 to 8.7 percent in 1973, 9.7 percent in 1981 and 10.3 percent in 1988. Within this category plastic products predominate, followed by synthetic resins and basic chemicals.

Even larger increases occurred in the export share of engineering products, which grew from 1.1 percent in 1963 to 26.2 percent in 1973, and again to 33.1 percent in 1981 and 43.7 percent in 1988. The largest items within this category were radio and television sets (10.4 percent), followed by fabricated metal products (6.1 percent), office and computing equipment (5.6 percent) and other electrical machinery (5.0 percent). Finally, the export share of the miscellaneous group of 'other industries' increased from nil in 1963 to 4.5 percent in 1973 and 6.9 percent in 1981, declining slightly to 6.2 percent in 1988.

The share of nonfuel primary products declined on the import side as well. This share was 45.5 percent in 1963, 32.6 percent in 1977, 21.9 percent in 1981 and 18.8 percent in 1988. Declines were shown in all categories, including food and live animals, beverages and tobacco and industrial materials (see Table 5.8).

In turn, as noted above, changes in the import shares of fuels varied largely with changes in oil prices. The relevant shares were: 1963, 7.3 percent; 1973, 4.1 percent; 1981, 25.7 percent; and 1988, 10.4 percent. Finally, the import share of manufactured products increased from 46.8 percent in 1963 to 62.3 percent in 1973, declined to 50.3 percent in 1981, and increased again to 68.1 percent in 1988.

Within the manufacturing sector, iron and steel led in 1963, followed by engineering products and by chemicals. By 1988, engineering products were in the lead, with a share of 39.8 percent, followed by chemicals (10.7 percent) and iron and steel (7.3 percent). These changes indicate the effects of import substitution in chemicals and iron and steel, with continued reliance on foreign machinery.

PROSPECTS FOR THE FUTURE

Economic growth in Taiwan has been projected at 8.0 percent a year for the 1987–2000 period. This is higher than the 7.6 percent growth

Table 5.8 Commodity composition of imports: major product groups: Taiwan (percent of total imports)

		1963	1973	1981	1988
Fuels	(SITC 3)	7.3	4.1	25.7	10.4
Nonfuel primary products		45.5	32.6	21.9	18.8
Food and live animals	(SITC 0)	10.3	8.0	6.7	
Beverages and tobacco	(SITC 1)	1.1	0.6	0.4	
Industrial materials	(SITC 2+4+68)	34.1	23.9	14.7	
Manufactures	(SITC 5+6+7+8–68)	46.8	62.3	50.3	68.1
Other	(SITC 9)	0.4	1.0	2.1	2.7
Total		100.0	100.0	100.0	100.0
Manufactures (industrial classification)		14.7	60.4	48.7	68.8
Textile, apparel, leather	(ISIC 32)	0.5	5.4	1.8	2.7
Wood product and furniture	(ISIC 33)	0.0	0.1	0.3	1.4
Paper and paper products	(ISIC 34)	0.1	0.5	0.5	5.5
Chemicals	(ISIC 35)	4.1	11.6	9.7	10.7
Nonmetallic mineral products	(ISIC 36)	0.1	0.6	0.7	1.4
Iron and steel	(ISIC 37)	5.6	6.4	5.2	7.3
Engineering products	(ISIC 38)	4.4	35.3	30.0	39.3
Other industries	(ISIC 39)	0.0	0.4	0.4	0.5

Source: UN, COMTRADE data base.

rate for 1981–7 period but lower than the growth rate of 9.2 percent reached in 1963–87. At the same time, population growth would decline from 1.4 percent in 1981–7 to 1.2 percent in 1986–2000, resulting in a per caput income growth rate of 6.7 percent for the period.

In order to attain these growth rates, however, appropriate policies would need to be followed. To begin with, Taiwan should eliminate quantitative import restrictions and reduce average tariffs to 5 percent. Also, export subsidies should be eliminated.

These changes would make only a small dent in Taiwan's large current account surplus. It will also be necessary to appreciate the exchange rate. While a substantial appreciation occurred between 1987 and 1989, this would have to continue in order to reduce Taiwan's current surplus further. Such a surplus is not desirable since higher returns can be obtained in domestic investment than abroad.

The appreciation of the exchange rate would have to be accompanied by appropriate steps to ensure increases in domestic investment and consumption. To begin with, there would be a need for substantial infrastructural investments to support private investment in Taiwan. Also, mortgage credit would need to be liberalized as today only 15-year mortgages are provided with a 60 percent downpayment. Finally, consumer credit should be liberalized.

Private investment would be further promoted through the reform of the financial system. It would be desirable to denationalize state-owned banks gradually, to establish more private banks and to promote investment banking.

Taiwan would also need to modify the tax system that excessively encourages saving (at present there is no tax liability on deposit interest and dividend income up to about $10,000). At the same time, it would be sensible to cut taxes, so as to encourage private investment as well as consumption.

Bibliography

Aikman, David, 1986. 'China's Periphery: Hong Kong and Taiwan', Chapter 5 in David Aikman, *Pacific Rim: Area of Change, Area of Opportunity*. Boston, Little, Brown.

Allen, Richard V. *et al.*, 1985. *U.S.–Taiwan Relations: Economic and Strategic Dimensions*. San Francisco, CA: Institute for Contemporary Studies.

Chou, Tein-Chen, 1986. 'Concentration, Profitability and Trade in a Simultaneous Equation Analysis: The Case of Taiwan', *The Journal of Industrial Economics*, vol. 34.

Emery, Robert F., 1987. 'Monetary Policy in Taiwan, China', unpublished paper.

Fei, John C. H., Gustav Ranis and Shirley W. Y. Kuo, 1979. *Growth with Equity: The Taiwanese Case*. A World Bank Research Publication. New York: Oxford University Press.

Fuh-sheng Hsieh, John, and Chung-lih Wu, 1988. 'Economic and Political Development in the Republic of China', in David M. Lampton and Catherine H. Keyser (eds), *China's Global Presence: Economics, Politics, and Security*. Washington, DC: American Enterprise Institute.

Galenson, Walter (ed.), 1979. *Economic Growth and Structural Change in Taiwan: The Post-War Experience of the Republic of China*. Ithaca, NY: Cornell University Press.

Gold, Thomas B., 1986. *Dependent Development in Taiwan*. Ann Arbor, MI: University Microfilms International.

Gold, Thomas B., 1986. *State and Society in the Taiwan Miracle*. Armonk, NY: M. E. Sharpe.

Grabowski, Richard, 1988. 'Taiwanese Economic Development: An Alternative Interpretation', *Development and Change*, vol. 19, pp. 53–67.

Haggard, Stephen and Tun-jen Cheng, 1987. 'Taiwan', Chapter III in Stephen Haggard and Tun-jen Cheng, *Newly Industrializing Asia in Transition: Policy Reform and American Response*. Policy Paper in International Affairs, no. 17. Berkeley, CA: University of California.

Hou, Chi-ming, 1987. 'Strategy for Industrial Development', *Industry of Free China* (October) vol. 68, no. 4.

International Commercial Bank of China, 1987. 'Perspective of the Taiwan Economy up to the Year of 2000', *Economic Review* (November–December), no. 240.

Kohsaka, Akira, 1987. 'Financial Liberalization in Asian NICs: A Comparative Study of Korea and Taiwan in the 1980s', *The Developing Economies*, vol. 25, no. 4.

Kuo, Shirley W. Y., 1983. *The Taiwan Economy in Transition*. Boulder, CO: Westview Press.

Kuo, Shirley W. Y. and John C. H. Fei, 1985. 'Causes and Roles of Export Expansion in the Republic of China', in Walter Galenson (ed.), *Foreign Trade and Investment: Economic Growth in the Newly Industrializing Asian Countries*. Madison, WI: University of Wisconsin Press.

Kuo, Shirley W. Y., Gustav Ranis and John C. H. Fei, 1981. *The Taiwan Success Story: Rapid Growth with Improved Distribution in the Republic of China, 1952–1979*. Boulder, CO: Westview Press.

Kuznets, Paul W., 1988. 'An East Asian Model of Economic Development: Japan, Taiwan, and South Korea', *Economic Development and Cultural Change*, vol. 36, no. 3.

Lau, Lawrence J. and Lawrence R. Klein (eds), 1986. *Models of Development: A Comparative Study of Economic Growth in South Korea and Taiwan*. San Francisco, CA: Institute for Contemporary Studies.

Li, K. T., 1976. *The Experience of Dynamic Economic Growth on Taiwan*. Taipei, Taiwan: Mei Ya.

Liang, Kuo-shu, 1988. 'Financial Reform, Trade and Foreign Exchange Liberalization in the Republic of China', *Economic Review* (March–April), no. 242, pp. 1–24.

Liang, Kuo-shu and Chin-ing Hou Liang, 1986. 'The Industrial Policy of Taiwan', in Sekiguchi Mutoh *et al.* (eds), *Industrial Policies for Pacific Economic Growth.* North Sydney, Australia: Allen & Unwin Australia Pty.

Liang, Kuo-shu, and Ching-ing Hou Liang, 1986. 'Trade Strategy and Industrial Policy in Taiwan', *Economic Review* (September–October), no. 233, pp. 1–28.

Lin, Ching-yuan, 1973. *Industrialization in Taiwan, 1946–72: Trade and Import Substitution Policies for Developing Countries.* New York: Praeger.

Liu, Alan P. L., 1987. *Phoenix and the Lame Lion: Modernization in Taiwan and Mainland China, 1950–1980.* Stanford, CA: The Hoover Institution.

Ranis, Gustav and Chi Schive, 1985. 'Direct Foreign Investment in Taiwan's Development', in Walter Galenson (ed.), *Foreign Trade and Investment: Economic Growth in the Newly Industrializing Asian Countries.* Madison, WI: University of Wisconsin Press.

Schive, Chi and Tze-zer Kao, 1986. 'A Measure of Secondary Import Substitution in Taiwan', *Economic Review* (September–October), no. 233, pp. 29–48.

Seabury, Paul, 1981. 'South Korea and Taiwan: Prospering but Threatened', Chapter 7 in Paul Seabury, *America's Stake in the Pacific.* Washington, DC: Ethics and Public Policy Center.

Simon, Dennis Fred and Chi Schive, 1986. 'Taiwan', in Frances W. Rushing and Carol Ganz Brown (eds), *National Policies for Developing High Technology Industries: International Comparisons.* Boulder, CO: Westview Press.

Sun, I-Shuan, 1969. 'Trade Policies and Economic Development in Taiwan', in Theodore Morgan and Nyle Spoelstra (eds), *Economic Interdependence in Southeast Asia.* Madison, WI: University of Wisconsin Press.

Tsiang, S. C., 1984. 'Taiwan's Economic Miracle: Lessons In Economic Development', in Arnold C. Harberger (ed.), *World Economic Growth: Case Studies of Developed and Developing Nations.* San Francisco, CA: Institute for Contemporary Studies.

US Congress, Joint Economic Committee, 1987. *Restoring International Balance: The Taiwan Economy and International Trade.* A Staff Study, 100th Congress, 1st session, Washington D.C. Superintendent of Documents.

Verbruggen, Harmen, 1985. 'The Case of the Taiwan', in Harmen Verbruggen, *Gains from Export-Oriented Industrialization in Developing Countries with Special Reference to South-East Asia.* Amsterdam, Netherlands: Free University Press.

Wheeler, Jimmy W. and Perry L. Wood, 1987. *Beyond Recrimination: Perspectives on U.S.–Taiwan Trade Tensions.* Indianapolis, IN: Hudson Institute.

Woronoff, Jon, 1986. 'Taiwan, Industrial Island', Chapter 2 in Jon Woronoff, *Asia's Miracle Economies.* New York: M. E. Sharpe.

Wu, Rong-I, 1971. *The Strategy of Economic Development: A Case Study of Taiwan.* Louvain: Vander.

Wu, Rong-I, 1988. 'The Distinctive Features of Taiwan's Development', in Peter L. Berger and Hsin-Huang Michael Hsiao (eds), *In Search of an East Asian Development Model.* New Brunswick, NJ: Transaction Books.

Wu, Yuan-li, 1985. *Becoming and Industrialized Nation: ROC's Development on Taiwan.* New York: Praeger.

6 Indonesia

INTRODUCTION

Indonesia has a population of 166.4 million in an area of 1 919 000 square kilometers. It was colonized by the Dutch in the seventeenth century and occupied by the Japanese during the Second World War. Following the declaration of independence on April 17, 1945, the Netherlands attempted to reimpose its colonial rule by force and only accepted Indonesia's independence after four years of armed struggle.

Indonesia consists of 13 600 islands, of which 3000 are inhabited. The five big islands, Java (together with Madura), Sumatra, Sulawesi (Celebes), Kalimantan (the Indonesian part of Borneo) and Irian Jaya (the Indonesian part of New Guinea) account for 92 percent of the area and 94 percent of the population. Over three-fifths of the population live on Java and Madura.

While there are 300 linguistic and ethnic groups, 95 percent of the population of Indonesia are ethnic Malays. The largest minority are the Chinese (2.5 million); other non-indigenous groups include Arabs, Indians and Europeans. Irian Jaya is inhabited by Papuans.

Indonesia straddles the equator. Java has fertile land while land in the other islands is erosion-prone. Primary exports of rubber, coffee, copper, copra, palm oil and spices are overshadowed by petroleum whose share has, however, been declining in recent years. Indonesia is an important exporter of tin and has other mineral resources as well.

After independence, pre-war production levels were re-established, but per caput incomes declined during the 'Guided Economy' period (1958–65) that left the Indonesian economy in a poor state, resulting in the depletion of foreign exchange reserves, a large external debt, the decline of the banking system, substantial budget deficits and high rates of inflation. The economy was consolidated in the subsequent period of stabilization under President Suharto, followed by rapid economic growth.

Growth was given further impetus by the quadrupling of oil prices in 1973. In turn, the decline in oil prices and the virtual exhaustion of possibilities for import substitution in manufacturing contributed to substantial decreases in growth rates during the first half of the 1980s.

The diversification of the economy and strong adjustment efforts have led, however, to improvements in the economic situation in recent years.

GOVERNMENT POLICIES

Under colonial rule, Indonesia's economy was based on primary activities, producing tin, rubber, coffee and other crops for export and foodstuffs for domestic consumption. Exports were exchanged for manufactured goods (of which Indonesia produced little beyond handicrafts) and for rice, in which domestic self-sufficiency was not achieved.

After independence, President Sukarno set out to develop heavy industry in the framework of the Five-Year Plan of 1955–60 and the Eight-Year Overall Development Plan initiated in 1960. These plans were largely unsuccessful and attention soon turned to inflation, which was but one manifestation of economic mismanagement.

Sukarno's 'Old Order' was replaced by Suharto's 'New Order' which stabilized and rehabilitated the economy. By 1969, annual rates of inflation were reduced from 650 percent to below 20 percent, the balance of payments was brought under control, and attention shifted to long-term development.

The first Five-Year Plan (Repelita I) of 1969–73 put emphasis on agriculture and infrastructure and on industry supporting agricultural production. Agriculture also received emphasis during Repelita II (1974–8) while industry grew rapidly in response to the increased revenues derived from higher oil earnings. Industrial infrastructure was the focus of Repelita III (1979–83); Repelita IV (1984–88) concentrated on basic industries; and Repelita V (1989–93) emphasized private sector development in nonoil industries.

Suharto introduced various measures to stimulate agricultural production. In particular, rice cultivation was assisted through improvements in irrigation, the subsidization of modern inputs (such as fertilizer and insecticides) and the provision of high-yielding seeds. These measures, together with more favorable prices for rice, contributed to the attainment of the long-cherished aim of self-sufficiency in rice, the principal staple of the Indonesian population.

Programs were introduced also for other food crops, tobacco and sugar cane. These programs generally aimed at providing modern inputs at subsidized rates. Finally, an extensive replanting effort was introduced for tree crops in the early 1980s.

The transmigration program from Java to the outer islands focused first on bringing into cultivation new lands for irrigated rice farming, followed by reclaiming swampland and, subsequently, opening areas for a combination of dryland food and tree crop farming. The number of migrants remained, however, below the natural increase of the population in Java.

In the manufacturing sector, President Sukarno discouraged the operation of market forces and relied largely on state enterprises for industrial development in a highly protected and regulated environment. The nationalization of Dutch-owned enterprises and controls on new investment also discouraged foreign direct investment.

President Suharto adopted a favorable attitude toward foreign direct investment and encouraged private activities, although the state enterprise sector continued to grow. At the same time industrial protection was maintained, with the chief reliance based on quantitative import restrictions. This led to the development of a high-cost industrial structure while discriminating against agriculture.

A variety of measures also promoted capital-intensive activities. They included overvalued exchange rates (which lowered the cost of capital goods), negative real interest rates and credit allocation favoring government-sponsored large projects, accelerated depreciation and other investment incentives, as well as the exemption of capital goods from import duties.

The policies applied contributed to the rapid expansion of industry in Indonesia's large domestic market without commensurate gains in employment. Industrial growth slowed down, however, towards the end of the 1970s, when import-substitution possibilities came to be largely exhausted. There followed a period of increased attention to exports.

In November 1978, export subsidies were granted to offset tariffs and taxes on imported inputs as well as the high cost of domestic inputs. Subsequently, in January 1982, export–import procedures were simplified, and subsidized export credits were provided.

In March 1985, under US pressure, Indonesia signed the GATT Code on Subsidies and Countervailing Measures and undertook the obligation to phase out export subsidies. In April 1986, these were replaced by duty drawbacks, followed by the abolition of the preferential credit scheme.

In the following years, several measures were taken to assist exports without infringing on Indonesia's GATT obligations. They included improvements in shipping, reductions in port charges, simplifications in port administration, the transfer of customs functions to the Swiss Société Générale de Surveillance, the establishment of an export insurance and guarantee company, and the creation of an export supporting board for small and medium-scale exporters.

In May 1986, 'producer exporters' who exported more than 85 percent of output were exempted from regulations requiring the use of domestic inputs. Producers exporting less than 85 percent of output, companies exporting their output indirectly through other companies, and suppliers of inputs to exporting companies were also given the chance of using imported inputs if these could be obtained more cheaply abroad than domestically. Finally, in 1987, several export bans and quotas were removed and most export licenses were abolished.

The first steps toward the dismantling of quantitative import restrictions were taken in 1986. These were followed by the removal or relaxation of import licensing on 548 items in October 1986 and January 1987, accounting for 37 percent of all items that had previously been restricted. As a result, the share of domestic production protected under import licensing declined from 66 percent to 38 percent.

Further measures of import liberalization were taken in 1988, reducing the share of domestic production subject to import quotas to 29 percent. Also, important tariff reductions were undertaken, lowering the average tariff rate from 37 percent in 1984 to 27 percent in 1985 and to 26 percent in 1989.

At the same time the state enterprise sector has assumed considerable importance in Indonesia. In 1957 there were only two state enterprises: a cement plant and a spinning mill. There followed the nationalization of Dutch enterprises and the establishment of state firms in heavy industry under Sukarno.

The New Order brought a change in the philosophy towards state enterprises. According to Decision XXIII of July 5, 1966, on the Reform of Basic Economic, Financial and Development Policy, state enterprises will be limited to projects which '(i) require investment too large for national capital; (ii) involve problems of management and skills too complex for private enterprise; (iii) are unprofitable; (iv) too risky; (v) provide infrastructure – harbors, bridges, irrigation, public utilities etc.'

In practice, this has meant continued expansion of state enterprises, which numbered 215 in 1986. Apart from plantations, mining, transportation, trade and banking, where such enterprises were entrenched under Sukarno, expansion also occurred in the manufacturing sector, although the share of state enterprises in this sector declined from 28 percent in 1975 to 20 percent in 1983. Oil refineries, petrochemicals, fertilizers, steel and aluminum are fully state-owned, and the state has a dominant position in cement, basic chemicals, capital goods manufacturing and shipbuilding.

In the private sector, the government has tried to expand pribumi (indigenous) enterprises. Following the anti-Chinese riots of 1974, various measures have been used for this purpose. State-owned banks have favored pribumi enterprises in credit allocation. Special credit programs, including the Small Investment Credit and Permanent Working Capital Credit, have been established to promote pribumi business. Finally, the government has reserved a large number of items on its procurement list for small-scale pribumi firms.

In 1981, the latest year for which data are available, in industrial ventures with foreign companies pribumi had a share of 13 percent, the Chinese 10 percent, the state 9 percent, and foreign owners 68 percent. In turn, in domestic enterprises, the pribumi share was 11 percent, the Chinese share 22 percent, and the share of state enterprises 62 percent.

Hostility towards foreign direct investment under Sukarno gave place to a favourable attitude under Suharto. This was expressed in the Foreign Capital Investment Law of January 1967 whose main provisions were:

1. a guarantee that there is no intention to nationalize foreign assets and a guarantee of compensation payments if nationalization does occur;
2. the duration of the operation of foreign enterprise for thirty years, with extensions beyond this period depending on renegotiation;
3. exemption of foreign investors from profit and dividend taxation for three years and the carryover of losses into the post tax-holiday period;
4. exemption from import duties on machinery and equipment and from import duties on raw materials for two years;
5. free transfer of profits, depreciation funds, and proceeds from sale of shares to Indonesian nationals;
6. full authority to select management and to recruit foreign technicians for jobs which Indonesian labor is not yet capable of doing.

More restrictive policies were adopted following the violent protests that accompanied the visit of the Japanese Prime Minister,

Tanaka, in January 1974. A declaration by President Suharto, outlining the principles to govern new foreign direct investments, stated that all new foreign investments were to be joint ventures; Indonesian equity should be increased to 51 percent within a certain period, later said to be ten years; the list of industries closed to foreign investment was to be extended; tax incentives were to be reduced; and the number of foreign personnel was to be restricted.

In response to a decline in foreign direct investment these restrictions have been liberalized in subsequent years. In particular, the ten-year deadline for Indonesian equity participation has never been enforced. Also, administrative procedures for foreign direct investment have been greatly simplified.

In May 1986, domestic equity requirements were liberalized: for export-oriented and for high-risk projects domestic equity obligations were reduced to 5 percent; for others a 20 percent share could be paid in over five years. Also, foreign firms could be licensed for an additional 30 years.

There is little foreign participation in the Indonesian banking system which is dominated by state banks. The five state banks, with their large branch banking systems, account for about 65 percent of the deposit liabilities and 70 percent of the total assets of deposit money banks (DMBs). The DMBs further include 59 domestic private commercial banks, 10 private Indonesian foreign exchange banks, 11 foreign banks that cannot operate outside Jakarta and 29 development banks. The DMBs hold 90 percent of the assets of the organized financial systems that also comprises two savings banks, 3581 rural banks and a number of nonbank financial institutions.

The nonbank financial institutions are the development finance companies, which are wholly or partly state-owned and are engaged principally in medium- and long-term lending and equity participation, and the investment finance companies, which are privately owned and deal primarily in short-term commercial paper and promissory notes, thus constituting an important segment of the domestic money market. Despite their rapid growth, the nonbank financial institutions account for only 6 percent of the assets of the organized financial system.

Indonesia undertook important financial reforms in June 1983. The reforms included the abolition of credit ceilings, the elimination of controls on the state banks' interest rates, the introduction of a new mechanism of monetary control that relies primarily on open market operations complemented by a system of rediscount facilities, and the adoption of measures to strengthen the money market.

Further important measures were taken in 1988. These measures permitted the entry of new private banks, including joint ventures with foreign banks, allowed domestic banks to open branches throughout Indonesia and foreign banks to open branches in seven major cities, allowed the establishment of new rural banks, eased the requirements to create foreign exchange banks, and liberalized the rules under which nonbank financial intermediaries operate.

Measures were also taken to promote the development of the bond and stock markets. Also, with the imposition of a 15 percent tax on bank interest, discriminatory tax regulations against bond and stock markets have been removed.

These changes in tax regulations followed the introduction of a far-reaching tax reform in 1984. The centerpiece of the tax reform was a 10 percent value added tax on manufactured goods, without exception, which is complemented by luxury taxes at rates of 10 and 20 percent. Also, income tax rates were set at 15, 25 and 35 percent, compared with a maximum rate of 45 percent for business and 50 percent for individuals under the earlier rules. At the same time, tax holidays and other investment incentives were abolished. Finally, property taxes were rationalized.

As a result of the measures taken, between 1983/84 and 1986/87 nonoil tax revenue increased by 87 percent, raising its share in GDP from 6.0 percent to 8.2 percent. Still, these increases provided only partial compensation for the decline in oil revenues from 14.5 percent of GDP in 1981 to 5.6 percent in 1986.

Compared with an average ratio of 72 percent in 1965, virtually 100 percent of school-age children attended primary school in Indonesia by 1986. In the same period, enrollment in secondary schools increased from 12 percent to 41 percent of the relevant age group; the change was from 1 to 7 percent in higher education.

ECONOMIC GROWTH

Per caput incomes in Indonesia increased at an average annual rate of 3.6 percent between 1963 and 1987. However, while per caput incomes rose by 4.0 percent a year between 1963 and 1973 and 5.2 percent a year between 1973 and 1981, the increase was only 1.0 percent between 1981 and 1987 (see Table 6.1). In turn, population growth rates were 2.2 percent during the 1963–87 period.

Table 6.1 Economic performance indicators: Indonesia

Growth rates	1963–73	1973–81	1981–7	1963–87
GDP	6.7	7.2	3.2	6.0
Population	2.6	1.9	2.2	2.2
GDP per caput	4.0	5.2	1.0	3.6
Investment	14.2	18.7	–1.0	11.7
Manufacturing production	6.7	14.4	7.3	9.4
Agricultural production	4.4	4.1	2.8	3.9
Exports	10.9	2.2	1.1	5.5
Imports	13.6	16.1	–0.3	10.7

Source: World Bank.

Table 6.2 Industrial composition and trade: Indonesia (percent of GDP)

	1963	1973	1981	1987
Industrial composition				
Agriculture	55.1	38.2	23.4	25.5
Mining and quarrying	3.3	11.4	22.6	13.1
Manufacturing	7.4	10.6	12.1	13.9
Gas, electricity and water	0.1	0.5	0.5	0.9
Construction	1.9	4.1	6.0	5.3
Transportation	2.3	4.3	4.1	6.5
Wholesale and retail trade	13.6	15.1	15.3	16.8
Banking, real estate	0.8	1.4	2.7	3.5
Ownership of dwellings	1.9	2.1	2.6	2.5
Public administration	3.7	6.0	7.2	7.8
Other services	9.7	6.4	3.6	4.1
Imputed bank service charge, duty	.	.	.	.
Trade				
Exports of goods and nonfactor services	9.2	20.3	28.1	26.0
Imports of goods and nonfactor services	8.9	18.6	24.0	23.2

Source: World Bank.

Manufacturing production increased 6.7 percent a year between 1963 and 1973; its growth accelerated to 14.4 percent in 1973–81 and decelerated again to 7.3 percent in 1981–7. As a result of these changes, the share of manufacturing in GDP rose from 7.4 percent in 1963 to 10.6 percent in 1973, 12.1 percent in 1981 and 13.9 percent in 1987 (see Table 6.2).

Even larger increases occurred in the share of the mining sector. With rising oil revenues, the share of mining in the GDP rose from 3.3 percent in 1963 to 11.4 percent in 1973 and to 22.6 percent in 1981. Its share declined, however, to 13.1 percent in 1987, following the fall of oil prices.

In turn, agriculture's share fell from 55.1 percent in 1963 to 38.2 percent in 1973 and to 23.4 percent in 1981, although it increased to 25.5 percent in 1987 as a counterpart to the decline in the share of mining. Yet agricultural production continued to grow at rates exceeding the rise of population by a substantial margin. It exhibited growth rates of 4.4 percent between 1963 and 1973, 4.1 percent between 1973 and 1981, and 2.8 percent between 1981 and 1987 when there were two poor harvests.

At the same time, the share of services in the GDP experienced uninterrupted increases over time. Their share was 34.2 percent in 1963, which rose to 39.8 percent in 1973, to 41.3 percent in 1981 and to 47.5 percent in 1987.

The data further show increases in the share of every service sector between 1963 and 1987, the only exception being the 'other services' category. Increases were especially large in construction, transportation and banking, followed by public administration. It is noteworthy that the share of public administration in GDP more than doubled during the period.

Exports rose more rapidly than GDP in the 1963–73 period (at a rate of 10.9 percent a year). Their growth rate declined to 2.2 percent a year in 1973–81 and 1.1 percent a year in 1981–7. In turn, imports grew at average annual rates of 13.6 percent in 1963–73 and 16.1 percent in 1973–81, but declined 0.3 percent a year between 1981 and 1987.

Export and import shares were further affected by changes in export and import prices. Thus, with rising oil prices, the share of exports of goods and services in GDP increased from 9.2 percent in 1963 to 20.3 percent in 1973 and to 28.1 percent in 1981. However, their share fell to 26.0 percent in 1987 as oil prices declined.

Changes in import shares show a similar pattern, except that the amplitude of fluctuations was smaller. The share of the imports of goods and services in GDP rose from 8.9 percent in 1963 to 18.6 percent in 1973 and to 24.0 percent in 1981, declining afterwards to 23.2 percent in 1987.

Domestic savings amounted to 22.5 percent of the GDP in 1973; they were in the 26–28 percent range between 1976 and 1978; and

Table 6.3 Savings and investment ratios: Indonesia (percent of GDP)

	1973	1974	1975	1976	1977	1978	1979	1980
Private savings	24.5	28.8	29.1	27.8	27.2	26.9	34.1	39.6
Government budget balance	–2.0	–0.9	–3.2	–1.5	1.0	–0.5	–0.5	–2.4
Domestic savings	22.5	27.9	25.9	26.3	28.2	26.3	33.6	37.2
Foreign savings	–1.7	–8.3	–2.2	–2.2	–4.8	–2.4	–7.0	–12.8
Domestic investment	20.8	19.5	23.7	24.1	23.4	23.9	26.6	24.3

	1981	1982	1983	1984	1985	1986	1987
Private savings	35.0	30.2	29.7	31.1	28.6	27.7	30.8
Government budget balance	–1.4	–2.3	–1.4	–0.6	–0.3	–2.8	–1.7
Domestic savings	33.7	27.9	28.3	30.5	28.3	24.9	29.1
Foreign savings	–4.1	–0.4	1.1	–5.0	–1.9	–0.3	–2.8
Domestic investment	29.6	27.5	29.4	25.5	26.4	24.6	26.3

Source: World Bank.

they surpassed 30 percent between 1978 and 1981 (see Table 6.3). In turn, domestic savings were slightly below 30 percent of GDP in 1982–7, except that they were 30.5 percent in 1984 and 24.9 percent in 1986.

Apart from 1977, the government budget was continuously in a deficit. The deficit reached 2.8 percent of the GDP in 1986, when the fall of oil prices substantially reduced government revenues, declining to 1.7 percent of GDP in 1987.

Domestic investment fluctuated to a lesser extent than domestic savings. From 20 percent in 1973–4, domestic investment grew to nearly 30 percent of GDP in the early 1980s but declined to 26.3 percent in 1987.

While oil exports gave rise to a positive trade balance, oil royalty payments contributed to a negative balance on the service account in Indonesia (see Table 6.4). It is further apparent that Indonesia had an inflow of foreign direct investment and long-term capital throughout this period. In turn, if one combines short-term capital and errors and omissions, an inflow is shown only for recent years.

INTERNATIONAL TRADE

In 1963, 68.6 percent of Indonesian exports were destined to the developed countries. This share increased to 79.5 percent in 1973,

Table 6.4 Balance of payments: Indonesia (million US$)

	1978	1979	1980	1981	1982	1983	1984	1985	1986	1987
Merchandise exports	11 035	15 154	21 795	23 348	19 747	18 689	20 754	18 527	14 396	17 206
Merchandise imports	-8 386	-9 245	-12 624	-16 542	-17 854	-17 726	-15 047	-12 705	-11 938	-12 710
Trade balance	2 649	5 909	9 171	6 806	1 893	963	5 707	5 822	2 458	4 496
Other goods, services, and income: credit	291	398	446	1 530	1 527	1 177	1 398	1 612	1 576	1 610
Other goods, services, and income: debit	-4 368	-5 357	-6 807	-9 152	-8 878	-8 592	-9 128	-9 445	-8 204	-8 484
Other goods, services, and income: net	-4 077	-4 959	-6 361	-7 622	-7 351	-7 415	-7 730	-7 833	-6 628	-6 874
Unrequited transfers	14	30	55	250	134	114	167	88	259	228
Current account balance	-1 414	980	2 865	-566	-5 324	-6 338	-1 856	-1 923	-3 911	-2 150
Direct investment	279	226	183	133	225	292	222	310	258	307
Long-term capital	1 317	1 094	1 973	2 018	4 871	5 031	2 759	1 570	2 624	2 265
Short-term capital	121	-454	-820	-290	526	731	476	-98	1 295	642
Capital account balance	1 717	866	1 336	1 861	5 622	6 054	3 457	1 782	4 177	3 214
Errors and omissions	-133	-402	-1 773	-1 669	-2 151	467	-620	651	-1 269	-435
Overall balance	170	1 444	2 428	-374	-1 853	183	981	510	-1 003	629
Net use of reserves	-117	-1 436	-2 155	353	1 879	-172	-972	-568	928	-876

Note: The overall balance is the sum of the current and capital account balances and errors and omissions. Net use of reserves was derived by adding the following items to overall balance: counterpart to the monetization and demonetization of gold, counterpart to SDR allocation, and counterpart to valuation changes.

Source: IMF, *International Financial Statistics*, various issues.

Table 6.5 Geographical composition of exports: Indonesia
(percent of total exports)

	1963	1973	1981	1988
Developed Countries	68.6	79.5	73.9	71.4
United States	15.8	14.5	18.3	16.2
Western Europe	35.0	10.1	4.7	11.3
Japan	8.5	53.2	47.9	41.7
Canada, Australia, New Zealand	9.3	1.7	2.9	2.2
Developing Countries	25.0	20.1	25.4	27.8
Pacific countries (other than China)	16.2	12.2	15.3	20.5
East Asian NICs	0.6	11.1	13.1	18.3
Hong Kong	0.5	0.4	0.6	2.9
Korea	NA	NA	1.2	4.4
Singapore	NA	10.6	9.7	8.5
Taiwan	0.0	0.0	1.5	2.5
East Asian NECs	15.7	1.1	2.2	2.2
Indonesia	–	–	–	–
Malaysia	12.2	1.1	0.2	0.9
Philippines	2.3	0.0	1.8	0.4
Thailand	1.2	0.0	0.2	0.8
China	5.8	0.0	0.0	2.5
Other developing countries	3.0	7.8	10.1	4.8
Other Asia	2.0	4.8	0.4	1.2
Africa	0.2	0.2	0.1	0.9
Southern Europe	0.0	0.7	0.5	0.2
Middle East	0.0	NA	0.6	2.2
Latin America	0.7	2.1	8.5	0.2
European Socialist Countries	6.3	0.5	0.7	0.7

Note: Taiwanese figures for 1981 and 1987 derived as difference between total exports, the regional aggregates, special categories, and other countries not included. Regional aggregates may not sum to 100 percent due to inclusion in denominator of special categories and other countries not specified.

Sources: IMF, *Direction of Trade Statistics*, various issues.

declined to 73.9 percent in 1981 but declined to 71.4 percent in 1988. Within this total, large shifts were experienced from Western Europe and from Canada, Australia and New Zealand to Japan, reflecting mainly a redirection of the exports of petroleum (see Table 6.5).

Thus, the share of Western Europe in Indonesia's exports declined from 35.0 percent in 1963 to 11.3 percent in 1988, while that of

Canada, Australia and New Zealand fell from 9.3 percent to 2.2 percent. By contrast, Japan's share increased from 8.5 percent in 1963 to 41.7 percent in 1988. Smaller changes were shown in the export share of the United States, which was 15.8 percent in 1963 and 16.2 percent in 1988.

In turn, the share of the developing countries in Indonesia's exports fell from 25.0 percent in 1963 to 20.1 percent in 1973, rose again to 25.4 percent in 1981 and to 27.8 percent in 1988. At the same time, divergent trends are shown in the export shares of various areas.

The East Asian NICs had a negligible share (0.6 percent) in Indonesian exports in 1963. Their share reached 11.1 percent in 1973, increasing further to 13.1 percent in 1981 and to 18.3 percent in 1988, largely on account of their petroleum imports. Singapore accounts for more than two-fifths of the total (8.5 percent), followed by Korea (4.4 percent), Hong Kong (2.9 percent) and Taiwan (2.5 percent).

By contrast, the export share of the East Asian NECs declined from 15.7 percent in 1963 to 1.1 percent in 1973; it was 2.2 percent in 1981 and 2.5 percent in 1988. The decline was concentrated in Malaysia; none of the countries of this group had an export share of even 1 percent in 1988.

The other developing countries showed considerable fluctuations, with their share in Indonesia's exports rising from 3.0 percent in 1963, to 7.8 percent in 1973 and to 10.1 percent in 1981, declining subsequently to 4.8 percent in 1988. The fluctuations were concentrated in Other Asia and Latin America. In 1988, these regions had export shares of 1.2 percent and 0.2 percent, respectively. The export shares of the other regions were: Africa, 0.9 percent; Southern Europe, 0.2 percent; and Middle East, 2.2 percent.

China's export share was 5.8 percent in 1963 when it had close political ties with Indonesia. Its share was nil in 1973 and in 1981 but reached 2.5 percent in 1988. For similar reasons the European socialist countries took 6.3 percent of Indonesia's exports in 1963; their share declined to 0.5 percent in 1973 and it was 0.7 percent in 1981 and 1988.

The share of the developed countries in Indonesia's imports varied little over time. It was 68.2 percent in 1963, increased to 69.1 percent in 1973, declined to 66.9 percent in 1981, and rose again to 67.8 percent in 1988 (see Table 6.6). The major changes were declines in the US share and increases in the shares of Japan and of Canada, Australia and New Zealand.

Table 6.6 Geographical composition of imports: Indonesia
(percent of total imports)

	1963	1973	1981	1988
Developed Countries	68.2	69.1	66.9	67.8
United States	33.1	18.8	13.5	12.9
Western Europe	24.3	17.5	19.1	22.4
Japan	10.5	29.3	30.1	25.4
Canada, Australia, New Zealand	0.3	3.5	4.2	7.2
Developing Countries	24.6	29.9	31.9	30.8
Pacific countries (other than China)	9.2	14.8	20.1	18.7
East Asian NICs	1.5	11.0	16.6	15.5
Hong Kong	1.5	6.1	0.5	1.0
Korea	NA	NA	3.7	3.3
Singapore	NA	4.9	9.4	6.6
Taiwan	NA	0.0	3.1	4.6
East Asian NECs	7.7	3.8	3.5	3.2
Indonesia	–	–	–	–
Malaysia	4.2	0.5	0.5	2.2
Philippines	NA	0.5	1.9	0.3
Thailand	3.5	2.8	1.1	0.7
China	6.8	1.8	1.9	3.0
Other developing countries	8.6	13.4	9.9	9.0
Other Asia	6.8	9.5	0.9	0.9
Africa	NA	1.6	1.7	1.3
Southern Europe	0.0	1.2	0.0	0.2
Middle East	0.0	NA	5.3	5.0
Latin America	1.8	0.9	2.0	1.6
European Socialist Countries	7.2	1.0	1.0	0.9

Note: Taiwanese figures for 1981 and 1987 derived as difference between total imports, the regional aggregates, special categories, and other countries not included. Regional aggregates may not sum to 100 percent due to inclusion in denominator of special categories and other countries not specified.

Sources: IMF, *Direction of Trade Statistics*, various issues.

The US share of Indonesia's imports fell from 33.1 percent in 1963 to 18.8 percent in 1973, declining further to 13.5 percent in 1981 and to 12.9 percent in 1988. In turn, after earlier decreases from 24.3 percent in 1963 to 17.5 percent in 1973, the share of Western Europe increased to 19.1 percent in 1981 and to 22.4 percent in 1988.

The import share of Japan rose from 10.5 percent in 1963 to 29.3

percent in 1973 and 30.1 percent in 1981 declining to 25.4 percent in 1988. Finally, the share of Canada, Australia and New Zealand increased from 0.3 percent in 1963 to 3.5 percent in 1973, 4.2 percent in 1981 and 7.2 percent in 1988.

The developing countries' share in Indonesia's imports underwent little change during the period under consideration. It was 24.6 percent in 1963, 29.9 percent in 1973, 31.9 percent in 1981 and 30.8 percent in 1988. Within the total, however, considerable fluctuations were observed.

While the import share of the East Asian NICs increased from 1.5 percent in 1963 to 15.5 percent in 1988, that of the East Asian NECs declined from 7.7 percent to 3.2 percent. The 1988 shares of individual countries were: Hong Kong, 1.0 percent; Korea, 3.3 percent; Singapore, 6.6 percent; Taiwan, 4.6 percent; Malaysia, 2.2 percent; the Philippines, 0.3 percent; and Thailand, 0.7 percent.

In turn, the share of other developing countries in Indonesia's imports increased from 8.6 percent in 1963 to 13.4 percent in 1973, declining afterwards to 9.9 percent in 1981 and to 9.0 percent in 1988. Much of the fluctuations originated in Other Asia, whose 1988 import share was 0.9 percent. The corresponding figures are: Africa, 1.3 percent; Southern Europe, 0.2 percent; Middle East, 5.0 percent; and Latin America, 1.6 percent.

Finally, with the ending of political ties, the import share of China and the European socialist countries declined from the 1963 peak of 6.8 percent and 7.2 percent, respectively. Their shares in 1988 were China, 3.0 percent, and the European socialist countries, 0.9 percent.

The commodity composition of Indonesian exports changed to a considerable extent during the period under review. The share of fuels increased from 38.5 percent in 1963 to 50.1 percent in 1973 and to 79.8 percent in 1981, declining to 48.9 percent in 1988 in response to lower petroleum prices (see Table 6.7). Initially, all fuel exports consisted of petroleum; since 1980 natural gas has also assumed importance.

In turn, the export share of nonfuel primary products declined from 61.2 percent in 1963 to 47.8 percent in 1973 and to 16.9 percent in 1981, increasing subsequently to 26.0 percent in 1988. Within this category, the share of food and live animals decreased slightly, from 12.1 percent in 1963 to 10.0 percent in 1988, while the share of beverages and tobacco fell from 2.7 percent in 1963 to 0.4 percent in 1988 and that of industrial materials declined from 46.3 percent to 15.6 percent.

Table 6.7 Commodity composition of exports: major product groups: Indonesia (percent of total exports)

		1963	1973	1981	1988
Fuels	(SITC 3)	38.5	50.1	79.8	68.9
Nonfuel primary products		61.2	47.8	16.9	26.0
Food and live animals	(SITC 0)	12.1	8.3	4.2	10.0
Beverages and tobacco	(SITC 1)	2.7	1.3	0.2	0.4
Industrial materials	(SITC 2+4+68)	46.3	38.2	12.5	15.6
Manufactures	(SITC 5+6+7+8–68)	0.3	1.9	3.0	25.0
Other	(SITC 9)	0.0	0.3	0.3	0.1
Total		100.0	100.0	100.0	100.0
Manufactures (industrial classification)		0.0	1.0	3.0	25.1
Textile, apparel, leather	(ISIC 32)	0.0	0.2	0.7	6.9
Wood product and furniture	(ISIC 33)	0.0	0.1	0.9	14.0
Paper and paper products	(ISIC 34)	0.0	0.0	0.0	0.6
Chemicals	(ISIC 35)	0.0	0.4	0.3	1.2
Nonmetallic mineral products	(ISIC 36)	0.0	0.0	0.1	0.6
Iron and steel	(ISIC 37)	0.0	0.0	0.1	1.1
Engineering products	(ISIC 38)	0.0	0.3	0.9	0.7
Other industries	(ISIC 39)	0.0	0.0	0.0	0.1

Source: UN, COMTRADE data base.

Among foodstuffs, coffee is of greatest importance (5.6 percent in 1987), followed by shellfish (2.0 percent), which represents a recent development. Among industrial materials, the share of natural rubber declined from 35.4 percent to 4.8 percent in 1987 and Indonesia does not export copra and raw wood any more. In the latter case, an export ban has been imposed in order to promote the exports of plywood.

In fact, plywood exports increased from nil to 6.9 percent of total exports in 1987. They account for over one-third of the manufactured exports that came to provide 25.0 percent of total exports in 1988, compared with 0.3 percent in 1963, 1.9 percent in 1973 and 3.0 percent in 1981. Other important manufactured exports in 1987 included clothing (3.5 percent of total exports) and textile yarn and fabrics (1.8 percent).

Data on the product composition of imports are not available for 1963. Between 1973 and 1988 the import shares of fuels and nonfuel primary products increased from 1.8 percent to 9.0 percent and from 14.9 percent to 15.5 percent, respectively. In turn, the import share

Table 6.8 Commodity composition of imports: major product groups: Indonesia (percent of total imports)

		1963	1973	1981	1988
Fuels	(SITC 3)	0.0	1.8	13.3	9.0
Nonfuel primary products		0.0	14.9	17.2	15.5
Food and live animals	(SITC 0)	0.0	9.9	10.4	3.9
Beverages and tobacco	(SITC 1)	0.0	0.3	0.3	6.3
Industrial materials	(SITC 2+4+68)	0.0	4.7	6.5	11.3
Manufactures	(SITC 5+6+7+8–68)	0.0	83.3	68.9	75.1
Other	(SITC 9)	0.0	0.0	0.5	0.4
Total		0.0	100.0	100.0	100.0
Manufactures (industrial classification)		0.0	82.5	68.9	74.9
Textile, apparel, leather	(ISIC 32)	0.0	7.6	2.1	1.8
Wood product and furniture	(ISIC 33)	0.0	0.3	0.1	0.1
Paper and paper products	(ISIC 34)	0.0	2.2	1.6	2.9
Chemicals	(ISIC 35)	0.0	14.0	14.0	19.6
Nonmetallic mineral products	(ISIC 36)	0.0	2.5	1.5	1.3
Iron and steel	(ISIC 37)	0.0	10.2	8.7	3.6
Engineering products	(ISIC 38)	0.0	45.4	40.6	42.8
Other industries	(ISIC 39)	0.0	0.3	0.3	0.4

Source: UN, COMTRADE data base.

of manufactured goods declined from 83.3 percent to 75.1 percent (see Table 6.8).

Among nonfuel primary products, the share of industrial materials increased at the expense of food and live animals. Among manufactured goods, increases in the share of paper and its products, chemicals and other industries were more than offset by declines in the shares of textiles, apparel and leather products, wood products and furniture, nonmetallic mineral products, iron and steel, and engineering products.

PROSPECTS FOR THE FUTURE

Economic growth in Indonesia has been projected at 5.8 percent for the period 1987–2000. This represents a slight decline compared with a GDP growth rate of 6.0 percent in the 1963–87 period and a substantial acceleration compared with annual increases of 3.2 percent between 1981 and 1987.

Population is projected to rise at an average annual rate of 2.0 percent, compared with 2.2 percent in 1963–87. Correspondingly, per caput incomes would increase by 3.8 percent a year, slightly exceeding the growth rate of 3.6 percent in 1963–87.

The acceleration of economic growth relative to the low growth rates of the 1981–7 period reflects the assumption of stable and, eventually, rising oil prices. It further assumes improvements in economic policies.

The good performance of Indonesian agriculture had to do in large part with a rapid rise in the production of rice which cannot be expected to continue in the future. This would not be desirable anyway since Indonesia has reached self-sufficiency and its rice quality does not have a ready international market.

Correspondingly, in the future emphasis should be given to agricultural diversification in Java and to the exploitation of agricultural potential in the outer islands. Various measures may be used to ensure agricultural growth.

There is a need to reduce input subsidies which have contributed to the wasteful use of inputs. At the same time, it would be sensible to increase support to agricultural research and to expand extension services. Also, the irrigation system in operation would need to be improved and rural road building promoted.

Administrative regulation of cropping patterns should give place to greater reliance on price incentives. The government should also encourage private-sector participation in agricultural marketing, including domestic trade as well as exports.

The private sector should be given a greater role in the manufacturing sector as well. This would mean forgoing the establishment of additional state enterprises together with the gradual denationalization of enterprises in individual sectors. In addition, the operation of the remaining state enterprises should be streamlined, limiting the government's role to setting the policy framework and performance targets, and monitoring and rewarding the performance of managers who should have freedom of action within the policy framework.

At the same time, the incentive system would need improvement. It would be desirable if import bans and quotas were abolished at an early date and if import licensing were phased out over time, with the remaining protection taking the form of tariffs. In turn, the tariff structure should be rationalized, with the range of tariffs reduced and tariff levels lowered. Also, export licensing and controls should be eliminated and all exporters should be given the choice between domestic and imported inputs.

The focus of investment policy should be shifted from regulation to promotion. At the same time, the domestic content program should be reduced in scope and rationalized, limiting the number of products subject to such programs, eliminating the specification of components to be supplied by domestic production, and including exports in the calculation of the fulfillment of domestic content requirements.

There is further need to reduce the deficit of the government budget. Apart from reversing the doubling of the share of public administration, this would necessitate an improvement in the tax collection effort that should permit raising the ratio of nonoil taxes to GDP from 8 percent to 10–11 percent.

Further efforts should be made to develop the bond and the stock market which would require liberalizing existing regulations. Regulations on the money market should also be liberalized and a greater role be given to market forces in the determination of interest rates.

Indonesia further needs improvements in its educational system. In this connection, emphasis should be given to upgrading primary education, improving the quality of secondary education and emphasizing technical education at the universities.

For the future, Indonesia should place increased reliance on foreign direct investment that brings with it technological, management and marketing knowledge. This would necessitate further liberalization of the conditions for joint ventures.

Bibliography

Arndt, H. W., 1984. *The Indonesian Economy: Collected Papers*. Singapore: Chopmen.

Arndt, H. W., 1987. 'The Financial System of Indonesia', *Savings and Development*, vol. 11, no. 3.

Bunge, Frederica (ed.), 1982. *Indonesia: A Country Study*. Washington, DC: US Government Printing Office.

Economist Intelligence Unit, 1987. *Country Profile: Indonesia, 1987–88*. London: The Economist.

Economist Intelligence Unit, 1987. *Indonesia to 1991: Can Momentum be Regained?* London: The Economist.

Erquiaga, Philip, 1987. 'Improving Domestic Resource Mobilization through

Financial Development – Indonesia'. Asian Development Bank Economic Staff Paper, no. 40. Manila: Asian Development Bank.

Fitzgerald, Bruce, 1986. 'An Analysis of Indonesian Trade Policies: Countertrade, Downstream Processing, Import Restrictions, and the Deletion Problem'. CPD Discussion Paper, no. 1986–22. Washington, DC: World Bank.

Fryer, Donald W. and James C. Jackson, *Indonesia*. London: Ernest Benn.

Gillis, Malcolm, 1984. 'Episodes in Indonesian Economic Growth', in Arnold C. Harberger (ed.), *World Economic Growth: Case Studies of Developed and Developing Nations*. San Francisco, CA: Institute for Contemporary Studies.

Gillis, Malcolm, 1985. 'Micro and Macroeconomics of Tax Reform: Indonesia', *Journal of Development Economics*, vol. 19, no. 3.

Glassburner, Bruce (ed.), 1971. *The Economy of Indonesia: Selected Readings*. Ithaca, NY: Cornell University Press.

Glassburner, Bruce, 1985. *Macroeconomics and the Agricultural Sector'*, *Bulletin of Indonesian Economic Studies*, vol. 21, no. 2.

Higgins, Benjamin, 1957. *Indonesia's Economic Stabilization and Development*. New York: Institute of Pacific Relations.

Hill, Hal, 1988. *Foreign Investment and Industrialization in Indonesia*. Singapore: Oxford University Press.

Myint, Hla, 1984. 'Inward and Outward-Looking Countries Revisited: The Case of Indonesia', *Bulletin of Indonesian Economic Studies*, vol. 20, no. 2.

Panglaykim, J. and Kenneth Thomas, 1969. 'Indonesian Exports: Performance and Prospects', in Theodore Morgan and Nyle Spoelstra (eds), *Economic Interdependence in Southeast Asia*. Madison, WI: University of Wisconsin Press.

Regional and Country Studies Branch, 1987. *Indonesia: Changing Industrial Priorities*. New York: UN Industrial Development Organization.

Robinson, Richard, 1986. *Indonesia: The Rise of Capital*. North Sydney, Australia: Allen & Unwin Pty.

Sundararajan, V. and Lazaros Molho, 1988. 'Financial Reform and Monetary Control in Indonesia'. IMF Working Paper. Washington, DC: IMF.

Sundrum, R. M., 1988. 'Indonesia's Slow Economic Growth: 1981–86', *Bulletin of Indonesian Economic Studies*, vol. 24, no. 1.

Timmer, C. Peter, 1987. 'Food Price Policy in Indonesia'. Development Discussion Paper, No. 250 AFP. Cambridge, MA: Harvard Institute for International Development.

Verbruggen, Harmen, 1985. 'The Case of Indonesia', in Harmen Verbruggen, *Gains from Export-Oriented Industrialization in Developing Countries with Special Reference to South-East Asia*. Amsterdam, Netherlands: Free University Press.

7 Malaysia

INTRODUCTION

Malaysia has a population of 16.1 million in an area of 337 000 square kilometers. About 85 percent of the population resides in West Malaysia, which is located on the long and narrow Malay Peninsula. East Malaysia, consisting of the Borneo territories of Sabah and Sarawak, is 650 kilometers to the east and is separated from West Malaysia by the South China Sea.

West Malaysia's population is comprised of Malays (54 percent), Chinese (35 percent) and Indians (11 percent). East Malaysia has a population consisting largely of Malays and various ethnic groups.

West Malaysia (Federation of Malaya) became independent in 1957. Malaysia was formed in 1963 with the participation of the Federation of Malaya, Singapore, Sabah, and Sarawak. Differences over political and economic issues led to the separation of Singapore from Malaysia in August 1965.

West Malaysia is rich in natural resources. It has rubber and palm oil plantations and has developed rice cultivation; it also has extensive tin deposits. Sabah and Sarawak are covered by tropical forests; the latter and, to a lesser extent, the former are petroleum producers; both have deposits of natural gas.

Manufacturing activities in Malaysia are of recent origin. They accounted for only 7.8 percent of the GDP in 1957. The development of manufacturing began with the Pioneer Industries Ordinance of 1958 that provided tax exemptions to firms qualifying for pioneer status. The Investment Incentives Act of 1968 increased the period of tax exemption and provided additional exemptions to firms located in development areas, to priority industries, and to firms having high domestic content. Furthermore, protection levels were raised, although Malaysia avoided the excesses of protection observed in Latin America, India and the Philippines.

By the early 1970s, domestic production accounted for 90 percent of the sales of consumer goods. With the possibilities of import substitution in consumer goods being practically exhausted in Malaysia's small domestic market, new policies were adopted to promote exports, in large part through the development of free trade zones (FTZs). As a result of these policies, Malaysia has attracted labor-intensive industries in electronics and, to a lesser extent, textiles which have permitted the rapid expansion of manufactured exports. In the mid-1980s, the government of Malaysia proposed to complement the development of manufactured exports by the establishment of selected heavy industries, including iron and steel and car manufacturing.

GOVERNMENTAL POLICIES

Before independence, Malaysia's exports consisted largely of rubber and tin, with rubber accounting for two-thirds and tin for one-fifth of the total. Subsequently, governmental policies in agriculture concentrated on the development of palm oil exports and on import substitution in rice. Palm oil was given particular importance in the framework of land development programs, while increased irrigation permitted the double cropping of rice.

Agricultural policies were complemented by industrial policies as manufacturing became the principal focus of governmental activities. The Pioneer Industries Ordinance of 1958 provided income tax exemptions to new manufacturing establishments approved as 'pioneer'. Furthermore, dividends paid from exempted income were also exempted from income taxes by shareholders.

The period of tax exemption depended on the size of the firm. Small firms received exemptions for two years, medium-sized firms for three years, and large firms for five years. The Pioneer Industries Act of 1965 added a further category of four years' tax exemption. Losses incurred during the tax exemption period could be carried forward to the post-exemption period.

The Investment Incentives Act of 1968 increased the period of tax exemption. An extension of an additional year was granted to firms fulfilling any of the following conditions, bringing the maximum period of tax exemption to eight years: (a) the manufacturing establishment was located in a development area; (b) it produced a priority product; or (c) it incorporated, by value, at least 50 percent of raw materials and parts and components produced in Malaysia.

The qualifying conditions for pioneer status were broadly defined, leading to the establishment of a large number of pioneer firms. In 1969 the share of pioneer approvals in total approvals was 80 percent and, while this share declined to 32 percent by 1986, it remained 60 percent in terms of capital as small companies often did not apply for pioneer status.

The number of pioneer firms increased from 18 in 1958 to 399 in 1984, producing one-third of manufacturing output in that year. Priority firms were established in a wide variety of industries, including food products, wood manufacture, textiles, petroleum and coal products, chemicals and metal products.

The Investment Incentives Act of 1968 also provided tax incentives for firms that did not qualify for pioneeer status. A tax credit was granted for 25 percent of the capital expenditure, with an additional 5 percent if the plant was located in a development area, if it manufactured a priority product, or if it had a 50 percent Malaysian content.

Furthermore, a tax incentive entitled 'increased capital allowance' was established to encourage the setting-up of modern factories. For qualifying plant expenditure, the rate of capital allowance was set at 60 percent. Finally, accelerated depreciation allowances were introduced.

The measures described encouraged the use of capital. In turn, the 1971 Labor Utilization Relief Act provided tax exemptions on the basis of the number of workers employed. The tax exemption period was set at two years for firms with 51–100 employees, three years for firms with 101–200 employees, four years for firms with 201–350 employees, and five years for firms with more than 350 employees. An additional year of tax exemption was provided if the factory was located in a development area, it manufactured a priority product, or it had a 50 percent Malaysian content.

These regulations continue to be in effect. Qualifying firms have a choice between pioneer status and labor utilization relief. In both cases, they can receive tax exemption for up to ten years if they locate in a Locational Incentives Area.

While investment incentives do not discriminate between production for domestic and for foreign markets, trade policies have such an effect. Until independence, tariffs served only revenue purposes. The first step towards tariff protection as an instrument of trade policy was taken with the establishment of the Tariff Advisory Committee in 1959. Nevertheless, the committee followed a cautious approach towards tariff protection and tariffs were granted only to a few pioneer industries. The Tariff Advisory Board, established in 1963, set moderate duties on about 200 items. Excluding alcoholic beverages and tobacco products that bear high tariffs for revenue purposes, in 1965 tariffs on manufactured goods averaged 7 percent.

In the first Malaysia Plan (1966–70), the government made a commitment to use tariffs to protect infant industries. Tariffs were to be moderate and levied on a temporary basis. In particular, the Plan recognized the need for efficient production for eventual exportation:

> In recognition of the problems of infant industries and those which arise from the limited industrial experience of the country, major attention will be given to the imposition of protective tariffs . . . The government, however, is intent on ensuring that no more protection than is necessary will be accorded, for the cost of industrialization to the domestic consumer must be minimized. The government is also intent that tariff protection will not be afforded for periods longer than are absolutely necessary. The growth of the industrial sector in the long run will demand that eventually production be extended to supply not only the domestic market but also markets overseas. This makes it essential that domestic enterprise be constantly prodded to increase efficiency so that there will be progressive reductions in production costs. (pp. 132–3).

In 1966, the Federal Industrial Development Authority (FIDA) was established under the aegis of the Ministry of Commerce and Trade. FIDA gradually took over the functions of the Tariff Advisory Board, which was subsequently abolished. In 1967, a 2 percent surtax was levied on all imports and the duty on automobiles was raised from 5 to 35 percent in order to encourage the establishment of car assembly plants.

In 1969, the Capital Investment Committee (CIC) was established. A report of FIDA, entitled 'Tariffs: Structure for an Efficient Utilization of Resources for 1971–1975' and published in 1970, described CIC's policy as follows: 'In the present context of creating more employment opportunities as a national objective, tariff policy should be radically modified to give positive assurance and encouragement not only to established industries but more particularly to industries not yet established but possessing good prospects for becoming viable' (p. 7).

Furthermore, import quotas were used for protective purposes. But quotas were meant to be temporary and only relatively few products received continuing quota protection, including animal feeds, leather, automobiles, motorcycles and bicycles. In 1984, some 80 products were imported under quotas.

Tariffs also remained moderate compared with most other developing countries. In 1980 the unweighted average of tariffs was 11.6

percent, compared with 63.1 percent in the Philippines. And although the subsequent emphasis on heavy industry led to increases in tariffs, while tariffs were reduced to a considerable extent in the Philippines, in 1985 average tariffs remained considerably lower in Malaysia (13.6 percent) than in the Philippines (28.1 percent).

As import substitution in consumer goods was nearly complete and primary products did not promise a sufficiently rapid expansion of exports, around 1970 Malaysia turned toward the promotion of manufactured exports. The 1968 Investment Incentives Act provided tax reductions based on a formula including last year's exports and increments in exports, with a large weight given to the latter; tax deductions for promotional expenditures abroad; and accelerated depreciation.

These measures were of no value, however, to pioneer firms except for carry forward provisions for the time pioneer status expired. However, after 1970 export-oriented projects were strongly represented in approvals for pioneer status while import substitution projects often received approval without incentives.

Furthermore, in 1977 an export refinancing facility was established which provided credit facilities for Malaysian exporters at preferential interest rates. Under this scheme, all exports other than petroleum products are eligible for the discounting of export bills for a period not exceeding 90 days at an interest rate of 7 percent. The financing is done by commercial banks which receive refinancing at 5.5 percent from the central bank.

Exporters can also claim drawbacks for import duties on imported raw materials and parts and components, and do not pay excise taxes and sales taxes. At the same time, drawbacks are subject to long bureaucratic delays.

Such bureaucracy is avoided by firms established in free trade zones. In Malaysia, more than anywhere else, FTZs assumed importance in promoting manufactured exports. FTZs have been established in the states of Penang, Selangor and Melaka. Use has also been made of licensed manufacturing warehouses (LMWs).

The FTZ incentive package has included the provision of duty-free imports of raw materials, parts and components, and capital equipment; streamlined customs formalities; infrastructure facilities, with land leased well below market rates; and tax exemptions, as firms in FTZs have the choice between pioneer status and labor utilization relief.

In 1982, the only year for which complete data are available, the

FTZs accounted for 51 percent of the manufactured exports of Malaysia; their share was 89 percent for electronics exports. In the exports by FTZs, electronics had a share of 85 percent, followed by textiles (10 percent) and electrical equipment (3 percent).

Raw materials, parts and components, and capital equipment may enter duty-free in LMWs. In undertaking in-bound production, the firms in question escape the red tape involved in getting drawbacks. LMW firms tend to be smaller and to engage in labor-intensive production.

In 1982, LMW firms provided 10 percent of Malaysia's manufactured exports. Within LMW exports, the share of electronics was 60 percent, followed by electrical goods (21 percent), clothing (19 percent) and textiles (9 percent).

In the early 1980s, the Malaysian government embarked on the promotion of heavy manufacturing establishments. They included two petroleum refineries, a petrochemical complex, a methanol plant, a urea-ammonia plant, two cement plants, two sponge iron plants, a cold rolling steel mill, a paper-pulp plant and a factory producing the Malaysian car, the Proton Saga.

Some of these plants (such as the cement plants) represent competition to existing factories in Malaysia. For other plants, the Malaysian market is not sufficiently large for efficient operations. And while the urea-ammonia plant is an integration industry, established in the ASEAN context, other plants are not competitive in export markets. A case in point is the Proton Saga which can be exported only at a considerable subsidy.

Following the riots of the previous year, in 1970 the New Economic Policy (NEP) was introduced in Malaysia, with the twin objectives of eradicating poverty and 'restructuring Malaysian society to eliminate identification of race with economic function and geographical location'. The latter statement refers to the fact that Malays were generally engaged in agriculture while the Chinese and Indians dominated industries and commerce in the cities.

NEP gave special rights and privileges to Malays in the framework of an affirmative action program that included subsidies, quotas, scholarships and investment licensing. In addition, trustee agencies were established to invest on behalf of Malays. Finally, Malays were the main beneficiaries of the poverty eradication program that included land development and settlement schemes for rubber and palm oil, and modernization and commercialization schemes for rice cultivation.

The poverty eradication scheme set out to reduce the number of households below the poverty level from 7 918 000 in 1970 to 5 139 000 by 1990. By 1980, more than half of the target was met as the number of households below the poverty line was 6 359 000 in that year. However, poor economic conditions in the early 1980s led to an increase in the number of households below the poverty line to 7 176 000 by 1983.

The NEP also projected a decline in the share of Malay employment in the agricultural sector from 67.6 percent in 1970 to 61.6 percent in 1990, with a corresponding increase in the nonagricultural share, from 38.0 percent to 49.8 percent. In fact, the share of Malay employment in nonagricultural occupations increased to a considerable extent, to 43.7 percent, by 1980. However, little decline was experienced in the Malay employment share in the agricultural sector where the Malay share remained 66.3 percent in 1980. These results may be explained by the rapid growth of the Malay population which was apparently not fully reflected in the projections.

Another area of NEP targets is capital shares in the corporate sector. In 1970, the Bumiputra (Malays and other indigenous people) share was only 2.4 percent, compared to a 34.3 percent share for Chinese and Indians and a 63.3 percent foreign share. For 1990, the targets are 30 percent, 40 percent, and 30 percent. *The Economist* (March 11, 1989) reported that by 1988 the Bumiputra share had reached 20 percent. This was achieved largely through the establishment of trust agencies, which invested on behalf of the Bumiputra.

Investments by the trust agencies have been undertaken mainly in public firms. By 1983, the government had set up 115 enterprises, statutory authorities, research institutes and other agencies under the control of various ministries. The Ministry of Public Enterprises, established in 1974, presently oversees the activities of 26 enterprises and trust agencies that control, in turn, some 500 companies employing chiefly Bumiputra managers.

The establishment of public enterprises increased the share of public investment in the total to one-third. At the same time, it has been reported that over one-half of all public enterprises had losses in 1986. These losses reflect inefficiencies of operation as well as excessive employment. Inefficiencies of operation, in turn, may be due to poor management, inappropriate technology or unsuitable location.

Privatization has been suggested as a remedy to the problems of public enterprises, but privatization cannot remedy the choice of poor technology and location. In such instances, it has been proposed to consider liquidation.

Privatization may extend to public firms that were established in earlier years. The first stage of privatization would include the Malaysian Airline System, the Malaysian International Shipping Cooperation, Telecoms and the Port Khang container terminal. The Malaysian Railway and Penang Port have also been proposed for privatization.

Foreign direct investment increased rapidly in Malaysia until the early 1980s but declined afterwards. According to balance-of-payments statistics, it was $500 million in 1978 and surpassed 1 billion dollars in 1981–3, but declined to $797 million in 1984, $695 million in 1985, and $489 million in 1986, increasing again to $575 million in 1987.

Foreign direct investment in Malaysia has been comparable to that in Singapore and much exceeded that in the other East Asian developing countries. Malaysia, however, has not been a favored location for Japanese direct investment, which accounts for an increasing proportion of foreign direct investment in East Asia. According to official Japanese data, in recent years Japanese direct investment was oriented largely to the four East Asian NICs and to Indonesia, with Malaysia far behind.

Malaysia provides primary education for everyone, and enrollment rates exceed 50 percent for the relevant age group in secondary education. However, only 6 percent of people in the corresponding age group are enrolled in establishments of higher education, compared with 38 percent in the Philippines, 20 percent in Thailand and 7 percent in Indonesia.

The relative backwardness of Malaysia in higher education is apparent in the small share of engineers in the labor force: 0.2 percent in the early 1980s compared with 0.6 percent in Singapore and 0.7 percent in Korea. Malaysia also produces only 400 engineers and 1500 diploma level technicians a year.

Malaysia's banking system is well developed. There are 39 commercial banks, 12 merchant banks and 42 finance companies under the supervision of the central bank (Bank Negara Malaysia). There are also financial cooperatives that play the role of 'secondary' banks.

Before independence, banks in Malaysia were largely foreign-owned and were closely linked to the London financial market. After independence, the government encouraged the development of indigenous banking and by the mid-1980s domestic banks accounted for about two-thirds of commercial bank credit.

Commercial banks provide credit largely in the form of overdrafts and short-term advances; merchant banks provide wholesale banking and corporate finance services; and finance companies provide consumer finance and installment credit facilities. Commercial banks also issue negotiable certificates of deposit while both commercial and merchant banks deal in bankers' acceptances.

The extent of financial intermediation in Malaysia approaches that of Singapore and much exceeds that of Korea. In 1988, the ratio of M2 to the GDP was 66 percent in Malaysia, compared with 87 percent in Singapore and 39 percent in Korea.

The development of the domestic stock exchange has also been impressive. The market value of listed shares of Malaysian firms in the Kuala Lumpur stock exchange reached 78 percent in GDP in 1987; the comparable figure for Korea is 5 percent. Unlike Korea, however, Malaysia has not developed a primary debt market.

The rapid development of the financial system in Malaysia has not been without costs. In 1986, the central bank had to suspend the operations of 24 financial cooperatives that went into receivership and the stock exchange was temporarily closed. In 1987, the central bank had to assist the sixth and seventh largest commercial banks to underwrite a rights issue, boosting paid-in capital to offset large loan write-offs. Since that time, however, the financial sector has regained its health.

ECONOMIC GROWTH

Per caput incomes in Malaysia increased nearly three times between 1963 and 1987, reaching $1886 per head in the latter year (Table 1.1). At the same time, growth has been rather uneven. The GDP increased by 7.0 percent a year between 1963 and 1973, 7.3 percent between 1973 and 1981 and 4.2 percent between 1981 and 1987 (see Table 7.1). The latter period included two recessions, in 1981–2 and in 1985–6. The recessions were related to adverse developments in the terms of trade and in export markets. A strong recovery after the second recession began in 1987.

Economic growth in Malaysia was accompanied by considerable changes in the sectoral composition of GDP. The share of the manufacturing sector increased from 8.3 percent in 1963 to 15.0 percent in 1973 and 20.0 percent in 1981, but declined to 18.6 percent in 1983; data for later years are not available. In turn, the share of agriculture fell from 31.5 percent in 1973 to 26.4 percent in 1972, 20.8 percent in 1981, and again to 19.5 percent in 1983 (see Table 7.2).

Table 7.1 Economic performance indicators: Malaysia

Growth rates	1963–73	1973–81	1981–7	1963–87
GDP	7.0	7.3	4.2	6.4
Population	2.5	2.8	2.7	2.7
GDP per caput	4.4	4.4	1.5	3.6
Investment	9.1	11.6	–2.2	7.0
Manufacturing production	.	9.5	6.9	.
Agricultural production	.	3.9	3.7	.
Exports	5.9	7.5	10.9	7.7
Imports	4.0	12.0	3.5	6.5

Source: World Bank.

Table 7.2 Industrial composition and trade: Malaysia (percent of GDP)

	1963	1973	1981	1987*
Industrial composition				
Agriculture	31.5	26.4	20.8	19.5
Mining and quarrying	9.6	6.9	9.8	9.4
Manufacturing	8.3	15.0	20.0	18.6
Gas, electricity and water	1.1	1.2	2.5	2.4
Construction	4.1	3.9	4.8	5.2
Transportation	4.4	4.2	5.9	5.7
Wholesale and retail trade	15.6	12.2	12.1	13.0
Banking, real estate	10.6	9.4	8.4	9.0
Ownership of dwellings	.	.	.	.
Public administration	.	.	.	.
Other services	14.9	20.9	15.7	17.1
Imputed bank service charge, duty	.	.	.	.
Trade				
Exports of goods and nonfactor services	43.2	39.8	52.3	64.2
Imports of goods and nonfactor services	41.5	34.3	58.5	50.6

* Industrial composition is for 1983.

Source: World Bank.

These results reflect the differential growth performance of the two sectors. Available data from 1973 onwards show that manufacturing output rose 9.5 percent a year between 1973 and 1981 and 6.9 percent a year between 1981 and 1987; the corresponding growth rates for agriculture were 3.9 percent and 3.7 percent (see Table 7.1).

Table 7.3 Savings and investment ratios: Malaysia (percent of GDP)

	1973	1974	1975	1976	1977	1978	1979	1980
Private savings	36.6	37.1	34.3	40.8	41.6	39.9	45.7	46.1
Government budget balance	−5.6	−6.0	−8.5	−7.1	−8.6	−7.6	−7.9	−13.2
Domestic savings	31.0	31.1	25.8	33.7	33.1	32.2	37.8	32.9
Foreign savings	−5.5	−0.3	−0.5	−10.1	−7.3	−5.6	−8.9	−2.5
Domestic investment	25.5	30.8	25.3	23.6	25.8	26.7	28.9	30.4

	1981	1982	1983	1984	1985	1986	1987
Private savings	47.9	46.4	43.9	44.4	40.0	42.1	44.5
Government budget balance	−19.1	−17.9	−13.1	−8.9	−7.4	−10.6	−7.6
Domestic savings	28.8	28.6	30.8	35.5	32.7	31.5	36.9
Foreign savings	6.2	8.7	5.3	−1.9	−5.2	−6.4	−13.6
Domestic investment	35.0	37.3	36.1	33.6	27.5	25.1	23.3

Source: World Bank.

The share of mining and quarrying fluctuated over time, reflecting to a large extent variations in tin prices. The relevant shares were: 1963, 9.6 percent; 1973, 6.9 percent; 1981, 9.8 percent; and 1983, 9.4 percent.

The share of the services sector fluctuated around 50 percent during the period under consideration. Increases in GDP shares were experienced in gas, electricity and water; construction; transportation; and the 'other services' category, which includes public administration. In turn, declines were observed in wholesale and retail trade and in banking.

Export expansion importantly contributed to economic growth after 1973. Having declined from 43.2 percent in 1963 to 39.8 percent in 1973, the share of the exports of goods and services in the GDP reached 52.3 percent in 1981 and 64.2 percent in 1987. Import shares also declined between 1963 and 1973, from 41.5 percent to 34.3 percent, increasing afterwards to 58.5 percent in 1981 and falling again to 50.6 percent in 1987.

The export and import figures are indicative of the changes in foreign savings. As shown in Table 7.3, Malaysia had an outflow of savings until 1980, followed by an inflow between 1981 and 1983, and an outflow again in 1984–7. Domestic savings, too, showed considerable fluctuations, varying between 25.8 percent (1975) and 37.8

percent (1979) of GDP. The domestic savings ratio was 35.5 percent in 1984, 32.7 percent in 1985, 31.5 percent in 1986, and 36.9 percent in 1987.

Apart from the high ratio in 1974 (30.8 percent of GDP), domestic investment varied between 23 and 25 percent in 1973–6. It increased rapidly in subsequent years, with a peak of 37.3 percent in 1982, falling afterwards to 23.3 percent in 1987.

The government budget deficit increased during the 1985–6 recession, reaching 10.6 percent of GDP in 1986, although it declined to 7.6 percent in 1987. It was considerably higher in the 1981–2 recession when the peak was 19.1 percent. In general, public sector deficits were much larger in the 1980s than in the 1970s, when they fluctuated between 5 percent and 8 percent.

Malaysia traditionally had a surplus on the trade account, the 1981 and 1982 recession years being exceptions (see Table 7.4). In turn, it had an increasing deficit on the service account (the current account figures do not match foreign savings in the national accounts because of differences in definitions).

In the capital account, both direct investment and long-term capital show an inflow except for the outflow of long-term capital in 1987. Short-term capital flows were positive in some years and negative in others. In recent years Malaysia's reserves increased to a considerable extent.

INTERNATIONAL TRADE

Data on the geographical composition of Malaysia's exports and imports are distorted because trade with Singapore is not shown in the figures for 1966 (1963 data are not available). Correspondingly, the discussion will be limited to the years 1973, 1981 and 1988.

The combined shares of developed countries in Malaysia's exports varied between 53 percent and 56 percent during the period under consideration (see Table 7.5). Within this total, the United States showed a substantial increase, from 10.6 percent in 1973 to 17.3 percent in 1988. The share of Japan declined, from 17.7 percent to 16.9 percent as did that of Western Europe, from 23.0 percent to 14.9 percent. The corresponding figures are 4.0 percent and 3.3 percent for Canada, Australia and New Zealand.

Singapore dominates Malaysia's exports to developing countries, with a 22.8 percent share in 1973 and 1981 and 19.3 percent in 1988.

Table 7.4 Balance of payments: Malaysia (million US$)

	1978	1979	1980	1981	1982	1983	1984	1985	1986	1987
Merchandise exports	7 311	10 994	12 868	11 675	11 966	13 683	16 407	15 133	13 703	17 706
Merchandise imports	−5 718	−7 838	−10 462	−11 780	−12 719	−13 251	−13 426	−11 556	−10 301	−11 820
Trade balance	1 593	3 156	2 406	−105	−753	432	2 981	3 577	3 402	5 886
Other goods, services, and income: credit	1 075	1 424	1 968	2 204	2 332	2 534	2 660	2 643	2 638	3 158
Other goods, services, and income: debit	−2 516	−3 644	−4 638	−4 551	−5 148	−6 454	−7 274	−6 828	−6 157	−6 764
Other goods, services, and income: net	−1 441	−2 220	−2 670	−2 347	−2 816	−3 920	−4 614	−4 185	−3 519	−3 606
Unrequited transfers	−45	−8	−20	−34	−32	−9	−39	−6	37	144
Current account balance	107	928	−284	−2 486	−3 601	−3 497	−1 672	−614	−80	2 424
Direct investment	500	573	934	1 265	1 397	1 261	797	695	489	575
Long-term capital	190	352	87	1 309	2 208	2 706	2 346	887	630	−992
Short-term capital	−63	−724	414	42	140	−113	−123	350	−18	−955
Capital account balance	627	201	1 435	2 616	3 745	3 854	3 020	1 932	1 101	−1 372
Errors and omissions	−455	−329	−682	−582	−406	−372	−863	−168	435	67
Overall balance	279	800	469	−452	−262	−15	485	1 150	1 456	1 119
Net use of reserves	−473	−658	−475	515	390	42	−343	−1 204	−1 027	−1 418

Note: The overall balance is the sum of the current and capital account balances and errors and omissions. Net use of reserves was derived by adding the following items to overall balance: counterpart to the monetization and demonetization of gold, counterpart to SDR allocation, and counterpart to valuation changes.

Source: IMF, *International Financial Statistics*, various issues.

Table 7.5 Geographical composition of exports: Malaysia (percent of total exports)

	1966	1973	1981	1988
Developed Countries	83.4	55.4	53.0	52.5
United States	18.2	10.6	13.1	17.3
Western Europe	29.5	23.0	16.2	14.9
Japan	27.9	17.7	21.1	16.9
Canada, Australia, New Zealand	7.8	4.0	2.6	3.3
Developing Countries	16.4	39.6	43.6	46.4
Pacific countries (other than China)	5.7	29.2	34.5	35.2
East Asian NICs	3.5	27.6	30.7	30.4
Hong Kong	1.0	1.4	2.0	3.4
Korea	1.3	2.2	3.6	4.8
Singapore	NA	22.8	22.8	19.3
Taiwan	1.2	1.2	2.3	2.9
East Asian NECs	2.2	1.6	3.7	4.8
Indonesia	NA	0.5	0.5	1.3
Malaysia	–	–	–	–
Philippines	1.2	0.6	1.6	1.5
Thailand	1.0	0.5	1.7	2.0
China	NA	2.6	0.7	2.0
Other developing countries	10.7	7.7	8.4	9.2
Other Asia	4.9	1.9	4.6	4.7
Africa	1.0	0.7	0.9	0.6
Southern Europe	0.6	2.8	0.3	0.6
Middle East	1.6	1.2	2.1	2.5
Latin America	2.5	1.2	0.5	0.8
European Socialist Countries	NA	5.1	3.3	1.1

Note: Taiwanese figures for 1981 and 1988 derived as difference between total exports, the regional aggregates, special categories, and other countries not included. Regional aggregates may not sum to 100 percent due to inclusion in denominator of special categories, and other countries not specified.

Sources: IMF, *Direction of Trade Statistics*, various issues.

This is largely entrepôt trade, with Singapore re-exporting its imports of primary products from Malaysia.

Among the East Asian NICs, Korea assumed importance as a market for Malaysia. It accounted for 4.8 percent of Malaysian exports in 1988, compared with 3.4 percent for Hong Kong and 2.9 percent for Taiwan. But all three countries increased their shares in Malaysian exports over time to a considerable extent.

Substantial increases were also shown in the shares of the Philippines and Thailand as markets for Malaysian exports, reaching 1.5 percent and 2.0 percent, respectively, in 1988. In the same year, Indonesia's share was 1.3 percent. Still, the combined share of these three member countries of ASEAN remained rather small, disappointing optimistic expectations as to the effects of economic integration.

Despite increases in recent years, China experienced a decline in its share in Malaysian exports between 1973 (2.6 percent) and 1988 (2.0 percent). The decline was even larger for the European socialist countries, from 5.1 percent in 1973 to 1.1 percent in 1988. Finally, the combined share of the rest of the developing world in Malaysian exports remained around 8–10 percent, with the Middle East gaining, and Other Asia, Africa, Southern Europe and Latin America losing market shares.

The combined share of the developed countries in Malaysian imports remained around 62 percent during the 1973–88 period (see Table 7.6). The share of the United States in the total increased to a considerable extent, from 8.2 percent in 1973 to 17.7 percent in 1988, while that of Japan remained approximately unchanged at around 22–24 percent. A large decline is shown for Western Europe, from 22.9 percent to 15.3 percent, and for Canada, Australia and New Zealand, from 9.1 percent to 6.2 percent.

Imports from developing countries are again dominated by Singapore, whose share in Malaysian imports – representing to a large extent entrepôt trade – increased over time, from 7.5 percent in 1973 to 13.2 percent in 1988. The other East Asian NICs also showed increases during this period: from 1.8 percent to 2.3 percent for Hong Kong, from 0.3 percent to 2.6 percent for Korea and from 2.2 percent to 4.6 percent in Taiwan.

Among the East Asian NECs, only the Philippines experienced an increase in market share, from 0.3 percent in 1973 to 0.8 percent in 1988; the shares of Indonesia and Thailand in Malaysian imports declined from 2.4 percent to 1.7 percent and from 4.2 percent to 3.0 percent, respectively. Even larger declines were experienced in the share of China (from 5.9 percent in 1973 to 2.9 percent in 1988), while that of the European socialist countries remained of 0.7 percent.

The rest of the developing world also experienced decreases in their share in Malaysian imports, from 8.3 percent in 1973 to 5.8 percent in 1988. Only Latin America and Africa went against the trend; Southern Europe, the Middle East and especially Other Asia exhibited declines.

Table 7.6 Geographical composition of imports: Malaysia
(percent of total imports)

	1966	1973	1981	1988
Developed Countries	68.3	61.8	62.7	62.2
United States	6.2	8.2	14.6	17.7
Western Europe	39.3	22.9	16.1	15.3
Japan	12.8	21.6	24.4	23.0
Canada, Australia, New Zealand	10.1	9.1	7.6	6.2
Developing Countries	31.8	32.9	36.3	37.0
Pacific Countries (other than China)	13.9	18.7	22.8	28.2
East Asian NICs	5.6	11.7	18.0	22.7
Hong Kong	4.9	1.8	1.3	2.3
Korea	0.1	0.3	1.4	2.6
Singapore	NA	7.5	13.1	13.2
Taiwan	0.6	2.2	2.2	4.6
East Asian NECs	8.3	7.0	4.8	5.6
Indonesia	NA	2.4	0.6	1.7
Malaysia	–	–	–	–
Philippines	0.7	0.3	0.8	0.8
Thailand	7.6	4.2	3.4	3.0
China	NA	5.9	2.4	2.9
Other developing countries	18.0	8.3	11.1	5.8
Other Asia	15.9	4.0	1.6	1.6
Africa	0.5	0.6	0.5	0.7
Southern Europe	0.0	0.2	0.1	0.1
Middle East	1.3	2.7	8.3	1.7
Latin America	0.3	0.8	0.6	1.7
European Socialist Countries	NA	0.7	1.0	0.7

Note: Taiwanese figures for 1981 and 1988 derived as difference between total imports, the regional aggregates, special categories, and other countries not included. Regional aggregates may not sum to 100 percent due to inclusion in denominator of special categories and other countries not specified.

Sources: IMF, *Direction of Trade Statistics*, various issues.

The commodity composition of Malaysia's exports underwent considerable changes during the period under consideration. Nonfuel primary products experienced a large decline in shares, from 90.3 percent in 1963 to 40.6 percent in 1987, with fuels (from 4.1 percent to 19.9 percent) and manufactured goods especially exhibiting substantial increases, from 4.7 percent to 39.3 percent (see Table 7.7).

Among nonfuel primary products, decreases were concentrated in

Table 7.7 Commodity composition of exports: major product groups: Malaysia (percent of total exports)

		1963	1973	1981	1987
Fuels	(SITC 3)	4.1	5.4	26.6	19.9
Nonfuel primary products		90.3	82.6	53.3	40.6
Food and live animals	(SITC 0)	4.5	6.0	4.2	5.4
Beverages and tobacco	(SITC 1)	1.4	0.3	0.1	0.1
Industrial materials	(SITC 2+4+68)	84.4	76.3	49.0	35.0
Manufactures	(SITC 5+6+7+8–68)	4.7	11.4	19.6	39.3
Other	(SITC 9)	0.9	0.6	0.5	0.2
Total		100.0	100.0	100.0	100.0
Manufactures (industrial classification)		3.0	11.4	19.4	39.2
Textile, apparel, leather	(ISIC 32)	0.3	1.6	2.7	4.9
Wood product and furniture	(ISIC 33)	0.1	3.8	1.9	2.0
Paper and paper products	(ISIC 34)	0.1	0.2	0.1	0.3
Chemicals	(ISIC 35)	0.9	1.4	1.3	2.7
Nonmetallic mineral products	(ISIC 36)	0.0	0.2	0.2	0.5
Iron and steel	(ISIC 37)	0.1	0.1	0.1	0.9
Engineering products	(ISIC 38)	1.3	4.1	12.9	27.1
Other industries	(ISIC 39)	0.1	0.1	0.3	0.7

Source: UN, COMTRADE data base.

industrial materials, from 84.4 percent in 1963 to 35.0 percent in 1987. The share of rubber declined from 44.5 percent to 8.7 percent and that of tin from 19.7 percent to 1.9 percent during this period. These declines were only partially offset by increases in the shares of palm oil, sawlogs and sawn timber, from 2.1 percent to 6.3 percent, from 6.3 percent to 9.5 percent and from 2.0 percent to 3.9 percent, respectively.

Manufacturing exports are dominated by engineering products and, within engineering products, by electronics. The share of electronics in Malaysian exports increased from 0.1 percent in 1963 and 0.3 percent in 1973 to 10.2 percent in 1981, and to 20.3 percent in 1987. It consists largely of semiconductors, as Malaysia has benefited from relatively low labor costs and the availability of high-quality testing facilities.

Another commodity group where considerable increases were experienced are textiles, apparel and leather products, whose share in Malaysian exports rose from 0.3 percent in 1963 to 4.9 percent in 1987. Increases were concentrated in wearing apparel, followed by textiles and by textile products.

Table 7.8 Commodity composition of imports: major product groups: Malaysia (percent of total imports)

		1963	1973	1981	1987
Fuels	(SITC 3)	11.1	6.6	17.2	7.1
Nonfuel primary products		38.8	27.8	18.1	16.3
Food and live animals	(SITC 0)	24.2	18.2	11.1	9.3
Beverages and tobacco	(SITC 1)	4.1	1.6	1.0	0.6
Industrial materials	(SITC 2+4+68)	10.6	8.0	6.1	6.4
Manufactures	(SITC 5+6+7+8–68)	47.8	64.5	64.0	76.2
Other	(SITC 9)	2.3	1.1	0.7	0.3
Total		100.0	100.0	100.0	100.0
Manufactures (industrial classification)		31.1	64.2	63.8	75.1
Textile, apparel, leather	(ISIC 32)	4.1	6.2	3.0	4.3
Wood product and furniture	(ISIC 33)	0.1	0.3	0.1	0.2
Paper and paper products	(ISIC 34)	1.6	3.2	2.2	2.8
Chemicals	(ISIC 35)	5.5	9.6	8.8	11.8
Nonmetallic mineral products	(ISIC 36)	1.3	1.6	1.6	0.8
Iron and steel	(ISIC 37)	3.4	6.5	5.5	4.2
Engineering products	(ISIC 38)	14.6	36.2	41.6	50.0
Other industries	(ISIC 39)	0.4	0.7	0.9	1.0

Source: UN, COMTRADE data base.

In the case of imports, the share of the nonfuel primary products category declined from 38.8 percent in 1963 to 16.3 percent in 1987, while the share of manufactured goods increased from 47.8 percent to 75.1 percent and that of fuels fell from 11.1 percent to 7.1 percent. (In the case of fuels, the imports are crude petroleum purchased from Brunei for re-export.)

Increases in manufactured imports were concentrated in engineering products, whose share rose from 14.6 percent in 1963 to 50.0 percent in 1987. The shares of other major commodity groups, except for non-metallic minerals, also increased (see Table 7.8).

PROSPECTS FOR THE FUTURE

The rate of economic growth for Malaysia has been projected at 6.1 percent a year for the 1987–2000 period. This growth rate substantially exceeds that observed in the 1981–7 period while falling behind the 1963–87 average growth rate. Population is projected to rise 2.3 percent a year, resulting in a per caput growth rate of 3.7 percent. As a result of these changes, Malaysia would become an NIC by the end of the century.

For the projected growth rate to be reached, however, economic policy changes would be necessary. To begin with, there is a need to reduce the large government budget deficit which limits the availability of funds for private investment. While some revenue raising measures are possible through extending the coverage of the sales tax or transforming this into a value added tax, the principal change would have to be a cut in expenditure.

Apart from reducing current government expenditure, emphasis should be given to reforming the public enterprise system. This would involve privatizing public enterprises in the competitive industrial sector, closing down enterprises that cannot be salvaged, and improving efficiency in the rest.

Given the limitations of import substitution in Malaysia's small domestic market, economic growth would have to be based to a large extent on export expansion. As far as manufactured exports are concerned, Malaysia has to go beyond the FTZs that are to a considerable extent cut off from the rest of the economy. This would necessitate extending the duty-free treatment of imported inputs, enjoyed in the free trade areas, to domestic enterprises which do not export all of their production.

Furthermore, there is a need to reduce the existing anti-export bias of the incentive system. This would involve eliminating import quotas and reducing tariffs. In particular, all tariffs above 25 percent should be lowered to that level.

The granting of pioneer status should be limited to export-oriented firms and pioneer status for other enterprises should not be renewed. Rather, reliance should be based on cutting corporate income taxes which do not favor capital-intensive activities. For the same reason, contributions to the Employee Provident Fund should be reduced.

Economic growth would have to be accompanied by policies aimed at reducing poverty. But the extension of the New Economic Policy, which expires in 1990, would not be advisable because it would hold down the rate of economic growth.

Bibliography

Anand, Sudhir, 1983. *Inequality and Poverty in Malaysia: Measurement and Decomposition.* A World Bank Research Publication. New York: Oxford University Press.

Arief, Sritua and Jomo K. Sundaram (eds), 1983. *The Malaysian Economy and Finance*. East Balmain, Australia: Rosecons.

Bhatia, Kul B., 1987. 'Foreign Trade and Income Distribution: The Case of Malaysia'. Working Paper no. 8801C, Center for the Study of International Economic Relations. London, Canada: University of Western Ontario.

Bunge, Frederica M. (ed.), 1984. *Malaysia: A Country Study*. American University Foreign Area Studies. Washington, DC: US Government Printing Office.

Ee, Tan Siew and Lai Yew Wah, 1983. 'Protection and Employment in the West Malaysian Manufacturing Industries', *Weltwirtschaftliches Archiv (Review of World Economics)*, vol. 119, no. 2.

Freeman, Roger, 1968. *Socialism and Private Enterprise in Equatorial Asia: The Case of Malaysia and Indonesia*. Palo Alto, CA: The Hoover Institution.

Ghani, Mohammed Nor Abdul, Bernard T.H. Wang et. al. (eds), 1984. *Malaysia Incorporated and Privatisation: Towards National Unity*. Selangor, Malaysia: Pelanduk Publications (M) Sdn Bhd.

Gullick, J. M., 1981. *Malaysia: Economic Expansion and National Unity*. Boulder, CO: Westview Press.

Hoffman, Lutz and Tan Siew Ee, 1980. *Industrial Growth, Employment, and Foreign Investment in Peninsular Malaysia*. Selangor, Malaysia: Oxford University Press.

Jomo, N. (ed.), 1985. *Malaysia's New Economic Policies: Evaluation of the Mid-Term Review of the Fourth Malaysia Plan*. Kuala Lumpur: Malaysian Economic Association.

Kanapathy, V., 1970. *The Malaysian Economy: Problems and Prospects*. Singapore: Asia Pacific Press.

Kasper, Wolfgang, 1974. *Malaysia: A Study in Successful Economic Development*. Washington, DC: American Enterprise Institute.

Khor, Kok Peng, 1983. *The Malaysian Economy*. Kuala Lumpur: Marican & Sons.

Kimura, Fukunasi, 1986. *Industrial Development of Malaysia: A Study on Manufacturing Survey*. Tokyo: Industrial Development Center of Japan.

Lean, Lim Lin and Chee Pang Lim, 1984. *The Malaysian Economy at the*

Crossroads: Policy Adjustment or Structural Transformation. Kuala Lumpur: Malaysian Economic Association & Organization Resources Sdn. Bhd.

Lim, David, 1973. *Economic Growth and Development in West Malaysia, 1964–70*. London: Oxford University Press.

Lim, David (ed.), 1976. *Readings on Malaysian Economic Development*. New York: Oxford University Press.

Lim, David (ed.), 1983. *Further Readings on Malaysian Economic Development*. New York: Oxford University Press.

Meerman, Jacob, 1977. *Meeting Basic Needs in Malaysia: A Summary of Findings*. Washington, DC: The World Bank.

Meerman, Jacob, 1979. *Public Expenditure in Malaysia: Who Benefits and Why*. A World Bank Research Publication. New York: Oxford University Press.

Mehmet, Ozay, 1986. *Development in Malaysia: Poverty, Wealth, and Trusteeship*. London: Croom Helm.

Onn, Fong Chan, 1986. *New Economic Dynamo: Structures and Investment Opportunities in the Malaysian Economy*. North Sydney: Allen & Unwin Australia Pty.

Snodgrass, Donald R., 1980. *Inequality and Economic Development in Malaysia*. Kuala Lumpur: Oxford University Press.

Spinanger, Dean, 1983. *Industrialization Policies and Regional Economic Development in Malaysia: A Policy-Oriented Analysis*. Singapore: Oxford University Press.

Stern, Joseph J., 1984. 'Malaysia: Growth and Structural Change'. Development Discussion Paper, no. 184. Cambridge, MA: Harvard Institute for International Development.

Thoburn, John T., 1977. *Primary Commodity Exports and Economic Development: Theory, Evidence, and a Study of Malaysia*. Chichester: Wiley.

Verbruggen, Harmen, 1985. 'The Case of Malaysia', in Harmen Verbruggen, *Gains from Export-Oriented Industrialization in Developing Countries with Special Reference to South-East Asia*. Amsterdam: Free University Press.

Warr, Peter G., 1987. 'Malaysia's Industrial Enclaves: Benefits and Costs', *The Developing Economies*, vol. XXV, no. 1, pp. 30–55.

Yah, Lim Chong, 1969. 'West Malaysian External Trade, 1947–65', in Theodore Morgan and Nyle Spoelstra (eds), *Economic Interdependence in Southeast Asia*. Madison, WI: University of Wisconsin Press.

Young, Kevin, Wilem C. F. Bussink and Parvez Hassan, 1980. *Malaysia: Growth and Equity in a Multiracial Society*. A World Bank Country Economic Report. Baltimore, MD: The Johns Hopkins University Press.

8 The Philippines

INTRODUCTION

The Republic of Philippines has a population of 57.3 million in an area of 300 000 square kilometers. It was a colony of Spain for over 300 years. In the wake of the Spanish–American war of 1898, it became a colony of the United States. US rule was reinstated after the 1941–5 Japanese occupation, followed by independence on July 4, 1946. The Philippines had free trade with the United States until independence. Under the 1946 agreement, duty-free status was maintained until 1955 and full duty status was reached in steps by 1974.

The Philippines consists of 7100 islands, with 11 islands accounting for 96 percent of the land area. More than half of the population live on the two largest islands, Luzon and Mindanao. The population is of Malay–Polynesian origin; there are a large number of cultural and language groups.

The Philippines has a tropical climate, a year-round growing season and a high but variable rainfall. It has fertile land, but the soil has been eroded in several areas due to poor cropping. Approximately 42 percent of the area is covered by forest that is at places endangered by overcutting. The Philippines has copper ore deposits.

In colonial times, agricultural exports (chiefly copra and later sugar) were exchanged for industrial products. After independence, import-substituting industrialization was pursued behind high protective barriers. As this policy encountered market limitations, non-traditional exports were encouraged. However, despite several attempts at liberalization, protection has remained higher than in other South-east Asian countries. Protectionist policies, in turn, have contributed to relatively low rates of economic growth. As a result, the Philippines fell behind Thailand in terms of per caput incomes and it is being caught up by Indonesia.

The economic situation deteriorated after 1981, reflecting the joint effects of protectionist policies, high external indebtedness following extensive borrowing in response of external shocks, and corruption under the Marcos regime. Growth was resumed as Corazon Aquino came to power, but a consistent set of policies has yet to be adopted.

GOVERNMENT POLICIES

Agriculture was neglected in the course of import-substituting industrialization in the Philippines. The exception is rice since the provision of high-yielding varieties, credit facilities and fertilizer, together with extension services and price support, has led to near self-sufficiency. Improvements were also made in bananas, pineapple and palm oil, which are dominated by agribusiness multinational corporations. In turn, the major export crops, sugar and coconut, were unfavorably affected by the establishment of monopolistic organizations directed by Marcos's entourage.

The import-substitution policy evolved as foreign exchange and import controls were imposed in the wake of the Second World War. Consumer goods industries developed behind these barriers were further assisted by exemptions from industrial revenue taxes instituted in 1946, and these were extended to customs duties on their inputs in 1951. Also, tariffs were increased to a considerable extent, ranging up to 100 percent, with lower rates on capital goods and industrial materials.

Import-substituting industrialization led to the rapid growth of the manufacturing sector in the 1950s, but it did not solve the country's foreign exchange problem as the expansion of consumer goods industries required imports of capital goods and industrial materials. At the same time, incentives provided for the use of capital led to capital-intensive development.

Manufacturing growth slowed down once import substitution in consumer goods was completed. The government opted for decontrol and devaluation in 1962. However, tariffs were raised so that the average tariff on manufactured goods reached 51 percent. Also, by 1966, the Central Bank reintroduced import controls and additional controls were exercised by different ministries.

At the same time incentives were provided to nontraditional exports. Fiscal incentives were introduced in 1967, followed by the Export Incentives Act of 1970 which granted a direct subsidy to value added for firms which export more than 50 percent of their output. In addition, bonded warehouse schemes and partial drawbacks provided duty-free imported inputs for selected exporters whenever a domestic input was not available. Finally, beginning in 1972, export processing zones were established.

In 1973, tariffs on final goods were raised again. With tariffs reduced on inputs, effective protection of value added was increased to a considerable extent. As a result, import substitution took place in capital-intensive industries, such as paper, industrial chemicals, rubber products and metal products which had a poor productivity performance.

The situation was aggravated by the policies applied in response to the oil shocks. The Philippines adopted expansionary fiscal and monetary measures and permitted the exchange rate to become overvalued. Furthermore, there was a shift toward the public sector that had much lower productivity than the private sector.

The factors described contributed to the fall of manufacturing productivity. At the same time, the Philippines borrowed substantial amounts abroad which were not used productively but were invested largely in prestige projects. Correspondingly, the economy did not generate sufficient improvement in output to repay the loans. There ensued a decline in the GDP after 1981, and the 1983 economic crisis involved a debt moratorium that ended with the IMF stand-by agreement of 1985. Under the agreement, imports were liberalized and maximum tariff rates were reduced from 100 to 50 percent.

Reference has been made to the shift toward the public sector in the Philippines. The shift began with the institution of martial law in 1972, representing a reversal of earlier tendencies towards the increased role of the private sector in the national economy. Thus the relative shares of public corporations in the total assets of nonfinancial corporations declined from 18.2 percent in 1955 to 14.9 percent in 1960 and 13.5 percent in 1965, but increased subsequently to 27.1 percent in 1980 and to 37.4 percent in 1985.

After the declaration of martial law, the state took ownership of Philippines Airlines; some multinational oil companies sold their interests to the state-owned Philippines National Oil Company; and the military took over several privately held steel mills to create the National Steel Corporation. A number of private enterprises were also acquired during the financial crisis of 1981.

In mid-1985 there were 96 government corporations with 149 subsidiaries. This number does not include the takeover of financially distressed corporations from the private sector in 1983–4. The government owns mines, paper mills, textile factories, sugar mills, steel mills, construction companies, hotels and shipping lines.

The government also owns the Development Bank of the Philippines and two commercial banks: the Philippines National Bank and the Land Bank of the Philippines. These banks accumulated considerable amounts of nonperforming loans; as of the end of 1985, their share was 87 percent in the assets of the Development Bank of the Philippines and 58 percent in the assets of the Philippines National Bank (corresponding figures for the Land Bank of the Philippines are not available).

Apart from the two banks in the public sector, there are 31 commercial banks in the Philippines, of which four are foreign owned. There are also offshore banking units, affiliated with foreign banks, which are authorized to conduct offshore banking business in the country but not to trade domestically. As well as these, there are savings and mortgage banks, private development banks, savings and loan associations, rural banks, leasing companies and finance companies.

The financial sector was traditionally less developed in the Philippines than in other East Asian countries. In 1983 the ratio of the broadly defined money supply (M2) to the GNP was 25.5 percent in the Philippines, compared with 49.6 percent in Thailand and 64.4 percent in Malaysia. Moreover, the ratio fell to 20.9 percent in 1985 as extensive Central Bank borrowing led to a decline in time deposits. Subsequent increases brought back the ratio to 23.4 percent in 1988.

In the securities market, bond trading predominates. The stock market has not been a significant source of funds because most corporations are closely held. The money market is at an early stage of development.

The Philippines has reached high levels of education for its income level. In 1986, 68 percent of the relevant age group was enrolled in secondary schools and 38 percent of the relevant age groups in higher education. There is, nevertheless, a shortage of technicians and engineers.

ECONOMIC GROWTH

Per caput incomes in the Philippines increased by less than half between 1963 and 1987, putting it far behind the other East Asian countries. GDP growth rates of 5.3 percent in 1963–73 and 5.8 percent in 1973–81 were followed by no change between 1981 and 1987. At the same time, despite the decline that occurred, population growth rates are high, averaging 2.5 percent year in the 1981–7 period (see Table 8.1).

Manufacturing production grew rapidly in the period of import

Table 8.1 Economic performance indicators: Philippines

Growth rates	1963–73	1973–81	1981–7	1963–87
GDP	5.3	5.8	–0.0	4.1
Population	3.0	2.7	2.5	2.7
GDP per caput	2.3	3.0	–2.5	1.3
Investment	5.6	10.7	–12.5	2.3
Manufacturing production	8.1	5.2	–0.5	4.9
Agricultural production	4.1	4.7	1.8	3.7
Exports	4.5	5.9	4.5	5.0
Imports	5.8	7.4	2.5	5.5

Source: World Bank.

substitution in consumer goods, reaching 8.1 percent a year in 1963–73. The growth rate declined to 5.2 percent a year in 1973–81, followed by decreases in absolute terms between 1981 and 1987.

In conjunction with these developments, the share of the manufacturing sector in the GDP increased from 20.7 percent in 1963 to 25.2 percent in 1973, declining afterwards to 24.6 percent in 1981 and in 1987. In turn, agriculture's share rose from 26.1 percent in 1963 to 29.3 percent in 1973, declined to 22.7 percent in 1981 but increased again to 24.2 percent in 1987 (see Table 8.2).

For the entire 1963–87 period, agricultural production grew at an average annual rate of 3.7 percent, surpassing the rate of growth of population by a substantial margin. While agricultural production rose by only 1.8 percent a year in 1981–7, its growth rate was 4.1 percent a year in 1963–73 and 4.7 percent in 1973–81.

The share of mining varied to a considerable extent during the period under review, as did that of services. Thus, while services accounted for 52.0 percent of GDP in 1963, their share fell to 42.1 percent in 1973, increased again to 50.5 percent in 1981 and declined to 49.7 percent in 1987.

Among individual services, the relative shares of gas, electricity and water and of transportation experienced increases while declines are shown for construction (following a peak in 1981) and for wholesale and retail trade. The share of the catchall category of other services fluctuated between 10 and 17 percent.

Exports rose less rapidly than the GDP during the import-substitution phase (4.5 percent a year between 1963 and 1973) but surpassed GDP growth rates in the 1973–81 period (5.9 percent a year). And exports continued to rise at an average annual rate of 4.5

Table 8.2 Industrial composition and trade: Philippines (percent of GDP)

	1963	1973	1981	1987
Industrial composition				
Agriculture	26.1	29.3	22.7	24.2
Mining and quarrying	1.2	3.3	2.2	1.5
Manufacturing	20.7	25.2	24.6	24.6
Gas, electricity and water	0.9	0.8	1.1	2.5
Construction	5.5	3.9	8.6	4.0
Transportation	4.1	4.8	6.4	6.0
Wholesale and retail trade	25.7	21.0	23.7	19.5
Banking, real estate	.	.	.	.
Ownership of dwellings	.	.	.	.
Public administration	.	.	.	.
Other services	15.8	11.6	10.6	17.8
Imputed bank service charge, duty	.	.	.	.
Trade				
Exports of goods and nonfactor services	16.5	22.0	18.9	23.2
Imports of goods and nonfactor services	15.4	18.5	24.4	22.3

Source: World Bank.

percent between 1981 and 1987 when the GDP remained unchanged.

Imports rose 5.8 percent a year between 1963 and 1973, and 7.4 percent a year in the 1973–81 period. However, between 1981 and 1987 imports increased only 2.5 percent a year, reflecting the effects of economic stagnation and import controls imposed during the period.

Changes in export and import shares were further influenced by variations in export and import prices. In 1963, the share of the exports of goods and services in the GDP (16.5 percent) slightly exceeded that of the imports of goods and services (15.4 percent). Both shares increased between 1963 and 1973, but increases were larger in export shares (22.0 percent in 1973) than in import shares (18.5 percent).

In 1981, however, export shares (18.9 percent were much lower than import shares (24.4 percent), reflecting the extensive foreign borrowing of the Philippines. The situation was reversed in 1987, where the GDP share of the exports of goods and services reached 23.2 percent, compared with 22.1 percent for the imports and goods and services. This occurred as the Philippines was adjusting after the external borrowing of earlier years.

Table 8.3 Savings and investment ratios: Philippines (percent of GDP)

	1973	1974	1975	1976	1977	1978	1979	1980
Private savings	25.0	22.0	24.1	26.7	26.6	25.1	25.4	26.2
Government budget balance	−1.2	0.4	−1.2	−1.7	−1.8	−1.2	−0.2	−1.3
Domestic savings	23.9	22.4	22.9	25.0	24.8	23.9	25.2	24.9
Foreign savings	−3.5	3.2	6.9	6.4	3.8	5.0	5.5	5.7
Domestic investment	20.4	25.6	29.8	31.4	28.6	28.9	30.7	30.6

	1981	1982	1983	1984	1985	1986	1987
Private savings	28.9	26.0	22.4	19.1	18.6	23.8	18.2
Government budget balance	−4.0	−4.2	−1.9	−1.8	−1.8	−5.0	−2.4
Domestic savings	24.9	21.8	20.4	17.2	16.8	18.7	15.9
Foreign savings	5.4	6.9	7.0	0.1	−2.9	−6.0	−0.9
Domestic investment	30.3	28.6	27.4	17.3	13.8	12.7	15.0

Source: World Bank.

The described changes are apparent in the foreign savings figures of Table 8.3. While the Philippines experienced an outflow of savings in 1973, this was followed by an inflow in subsequent years as reliance was based on external borrowing to finance the higher oil bill. External borrowing continued, to a greater or lesser extent, through to 1984. In the following year, external borrowing stopped and it gave place to an outflow of savings in 1985, 1986 and 1987.

Domestic savings were in the 22–6 percent range between 1973 and 1982 but declined sharply afterwards. In 1984 and 1985, domestic savings barely surpassed 17 percent of GDP; they rebounded to 18.7 percent in 1986 but declined again to 15.9 percent in 1987.

Domestic savings were largely determined by private savings as the government budget balance fluctuated within a relatively narrow range. Apart from a slight surplus in 1974, the government budget was in deficit. The deficit was less than 2 percent of GDP, except for 1981, 1982 and 1986, when it was 4 percent or slightly higher, and 1987, when it was 2.4 percent.

The share of gross domestic investment in GDP increased from 20.4 percent in 1973 to 25.6 percent in 1974 and to 29.8 percent in 1975. It remained at about this level in subsequent years, exceeding 30 percent in 1976, 1979, 1980 and 1981.

Investment ratios declined to 28.6 percent in 1982 and 27.4 percent in 1983, followed by a precipitous fall. Thus gross domestic investment accounted for 17.3 percent of GDP in 1984, 13.8 percent in 1985 and 12.7 percent in 1986, increasing to 15.0 percent in 1987.

Table 8.4 shows that the improvement in the current account balance of the Philippines is associated with a substantial reduction in the merchandise trade deficit, from over $2.6 billion in 1982 to $0.2 billion in 1986, followed by an increase to $1 billion in 1987. In the same period, the service account shifted from a deficit of $1.0 billion to a surplus of $0.8 billion, followed by a deficit of $0.1 billion.

Apart from 1980, the Philippines experienced a net inflow of foreign direct investment. And while this inflow practically dried up in 1984 and 1985, it re-emerged again in 1986 and 1987.

There was also a long-term capital inflow throughout the period under review, although it fluctuated to a considerable extent from year to year. In turn, the inflow of short-term capital gave place to an outflow in 1983 and large outflows were observed in 1985 and 1986 as well. Finally, errors and omissions show a varied picture.

INTERNATIONAL TRADE

In 1963, 95.5 percent of Philippine exports were destined for developed countries, with the United States accounting for 45.5 percent, Western Europe for 22.3 percent and Japan for 27.3 percent. The export share of the developed countries declined to 89.8 percent in 1973 and 74.0 percent in 1981, followed by a slight rise to 77.4 percent in 1988 (see Table 8.5).

The United States experienced a larger than average decline, to 31.0 percent by 1981, followed by a rebound to 35.7 percent in 1988. In Western Europe, a trough of 15.8 percent was reached in 1973, with export shares rising again to 17.3 percent in 1981 and 18.3 percent in 1988. By contrast, Japan's export share rose to 36.0 percent in 1973, followed by a decline to 21.9 percent in 1981 and to 20.1 percent in 1988. In the same year, the combined share of Canada, Australia and New Zealand was 3.2 percent compared with 0.5 percent in 1963.

The share of the developing countries in the Philippines' exports rose from 4.2 percent in 1963 to 9.7 percent in 1973, and again to 22.9 percent in 1981, declining slightly to 22.2 percent in 1988. All major trading areas participated in the expansion.

The East Asian NICs emerged as the largest developing country

Table 8.4 Balance of payments: Philippines (million US$)

	1978	1979	1980	1981	1982	1983	1984	1985	1986	1987
Merchandise exports	3 425	4 601	5 788	5 722	5 021	5 005	5 391	4 629	4 842	5 720
Merchandise imports	-4 732	-6 142	-7 727	-7 946	-7 667	-7 490	-6 070	-5 111	-5 044	-6 737
Trade balance	-1 307	-1 541	-1 939	-2 224	-2 646	-2 485	-679	-482	-202	-1 017
Other goods, services, and income; credit	1 485	1 654	2 209	2 861	2 983	3 127	2 626	3 288	3 791	3 497
Other goods, services, and income: debit	-1 591	-1 964	-2 621	-3 205	-4 023	-3 865	-3 601	-3 203	-3 034	-3 573
Other goods, services, and income: net	-106	-310	-412	-344	-1 040	-738	-975	85	757	-76
Unrequited transfers	319	355	434	472	474	472	386	379	441	554
Current account balance	-1 094	-1 496	-1 917	-2 096	-3 212	-2 751	-1 268	-18	996	-539
Direct investment	101	7	-106	172	16	105	9	12	127	186
Long-term capital	830	1 103	984	1 134	1 549	1 051	282	3 056	1 171	269
Short-term capital	857	453	1 806	712	1 281	-1 550	474	-2 741	-1 059	-274
Capital account balance	1 788	1 563	2 684	2 018	2 846	-394	765	327	239	181
Errors and omissions	66	249	124	-490	-364	-356	100	643	-104	90
Overall balance	760	316	891	-568	-730	-3 501	-403	952	1 131	-268
Net use of reserves	-864	-439	-1 134	-177	629	1 918	-392	3	-1 351	35

Note: The overall balance is the sum of the current and capital account balances and errors and omissions. Net use of reserves was derived by adding the following items to overall balance: counterpart to the monetization and demonetization of gold, counterpart to SDR allocation, and counterpart to valuation changes.

Source: IMF, *International Financial Statistics*, various issues.

Table 8.5 Geographical composition of exports: Philippines (percent of total exports)

	1963	1973	1981	1988
Developed Countries	95.5	89.8	74.0	77.4
United States	45.5	36.4	31.0	35.7
Western Europe	22.3	15.8	17.3	18.3
Japan	27.3	36.0	21.9	20.1
Canada, Australia, New Zealand	0.5	1.6	3.8	3.2
Developing Countries	4.2	9.7	22.9	22.2
Pacific countries (other than China)	3.0	7.9	16.3	16.9
East Asian NICs	2.9	6.6	11.4	13.2
Hong Kong	0.4	2.0	3.9	4.9
Korea	0.9	1.4	3.5	2.3
Singapore	0.1	0.8	2.3	3.1
Taiwan	1.5	2.3	1.8	2.8
East Asian NECs	0.1	1.3	4.9	3.8
Indonesia	NA	0.8	2.7	0.4
Malaysia	0.0	0.3	1.8	1.7
Philippines	–	–	–	–
Thailand	0.1	0.2	0.4	1.8
China	NA	0.3	1.4	0.9
Other developing countries	1.2	1.5	5.2	4.3
Other Asia	0.5	0.7	1.5	1.9
Africa	0.3	0.4	0.6	0.2
Southern Europe	0.0	0.0	0.1	0.1
Middle East	0.0	0.2	1.8	1.4
Latin America	0.3	0.3	1.2	0.7
European Socialist Countries	NA	0.4	3.1	0.4

Note: Taiwanese figures for 1981 and 1988 derived as difference between total exports, the regional aggregates, special categories, and other countries not included. Regional aggregates may not sum to 100 percent due to inclusion in denominator of special categories, and other countries not specified.

Sources: IMF, *Direction of Trade Statistics*, various issues.

market for the Philippines, accounting for 13.2 percent of its exports in 1988, compared with 2.9 percent in 1963. The 1988 shares of the individual countries were: Hong Kong, 4.9 percent; Korea, 2.3 percent; Singapore, 3.1 percent; and Taiwan, 2.8 percent.

In 1988, the combined export share of the East Asian NECs was 3.8 percent, representing a large increase compared with the 0.1 percent share in 1963. Among these countries, Thailand leads with a share of 1.8 percent in 1988, followed by Malaysia (1.7 percent) and Indonesia (0.4 percent). In the same year, China had an export share of 0.9 percent.

The combined share of other developing countries in the Philippines' exports was 1.2 percent in 1963; it reached 5.2 percent in 1981 but declined to 4.3 percent in 1988. Within this group, Other Asia leads with 1.9 percent, followed by the Middle East (1.4 percent), Latin America (0.7 percent), Africa (0.2 percent), and Southern Europe (0.1 percent). Finally, data are not available for the European socialist countries in 1963, but their export share was 0.4 percent in 1973, 3.1 percent in 1981 and 0.4 percent in 1988.

Changes in the geographical composition of the Philippines' imports more or less mirror those of exports. The developed countries experienced a decline in their combined share from 81.8 percent in 1963 to 58.6 percent in 1981, and 57.4 percent in 1988. In turn, the combined share of the developing countries rose from 18.3 percent in 1963 to 41.1 percent in 1981 and 41.9 percent in 1988 (see Table 8.6).

Among developed countries, the United States had the largest fall in its import share during the period under consideration, from 41.1 percent in 1963 to 21.0 percent in 1988, compared with a decline from 18.1 percent to 13.6 percent in Western Europe and a rise from 17.0 percent to 17.4 percent in Japan. Finally, a small decrease, from 5.7 percent in 1963 to 5.4 percent in 1988, was experienced in the import share of Canada, Australia and New Zealand.

Among developing countries, the import share of the East Asian NICs increased to the greatest extent, from 2.0 percent in 1963 to 18.7 percent in 1988. Within this group, Taiwan led in 1988 (6.1 percent), followed by Hong Kong (4.5 percent), Singapore (4.1 percent) and Korea (4.0 percent). In turn, the import share of the East Asian NECs declined from 6.3 percent in 1963 to 5.4 percent in 1988, with Malaysia accounting for 2.9 percent, Indonesia for 1.9 percent and Thailand for 0.6 percent. In 1988 China had an import share of 3.1 percent.

The import share of the other developing countries increased from 10.0 percent in 1967 to 25.5 percent in 1981, falling afterwards to 14.7 percent in 1988. These changes are explained in large part by variations in the share of the Middle East in conjunction with increases and subsequent decreases in petroleum prices.

The commodity composition of Philippine exports changed to a considerable extent during the period under consideration. While the share of nonfuel primary products declined from 94.9 percent in 1963

Table 8.6 Geographical composition of imports: Philippines (percent of total imports)

	1963	1973	1981	1988
Developed Countries	81.8	81.1	58.6	57.4
United States	41.1	28.3	22.8	21.0
Western Europe	18.1	14.4	12.2	13.6
Japan	17.0	31.3	19.0	17.4
Canada, Australia, New Zealand	5.7	7.1	4.7	5.4
Developing Countries	18.3	18.9	41.1	41.9
Pacific countries (other than China)	8.3	4.9	13.2	24.1
East Asian NICs	2.0	3.3	7.9	18.7
Hong Kong	1.1	1.0	2.6	4.5
Korea	0.1	0.3	1.4	4.0
Singapore	0.3	0.5	1.3	4.1
Taiwan	0.5	1.5	2.5	6.1
East Asian NECs	6.3	1.6	5.2	5.4
Indonesia	3.0	0.1	2.7	1.9
Malaysia	2.1	0.9	2.2	2.6
Philippines	–	–	–	–
Thailand	1.2	0.6	0.3	0.6
China	NA	1.4	2.5	3.1
Other developing countries	10.0	12.7	25.5	14.7
Other Asia	3.6	0.3	1.7	1.8
Africa	1.1	0.4	0.1	1.1
Southern Europe	NA	0.3	0.0	0.2
Middle East	3.8	11.1	20.7	9.6
Latin America	1.4	0.5	2.9	2.0
European Socialist Countries	NA	0.1	0.2	0.8

Note: Taiwanese figures for 1981 and 1988 derived as difference between total imports, the regional aggregates, special categories, and other countries not included. Regional aggregates may not sum to 100 percent due to inclusion in denominator of special categories and other countries not specified.

Sources: IMF, *Direction of Trade Statistics*, various issues.

to 35.0 percent in 1988, that of manufactured goods increased from 4.6 percent to 36.7 percent (see Table 8.7). Large increases were also shown, from 0.1 percent to 26.3 percent, in the share of the 'other' category, which includes the processing of foreign materials (principally electronics).

Among nonfuel primary products, the largest declines occurred in industrial materials, from 64.9 percent in 1963 to 25.0 percent in

Table 8.7 Commodity composition of exports: major product groups: Philippines (percent of total exports)

		1963	1973	1981	1988
Fuels	(SITC 3)	0.4	0.9	0.7	2.0
Nonfuel primary products		94.9	83.1	54.6	35.0
Food and live animals	(SITC 0)	28.2	24.2	23.5	13.9
Beverages and tobacco	(SITC 1)	1.8	1.6	0.9	0.4
Industrial materials	(SITC 2+4+68)	64.9	57.3	30.2	20.7
Manufactures	(SITC 5+6+7+8–68)	4.6	12.2	23.3	36.7
Other	(SITC 9)	0.1	3.8	21.4	26.3
Total		100.0	100.0	100.0	100.0
Manufactures (industrial classification)		4.3	11.8	23.2	34.7
Textile, apparel, leather	(ISIC 32)	0.5	2.1	8.3	8.0
Wood product and furniture	(ISIC 33)	3.7	6.0	5.1	7.6
Paper and paper products	(ISIC 34)	0.0	0.5	0.1	0.3
Chemicals	(ISIC 35)	0.1	0.6	2.8	3.4
Nonmetallic mineral products	(ISIC 36)	0.0	1.4	0.9	0.5
Iron and steel	(ISIC 37)	0.0	0.0	0.5	1.0
Engineering products	(ISIC 38)	0.0	0.4	3.9	10.9
Other industries	(ISIC 39)	0.1	0.7	1.5	3.0

Source: UN, COMTRADE data base.

1988. Two products account for much of the decline: copra, whose export share fell from 23.4 percent in 1963 to 0.4 percent in 1987, and wood and lumber, whose share fell from 21.2 percent in 1963 to 3.0 percent in 1987.

Between 1963 and 1988, the share of food and live animals decreased from 28.2 percent to 13.9 percent and that of beverages and tobacco from 1.8 percent to 0.4 percent. The largest decline occurred in sugar, from 22.2 percent in 1963 to 2.2 percent in 1987.

In 1963, the Philippines exported wood products and furniture (3.7 percent of total exports), textiles, apparel and leather products (0.5 percent), some chemicals (0.1 percent) and the products of other industries (0.1 percent) in the manufacturing category. In 1988, engineering products were in the lead (10.9 percent), followed by textiles, apparel and leather products (8.0 percent), wood products and furniture (7.6 percent), chemicals (3.4 percent) 'and other industries' (2.1 percent).

Among major import categories, the share of fuels increased from 11.3 percent in 1963 to 30.1 percent in 1981, but declined afterwards

Table 8.8 Commodity composition of imports: major product groups: Philippines (percent of total imports)

		1963	1973	1981	1988
Fuels	(SITC 3)	11.3	12.9	30.1	17.8
Nonfuel primary products		23.4	21.9	12.1	20.8
Food and live animals	(SITC 0)	13.2	12.8	7.6	6.9
Beverages and tobacco	(SITC 1)	0.4	0.6	0.7	6.0
Industrial materials	(SITC 2+4+68)	9.8	8.5	3.9	8.0
Manufactures	(SITC 5+6+7+8–68)	64.1	61.7	44.9	58.6
Other	(SITC 9)	1.2	3.5	12.9	12.8
Total		100.0	100.0	100.0	100.0
Manufactures (industrial classification)		50.6	56.9	44.6	58.4
Textile, apparel, leather	(ISIC 32)	1.6	2.5	2.2	2.0
Wood product and furniture	(ISIC 33)	0.1	0.1	0.0	2.0
Paper and paper products	(ISIC 34)	2.9	2.2	1.0	8.2
Chemicals	(ISIC 35)	8.1	14.0	10.8	9.9
Nonmetallic mineral products	(ISIC 36)	1.5	1.1	0.7	1.6
Iron and steel	(ISIC 37)	6.4	6.3	4.3	8.7
Engineering products	(ISIC 38)	29.7	30.4	25.3	25.5
Other industries	(ISIC 39)	0.5	0.4	0.4	0.5

Source: UN, COMTRADE data base.

to 17.8 percent in 1988. In turn, the share of nonfuel primary products fell from 23.4 percent to 20.8 percent. Finally, decreases in the share of manufactured goods from 64.1 percent in 1963 to 58.6 percent in 1988 were more than offset by increases in the 'other' category, which also consists of manufactured products, from 1.2 percent to 12.8 percent (see Table 8.8).

Among nonfuel primary products, the observed decline was approximately evenly divided between food and live animals and industrial materials. In turn, the import share of beverages and tobacco increased.

Among manufactured goods, declines were experienced in engineering products, from 29.7 percent in 1963 to 25.5 percent in 1988, reflecting the fall of investment activity in the latter year. The shares of the remaining manufactured product categories increased, except for other industries that remained unchanged.

PROSPECTS FOR THE FUTURE

Economic growth in the Philippines has been projected at 4.9 percent for the period 1987–2000. This growth rate slightly exceeds that for 1963–87 (4.1 percent); it represents a turnaround from the stagnation of the GDP between 1981 and 1987; and it means that the improved growth performance of recent years would not remain temporary.

Population is projected to rise at an average annual rate of 2.3 percent between 1987 and 2000. Correspondingly, per caput incomes would increase 2.5 percent a year. This represents a substantial improvement compared with the 1.3 percent annual rate of growth of per caput incomes between 1963 and 1987.

Improved growth performance would, however, require more investment. Apart from establishing an appropriate climate for private savings and investment, this would necessitate eliminating the public sector deficit. To pursue this objective, measures would have to be taken in regard to both the government budget and public enterprises which have contributed to the public sector deficit in approximately equal measure.

The Philippines would have to reverse the increases in the number of government employees which have taken place in recent years and economize on current expenditures in general. This would have to be partly offset, however, by increases in infrastructural investment, particularly in energy and transportation where considerable needs exist.

Correspondingly, measures taken in regard to public expenditure cannot bear the brunt of reductions in the budget deficit and this will also require increases in taxes. Such increases are possible as the Philippines has the lowest ratio of government revenue to GDP (11.5 percent) among East Asian countries.

At the same time, increases in taxation should not be made at the expense of economic activity and savings. This could be accomplished by raising the rates of the newly-instituted value added tax. But such increases could be kept at modest levels if more attention were given to increasing compliance and enforcement in the tax system.

Much needs to be done in the public enterprise sector. The privatization of public trading companies and the Philippine Airlines should be completed; the privatization of public enterprises in the competitive sector should be accelerated; and financial controls should be instituted in regard to the enterprises that remain in the public sector.

It would further be necessary to increase the productivity of investment. This would require improving the system of incentives which exhibits an anti-export bias. It would be necessary to reduce and rationalize import protection, and to provide greater export incentives.

To begin with, it would be desirable to abolish import controls at an early date. Also, tariffs would need to be lowered and tariff disparities reduced. At the same time, a tariff ceiling may be set at 25 percent.

On the export side, the maintenance of competitive exchange rates is a first priority. All exporters should also receive tradable inputs at world market prices. This would mean allowing for the free entry of inputs into export production even if domestic substitutes are available. Furthermore exporters should have access to export financing at internationally competitive rates.

Improvements would also need to be made in the financial sector. This would involve providing assistance to commercial banks that are basically sound and encouraging the merger of those that could not be saved. Also, the scope of operations of the Philippines National Bank would need to be reduced and its privatization completed. Finally, the Development Bank of the Philippines could play an important role in channelling institutional savings into long-term investment by the private sector.

Under present conditions, the growth of financial intermediation in the Philippines is limited by high charges on banking operations. These charges should be reduced by lowering reserve requirements, increasing interest paid on reserves, eliminating forced investment in agricultural reform bonds, and abolishing the 5 percent tax on the gross receipts of financial intermediaries.

Reforms of the educational system are also overdue. These reforms should aim at increasing technical training in agriculture and engineering and shifting attention towards technical areas at the universities. These changes may be accompanied by the promotion of R & D through the establishment of research institutes and support to R & D spending by firms.

Bibliography

Aikman, David, 1986. 'The Philippines: Democracy's Return', Chapter 6 in David Aikman, *Pacific Rim: Area of Change, Area of Opportunity*. Boston: Little, Brown.

Alburo, Florian A., 1985. 'Philippine Trade in Manufactures: Structural

Change and Adjustment'. Discussion Paper, no. 8509. Quezon City, Manila: University of the Philippines.

Alburo, Florian A., 1986. 'Import Liberalization Revisited'. Discussion Paper No. 8611. Quezon City, Manila: University of the Philippines.

Alburo, Florian and Geoffrey Shepherd, 1985. 'Trade Liberalization Experience in the Philippines, 1960–84'. Working Paper, no. 86–01. Manila: Philippine Institute for Development Studies.

AYC Consultants, 1985. *Private Sector Opportunity Assessment (Agricultural Sector): An Overview of the Philippines and Its Agricultural Sector (Task One)*. Manila: AYC Consultants.

Baldwin, Robert E., 1975. *Foreign Trade Regimes and Economic Development: The Philippines*. New York: National Bureau of Economic Research.

Bautista, Romeo M., 1987. 'Production Incentives in Philippine Agriculture: Effects of Trade and Exchange Rate Policies'. Research Report 59. Washington, DC: International Food Policy Research Institute.

Bautista, Romeo, John Power and Associates, 1978. *Industrial Promotion Politics in the Philippines*. Manila: Philippines Institute for Development Studies.

Bresnan, John (ed.), 1986. *Crisis in the Philippines: The Marcos Era and Beyond*. Princeton, NJ: Princeton University Press.

Bunge, Frederica M., 1983. *Philippines: A Country Study*. Washington, DC: US Government Printing Office.

Castro, Amado A., 1969, 'Philippine Export Development, 1950–65', in Theodore Morgan and Nyle Spoelstra (eds), *Economic Interdependence in Southeast Asia*. Madison, WI: University of Wisconsin Press.

Cheetham, Russell J. and Edward K. Hawkins, 1976. *The Philippines: Priorities and Prospects for Development*. Report of a mission sent to the Philippines by the World Bank. Washington, DC: World Bank.

Daquila, Teofilo C., 1987. 'Macroeconomic Policy and its Impact on the Philippine Economy'. Working Papers in Trade and Development, no. 87/12. Canberra: National Centre for Development Studies.

Economist Intelligence Unit, 1987. *Country Profile: Philippines, 1987–88*. London: The Economist.

Hawes, Gary, 1987. *The Philippine State and the Marcos Regime: The Politics of Export*. Ithaca, NY: Cornell University Press.

Hicks, George L. and Geoffrey McNicoll, 1971. *Trade and Growth in the Philippines*. Ithaca, NY: Cornell University Press.

Hooley, Richard W., 1984, *Productivity Growth in Philippine Manufacturing: Retrospect and Future Prospects*. Monograph Series, no. 9. Manila: Philippines Institute for Development Studies.

Intal, Ponciano S., Jr, 1985. 'A Decomposition Analysis of Philippine Export and Import Performance, 1974–1982', Staff Paper Series, no. 85–02. Manila: Philippines Institute for Development Studies.

Manasan, Rosario G. and Corazon R. Buenaventura, 1986. 'A Macroeconomic Overview of Public Enterprise in the Philippines, 1975–1984'. Staff Paper Series, no. 86–03. Manila: Philippines Institute for Development Studies.

May, R. J. and Francisco Nemenzo, 1985. *The Philippines After Marcos*. New York: St Martin's Press.

Montes, Manuel F., 1987. *Country Study: The Philippines*. Helsinki: WIDER Publications.

Montes, Manuel F., 1987. *Macroeconomic Adjustment in the Philippines, 1983–85*. Working Paper Series, no. 8701. Manila: Philippines Institute for Development Studies.

Owen, Norman (ed.), 1983. *The Philippine Economy and the United States: Studies in Past and Present Interactions*. Ann Arbor, MI: University of Michigan.

Philippines Institute for Development Studies, 1986. *Assessment of the First Phase of Tariff Reform (TRP) and Other Trade Liberalization Measures*. Manila: Philippines Institute for Development Studies.

Philippines Institute for Development Studies, 1986. *Economic Recovery and Long-Run Growth: Agenda for Reforms*, vol. I. Main Report. Manila: Philippines Institute for Development Studies.

Senga, Kunio, 1983. 'A Note on Industrial Policies and Incentive Structures in the Philippines: 1949–80', *Philippine Review of Economics and Business*, vol. XX, nos 3 and 4, (September/December), pp. 299–305.

UN Industrial Development Organization, 1985. *The Philippines*. Industrial Development Review Series, UNIDO/IS.527. New York: UN.

Verbruggen, Harmen, 1985. 'The Case of the Philippines', in Harmen Verbruggen, *Gains from Export-Oriented Industrialization in Developing Countries with Special Reference to South-East Asia*. Amsterdam: Free University Press.

Warr, Peter G., 1985. 'Export Processing Zones in the Philippines'. ASEAN–Australia Economic Papers, no. 20. Kuala Lumpur and Canberra: ASEAN–Australia Joint Research Project.

World Bank, 1980. *Philippines: Industrial Development Strategy and Policies*. Washington, DC: World Bank.

World Bank, 1987. *Philippines: A Framework for Economic Recovery*. Washington, DC: World Bank.

9 Thailand

INTRODUCTION

In an area of 514 000 square kilometers, Thailand has a population of 52.6 million. It is characterized by considerable ethnic and cultural homogeneity. Among ethnic minorities Malays account for 3 percent of the population, while Chinese have a share of 7–8 percent but are increasingly assimilated in the Thai population.

Thailand is a constitutional monarchy. It was never colonized by the Western powers but lost some of its territories to French and British colonies and protectorates in the nineteenth century. Thailand became modernized under successive rulers in the second half of the nineteenth and the first half of the twentieth century.

Apart from tin, Thailand has no mineral deposits but natural gas and some petroleum have been found in the Gulf of Thailand. Its principal economic asset is agricultural land. Rice is the main agricultural product, with maize and cassava assuming importance in the north-east and rubber in the south.

Manufacturing industry was originally dominated by public enterprises. Private industries developed in response to the adoption of *laissez-faire* policies, together with the provision of basic infrastructure. This development was also aided by the promotional measures taken, in particular the establishment of the Board of Investment in 1958, the establishment of the Industrial Finance Corporation of Thailand (IFCT) in 1959, and the Industrial Promotion Act of 1962. Today, Thai industry is operated largely by private enterprise, with governmental participation limited to a relatively small number of firms. While manufacturing industries originally hoped to provide for domestic needs, industrial exports have assumed increasing importance in recent years.

By 1981, the share of manufacturing industries in the GDP came to exceed that of agriculture. Nevertheless, agriculture also developed rapidly as it was not subject to the extensive discrimination practised in many developing countries. As a result, Thailand has become one of the largest exporters of agricultural products in the developing world.

GOVERNMENTAL POLICIES

Agricultural production increased at a high rate during the postwar period, reflecting both increases in the area of cultivation and higher yields. Governmental measures contributing to agricultural development have included infrastructural investments and the introduction of nitrogen-resistant varieties of rice.

Rice continues to dominate Thai agriculture, utilizing about two-thirds of arable land. Nevertheless, a number of new crops have emerged in response to favorable prices while an export tax continues to apply to rice. Among these crops maize, cassava and kenaf are new to Thailand; rubber has long been cultivated in the south.

In the period before the Second World War, foreign interests and resident Chinese built plants producing cement, matches, soap, cigarettes, sugar and alcoholic beverages. After the Second World War the government established a number of public enterprises manufacturing products such as paper, sugar, gunny bags, plywood, cement, beer and pharmaceuticals.

Questions were raised, however, about the efficiency of public enterprises and in the 1950s it was decided to promote private enterprise in the future. While the first law in 1954 to promote private industry was not very effective, additional steps were taken in 1958 through the establishment of the Board of Investment, in 1959 through the establishment of the IFCT and in 1962 in the form of the Industrial Promotion Act.

Under the 1977 revision of the Industrial Promotion Act, the Board of Investment may provide (a) exemptions, or reductions up to 50 percent, of import duties and business taxes on imported machinery and of business taxes on domestically produced machinery; (b) reductions up to 90 percent of import duties and business taxes on imported materials and of business taxes on domestic materials; (c) exemptions of corporate income taxes for 3-8 years, with the carry-forward of losses for up to five years after the period of exemptions; (d) exclusions from taxable income of fees for goodwill, copyright and other rights for a period of five years after income is derived from the promoted activity; and (e) exclusions from taxable income of dividends derived from the promoted activity during the period of tax holiday. The Board may also impose import surcharges on competing imports.

The Board has considerable discretionary authority to determine the list of activities eligible for promotion; to select the investment projects that are to receive promotion privileges; to set the conditions for these projects; and to determine the extent and the length of duration of promotion privileges. Promotion is subject to minimum conditions as to the size of investment and, in selected instances, the share of exports in output. In 1983, new guidelines were issued to give emphasis to export-oriented and labor-intensive projects.

The IFCT was established as a privately-owned corporation but its largest shareholder, the Krung Thai Bank, is wholly owned by the government and IFCT in general attempts to follow government priorities. In particular, one of its objectives is to select projects on a broad geographical basis.

Before the 1960s, tariffs in Thailand served mainly revenue purposes and varied between 15 and 30 percent. In 1971, tariffs were raised on consumer goods to a range of 30–50 percent. In 1974, however, tariffs were reduced across the board to combat inflationary pressures.

Tariffs were increased again between 1974 and 1980. As the adverse effects of high tariffs came to be recognized, a tariff reform involving considerable reductions of duties was introduced in 1982. This was followed by the imposition of surcharges for revenue purposes that were subsequently removed. And while tariffs were raised in 1985, Thailand remains a relatively low tariff country. In fact, tariffs average 18 percent, with finished consumer goods and – in particular – automobiles being subject to higher duties. Automobiles are also protected by domestic content requirements.

Quantitative import restrictions apply to 65 products, including kraft paper, some automobile parts, cars and motorcycles, diesel engines, compressors and iron bars and rods. The policy is to reduce the scope of quantitative restrictions over time.

Apart from relatively low import protection, the efficient development of Thai industry has been helped by a *laissez-faire* atmosphere which limits governmental interventions in business affairs. This atmosphere has contributed to rapid export expansion that has further been assisted by the devaluations of 1981 and 1984 and by the granting of export incentives.

Exporters are exempted from import duties, business taxes and municipal taxes on imported inputs used directly or indirectly in export production, and receive rebates on indirect taxes paid on domestic materials. Exporters also receive a rebate of 20 percent on electricity. Finally, a preferential export credit scheme is in effect.

An export processing zone has been established by the Industrial

Estate Authority of Thailand. Exports through this zone have remained relatively small, however. This reflects largely the relative ease with which export incentives can be obtained and the virtual lack of bureaucratic obstacles to exports.

Thai industry is concentrated in the Bangkok area. While the successive five-year plans called for the decentralization of industry, and tax as well as credit incentives have been provided for this purpose, the effects have been minimal. However, infrastructural investments under the plans helped the agriculture of the disadvantaged regions, so that regional income differences have declined somewhat.

An important recent step towards reducing the preponderance of Bangkok in Thai manufacturing has been the Eastern Seaboard region program. This region, extending from east of Bangkok towards the Kampuchean border, has several advantages. They include proximity to raw materials and labor supplies from the north-east, direct access to the Gulf of Thailand, the deep-sea port at Sattalip, and road and communications infrastructure. The region will serve as a center for resource-based industries, in particular those utilizing natural gas, and aims to attract export-oriented light industries.

The Thai government wishes to increase the availability of energy supplies via offshore gas and oil exploration. Natural gas is at the basis of the petrochemicals complex and the fertilizer plant, which will account for a substantial part of industrial investments in the Eastern Seaboard region. The petrochemicals complex is to include plants to process ethane and propane into ethylene and propylene which, in turn, will supply the inputs for a number of downstream chemical plants. The fertilizer plant will produce urea and compound fertilizers from methane gas.

The petrochemicals complex and the fertilizer plant will benefit from the construction of a new deep-sea port and heavy industry estate. There are further plans for constructing a light industry estate and an export processing zone in the region, and a deep-sea port for the exportation of local foodstuffs.

Thailand has 68 majority-owned state economic enterprises, compared with 264 such enterprises in the Philippines. There were 104 state enterprises in Thailand in the early 1960s when it was decided to reduce their number. The largest state enterprises are public utilities, transport and communication companies, financial institutions and the Petroleum Organization of Thailand. There are a number of smaller state enterprises in the other sectors, including agriculture, manufacturing, commerce and services.

Profit-making state enterprises include the Electricity Generating Authority and Thai Airways International, while the railways and the Bangkok Public Transport Authority have traditionally incurred losses. There are also several loss-making state enterprises in the directly productive sectors.

The government aims to involve the private sector through equity participation in infrastructure projects. Furthermore, private companies will be allowed to provide bus services and to build toll roads and bridges. In addition, the privatization of state enterprises in the productive sectors is envisaged.

Thailand has taken a favorable attitude toward foreign direct investment. Following fluctuations over the years, this has led to substantial increases after 1986. Japanese investments have been especially large.

After financial liberalization reform in the late 1950s, the Thai economy became increasingly monetized. These tendencies continued in subsequent years as the financial system gained in sophistication. As a result, the percentage of money and quasi-money in the GDP increased from 23 percent in 1960 to 31 percent in 1970, to 37 percent in 1980 and again to 67 percent in 1987.

Thailand has 30 commercial banks (with 1800 branches) of which 16 are Thai and 14 are foreign (with 20 branches). The largest, the Bangkok Bank, is also the largest bank in South-east Asia. While formerly the banks lent mainly by way of overdraft, term loans and promissory notes have assumed increased importance in recent years.

No new commercial banks were permitted after the early 1970s but finance companies have proliferated during this period. Several of these companies were adversely affected by the stock market collapse of 1979 and were intervened by the government.

Other components of the financial system include life insurance companies, agricultural cooperatives, private money lenders and specialized development finance institutions. The latter comprise the Government Savings Bank, the Bank for Agriculture and Agricultural Cooperatives, the Government Housing Bank, the IFCT and the Small Industry Finance Corporation.

Money and capital markets are still underdeveloped in Thailand. The stock market has suffered boom and bust cycles. Secondary

Economic Policies in the Pacific Area

Table 9.1 Economic performance indicators: Thailand

Growth rates	1963–73	1973–81	1981–7	1963–87
GDP	7.9	6.9	5.6	7.0
Population	3.4	2.3	1.9	2.7
GDP per caput	4.4	4.5	3.6	4.2
Investment	11.4	5.7	2.5	7.2
Manufacturing production	12.4	8.4	6.0	9.5
Agricultural production	4.8	4.1	3.0	4.1
Exports	10.6	9.4	10.5	10.2
Imports	10.8	5.1	6.5	7.8

Source: World Bank.

markets in government bonds practically do not exist and Thailand has failed to develop a significant open market in short-term instruments.

At the same time, Thailand has a relatively open financial system with continued arbitrage between domestic and foreign financial markets. This has meant that Thailand could tap the resources of foreign financial markets. Nevertheless, Thailand's foreign indebtedness abroad has remained moderate.

Thailand has an almost universal primary educational system. At the same time, higher education is top heavy, with the rate of secondary education enrollment by the relevant age group being much lower in Thailand (29 percent) than in lower-middle-income countries on the average (51 percent), while the opposite is the case for university education (20 percent and 17 percent). University education is heavily skewed towards the humanities and social sciences to the detriment of technical education.

ECONOMIC GROWTH

Per caput incomes in Thailand increased more than 3 times between 1963 and 1988 (see Table 1.1). At the same, a deceleration of economic growth is shown, with GDP growth rates averaging 7.9 percent in 1963–73, 6.9 percent in 1973–81, and 5.6 percent in 1981–7 (Table 9.1). The slowdown of economic growth in the latter period has been related to unfavorable developments in the world economy, poor harvests and the deceleration of the growth of investment activity in Thailand. Nevertheless, Thai growth performance ex-

Table 9.2 Industrial composition and trade: Thailand (percent of GDP)

	1963	1973	1981	1987
Industrial composition				
Agriculture	33.1	27.7	21.4	16.1
Mining and quarrying	1.7	2.3	2.8	3.1
Manufacturing	14.2	19.2	22.3	23.9
Gas, electricity and water	0.6	1.3	1.4	2.6
Construction	4.6	4.1	5.0	5.1
Transportation	6.9	5.8	6.0	7.5
Wholesale and retail trade	15.8	17.6	18.1	15.6
Banking, real estate	1.4	2.5	3.0	3.9
Ownership of dwellings	7.2	4.9	3.4	4.0
Public administration	4.7	4.1	4.4	4.3
Other services	10.6	10.7	12.1	13.9
Imputed bank service charge, duty	.	.	.	.
Trade				
Exports of goods and nonfactor services	14.8	18.6	23.8	30.1
Imports of goods and nonfactor services	18.0	20.0	30.1	29.8

Source: World Bank.

ceeded that of other lower-middle-income countries by a considerable margin. Growth accelerated again, exceeding 8 percent, in 1988.

Manufacturing was the leading sector of the economy throughout the period under consideration, with output rising 12.4 percent a year between 1963 and 1973, 8.4 percent between 1973 and 1981 and 6.0 percent between 1981 and 1987. Notwithstanding poor harvests in the last subperiod, the growth of agricultural production substantially exceeded that of population during the entire period. The relevant growth rates are: 1963–73, 4.8 percent; 1973–81, 4.1 percent; and 1981–7, 3.0 percent.

The differential growth performance of agriculture and manufacturing led to substantial shifts in the sectoral composition of the GDP. While the share of agriculture was 33.1 percent in 1963, it declined to 16.1 percent by 1987. During the same period, the share of manufacturing rose from 14.2 percent to 23.9 percent. The share of mining and quarrying also increased, from 1.7 percent in 1963 to 3.1 percent in 1987 (see Table 9.2).

Increases were experienced in the share of services as well. While services accounted for 51.0 percent of the GDP in 1963, their com-

Table 9.3 Savings and investment ratios: Thailand (percent of GDP)

	1973	1974	1975	1976	1977	1978	1979	1980
Private savings	28.2	23.0	23.8	25.4	24.9	27.8	24.7	25.0
Government budget balance	-3.3	0.9	-2.1	-4.1	-3.3	-3.8	-3.7	-4.7
Domestic savings	25.0	23.9	21.7	21.3	21.6	24.0	21.0	20.3
Foreign savings	1.4	2.3	4.5	2.5	5.5	4.2	6.9	6.4
Domestic investment	26.4	26.2	26.2	23.7	27.0	28.3	27.9	26.7

	1981	1982	1983	1984	1985	1986	1987
Private savings	23.6	27.6	23.1	24.2	26.4	28.5	26.5
Government budget balance	-3.3	-6.4	-4.0	-3.4	-5.4	-4.4	-2.3
Domestic savings	20.3	21.2	19.2	20.7	21.1	24.1	24.1
Foreign savings	6.4	1.7	7.4	4.4	2.8	-2.1	-0.1
Domestic investment	26.7	23.0	26.6	25.1	23.9	22.0	24.0

Source: World Bank.

bined share rose to 56.9 percent by 1987. The largest increase occurred in banking, from 1.4 percent in 1963 to 3.9 percent in 1987. The shares of gas, electricity and water, construction, transportation, and other services rose also, while declines were experienced in the shares of wholesale and retail trade, ownership of dwellings and public administration.

Export expansion importantly contributed to economic growth in Thailand. Export growth rates exceeded the rate of growth of GDP throughout the period, with exports rising 10.6 percent a year between 1963 and 1973, 9.4 percent between 1973 and 1981 and 10.5 percent between 1981 and 1987. As a result, the share of the exports of goods and services in the GDP increased from 14.8 percent in 1963 to 18.6 percent in 1973, 23.8 percent in 1981 and 30.1 percent in 1987. The share of the imports of goods and services rose more or less in parallel until 1981, from 18.1 percent in 1963 to 20.0 percent in 1973 and to 30.1 percent in 1986 but declined to 29.8 percent in 1987.

As shown in Table 9.3, Thailand experienced a foreign capital inflow every year until 1986 when this gave place to an outflow. But, even before 1986, foreign savings fluctuated to a considerable extent in Thailand, with their share in GDP varying between 1.4 percent and 7.4 percent. Domestic savings fluctuated between 21.0 percent and 25.0 percent in the 1970s and declined afterwards, reaching a low point of 19.2 percent in 1983. Subsequently, however, domestic savings increased again, attaining 24.1 percent of GDP in 1987.

Domestic savings originate in the private sector. Apart from a small surplus in 1974, the government budget has been in deficit. The deficit increased over time, with a peak of 6.4 percent of GDP in 1982. The next two years showed decreases, followed by a rise in 1985 and a subsequent decline to 2.3 percent in 1987.

Domestic investment's share in the GDP was in the 23–7 percent range between 1973 and 1976 and in the 27–9 percent range between 1977 and 1980. It declined subsequently and, after fluctuating between 22 percent and 27 percent during the 1983–6 period, it was 24.0 percent of GDP in 1987.

Table 9.4 indicates that the turnaround in foreign savings was associated with an improvement in the merchandise trade account, although a small deficit was shown again in 1987. In turn, there continued to be a small deficit in the service account. At the same time, Thailand continued to receive unilateral transfers from abroad.

Thailand was the recipient of foreign direct investment throughout the period under consideration. Except for 1986, there was also an inflow of long-term capital. Finally, if errors and omissions are combined with short-term capital, an inflow is shown except for the years 1980 and 1982, both of which preceded a devaluation.

INTERNATIONAL TRADE

Thai exports to developing countries exceeded exports to developed countries in 1963. The opposite was the case in subsequent years, and in 1988 developed countries took 62.4 percent and developing countries 36.3 percent of Thai exports, with European socialist countries accounting for the remainder (see Table 9.5).

The United States assumed increasing importance as an export market for Thailand over time. Its share was 7.4 percent in 1963, 10.1 percent in 1973, 12.9 percent in 1981 and 20.0 percent in 1988. The export share of Western Europe increased until 1981 and declined afterwards. It was 17.7 percent in 1963, 19.3 percent in 1973, 23.9 percent in 1981 and 22.7 percent in 1988.

In turn, Japan's export share rose from 18.1 percent in 1963 to 26.1 percent in 1973 but fell to 14.2 percent in 1981; it was 15.9 percent in 1988. Finally, the combined export share of Canada, Australia and New Zealand was negligible in 1963 but reached 3.8 percent in 1988.

Table 9.4 Balance of payments: Thailand (million US$)

	1978	1979	1980	1981	1982	1983	1984	1985	1986	1987
Merchandise exports	4 045	5 234	6 449	6 902	6 835	6 308	7 338	7 059	8 803	11 595
Merchandise imports	-4 904	-6 785	-8 352	-8 931	-7 565	-9 169	-9 236	-8 391	-8 415	-11 981
Trade balance	-859	-1 551	-1 903	-2 029	-730	-2 861	-1 898	-1 332	388	-386
Other goods, services, and income: credit	1 088	1 428	2 125	2 352	2 580	2 919	3 077	3 163	3 333	4 009
Other goods, services, and income: debit	-1 423	-2 024	-2 509	-3 062	-3 036	-3 209	-3 463	-3 533	-3 700	-4 378
Other goods, services, and income: net	-335	-596	-384	-710	-456	-290	-386	-370	-367	-369
Unrequited transfers	40	60	217	169	183	277	174	165	225	225
Current account balance	-1 154	-2 087	-2 070	-2 570	-1 003	-2 874	-2 110	-1 537	246	-530
Direct investment	50	51	187	288	189	348	400	162	261	182
Long-term capital	596	1 426	1 920	1 597	1 046	952	1 386	1 453	-203	389
Short-term capital	715	499	-63	594	58	662	767	-99	-219	462
Capital account balance	1 361	1 976	2 044	2 479	1 293	1 962	2 553	1 516	-161	1 033
Errors and omissions	-232	20	-180	133	-521	587	71	103	598	408
Overall balance	-25	-91	-206	42	-231	-325	514	82	683	911
Net use of reserves	-188	22	170	46	120	188	-432	-228	-932	-1 252

Note: The overall balance is the sum of the current and capital account balances and errors and omissions. Net use of reserves was derived by adding the following items to overall balance: counterpart to the monetization and demonetization of gold, counterpart to SDR allocation, and counterpart to valuation changes.

Source: IMF, *International Financial Statistics*, various issues.

Table 9.5 Geographical composition of exports: Thailand
(percent of total exports)

	1963	1973	1981	1988
Developed Countries	43.5	56.6	52.7	62.4
United States	7.4	10.1	12.9	20.0
Western Europe	17.7	19.3	23.9	22.7
Japan	18.1	26.1	14.2	15.9
Canada, Australia, New Zealand	0.2	1.1	1.7	3.8
Developing Countries	55.6	42.6	42.0	36.3
Pacific countries (other than China)	45.1	32.2	22.9	19.4
East Asian NICs	19.4	20.7	16.1	15.5
Hong Kong	9.8	7.3	4.8	4.4
Korea	0.3	1.0	2.1	1.6
Singapore	8.0	8.3	7.8	7.7
Taiwan	1.3	4.1	1.3	1.8
East Asian NECs	25.7	11.5	6.8	3.9
Indonesia	8.2	4.6	1.9	0.5
Malaysia	15.9	6.0	4.6	3.0
Philippines	1.7	0.9	0.3	0.4
Thailand	–	–	–	–
China	NA	NA	2.6	3.0
Other developing countries	10.5	10.4	16.5	13.9
Other Asia	5.6	5.5	2.2	3.4
Africa	1.1	2.2	5.0	3.3
Southern Europe	0.3	0.2	0.2	0.4
Middle East	2.6	2.5	8.8	6.0
Latin America	0.9	0.1	0.4	0.7
European Socialist Countries	0.8	0.7	5.3	0.9

Note: Taiwanese figures for 1981 and 1987 derived as difference between total exports, the regional aggregates, special categories, and other countries not included. Regional aggregates may not sum to 100 percent due to inclusion in denominator of special categories, and other countries not specified.

Sources: IMF, *Direction of Trade Statistics*, various issues.

The decline in the share of the developing countries in Thai exports from 55.6 percent in 1963 to 36.3 percent in 1988 was concentrated in the Pacific Area where the corresponding shares were 45.1 percent and 19.4 percent. Within this total, the sharpest declines were experienced in the East Asian NECs: Indonesia from 8.2 percent to 0.5 percent, Malaysia from 15.9 percent to 3.0 percent, and the Philippines from 1.7 percent to 0.4 percent.

By comparison, only a small decline was experienced in the export shares of the East Asian NICs. This occurred as a large drop in the export share of Hong Kong was nearly offset by increases in Korea and Taiwan. In turn, China had a 3.0 percent share in Thai exports in 1988.

The other developing countries increased their market share in Thai exports from 10.5 percent in 1963 to 13.9 percent in 1988. The largest increases occurred in the Middle East followed by Africa and Southern Europe, while the shares of Other Asia and Latin America declined. Finally, the European socialist countries experienced a small increase in their share of Thai exports.

The developed countries lost market shares to the developing countries in Thai imports. Thus, the import share of the former declined from 83.5 percent in 1963 to 55.5 percent in 1988 while that of the latter increased from 15.6 percent to 41.6 percent (see Table 9.6). The import share of the European socialist countries was 0.9 percent in 1963 and 2.3 percent in 1988.

The United States, Western Europe and Japan all experienced declines in their share of Thai imports. The share of the United States decreased from 17.5 percent in 1963 to 13.0 percent in 1981, increasing again to 16.8 percent in 1988; Western Europe's share was 30.8 percent in 1963, 15.5 percent in 1981 and 22.9 percent in 1988; Japan's share was 32.9 percent in 1963, 24.2 percent in 1981 and 11.7 percent in 1988. In turn, the share of Canada, Australia and New Zealand increased from 2.3 percent in 1963 to 5.0 percent in 1973, declining to 3.8 percent in 1981 and rising to 4.1 percent in 1988.

Among developing countries, the import share of the East Asian NICs increased more than three times, from 6.1 percent in 1963 to 19.3 percent in 1988. Except for Hong Kong, which experienced a decline from 2.6 percent in 1963 to 1.5 percent in 1987, all the countries in this group participated in the increase. The relevant figures, for 1963 and 1988, are: Korea, 0.3 percent and 3.4 percent; Singapore, 0.9 percent and 9.2 percent; and Taiwan, 2.2 percent and 5.1 percent.

Despite increases in recent years, the East Asians NECs did not regain their 1963 market shares in Thai imports. The figures are: 1963, 6.9 percent; 1973, 1.3 percent; 1981, 3.1 percent; and 1988, 4.8 percent. This result was due entirely to the decline in Indonesia's import share, from 6.4 percent in 1963 to 1.1 percent in 1988. Thus Malaysia's share increased from 0.5 percent to 2.5 percent and the Philippines' share from nil to 1.2 percent.

Table 9.6 Geographical composition of imports: Thailand
(percent of total imports)

	1963	1973	1981	1988
Developed Countries	83.5	78.4	56.6	55.5
United States	17.5	13.3	13.0	16.8
Western Europe	30.8	24.0	15.5	22.9
Japan	32.9	36.0	24.2	11.7
Canada, Australia, New Zealand	2.3	5.0	3.8	4.1
Developing Countries	15.6	20.6	40.8	41.6
Pacific countries (other than China)	13.0	8.4	14.5	24.1
East Asian NICs	6.1	7.1	11.4	19.3
Hong Kong	2.6	1.4	0.9	1.5
Korea	0.3	0.9	1.4	3.4
Singapore	0.9	1.4	7.0	9.2
Taiwan	2.2	3.3	2.1	5.1
East Asian NECs	6.9	1.3	3.1	4.8
Indonesia	6.4	0.4	0.2	1.1
Malaysia	0.5	0.7	2.7	2.5
Philippines	0.0	0.2	0.2	1.2
Thailand	–	–	–	–
China	NA	NA	3.2	4.1
Other developing countries	2.6	12.2	23.0	13.4
Other Asia	0.6	1.4	2.5	3.9
Africa	0.2	4.2	0.5	2.0
Southern Europe	0.1	0.1	0.2	0.2
Middle East	1.7	5.8	18.6	4.9
Latin America	0.1	0.6	1.2	2.4
European Socialist Countries	0.9	0.7	1.2	2.3

Note: Taiwanese figures for 1981 and 1987 derived as difference between total imports, the regional aggregates, special categories, and other countries not included. Regional aggregates may not sum to 100 percent due to inclusion in denominator of special categories and other countries not specified.

Sources: IMF, *Direction of Trade Statistics*, various issues.

In turn, the import share of the other developing countries increased from 2.6 percent in 1963 to 12.2 percent in 1973 and 23.0 percent in 1981, declining afterwards to 13.4 percent in 1988. This pattern of change is explained in large part by changes in oil imports from the Middle East, whose share in Thai imports rose from 1.7 percent in 1963 to 5.8 percent in 1973, and again to 18.6 percent in 1981, subsequently decreasing to 4.9 percent in 1988. Between 1963

Table 9.7 Commodity composition of exports: major product groups: Thailand (percent of total exports)

		1963	1973	1981	1987
Fuels	(SITC 3)	0.0	1.3	0.0	0.7
Nonfuel primary products		96.5	78.6	72.7	46.8
Food and live animals	(SITC 0)	56.0	44.0	53.7	36.3
Beverages and tobacco	(SITC 1)	0.5	1.1	1.2	0.5
Industrial materials	(SITC 2+4+68)	40.1	33.6	17.8	10.0
Manufactures	(SITC 5+6+7+8–68)	2.5	16.0	25.5	51.6
Other	(SITC 9)	1.0	4.0	1.8	0.9
Total		100.0	100.0	100.0	100.0
Manufactures (industrial classification)		2.4	15.7	23.8	50.2
Textile, apparel, leather	(ISIC 32)	0.7	8.4	9.9	20.9
Wood product and furniture	(ISIC 33)	0.1	1.5	1.0	2.2
Paper and paper products	(ISIC 34)	0.1	0.2	0.2	0.5
Chemicals	(ISIC 35)	0.2	0.8	1.9	3.8
Nonmetallic mineral products	(ISIC 36)	0.7	1.2	0.5	0.8
Iron and steel	(ISIC 37)	0.1	0.4	0.5	0.8
Engineering products	(ISIC 38)	0.1	0.9	6.3	13.4
Other industries	(ISIC 39)	0.5	2.3	3.6	7.6

Source: UN, COMTRADE data base.

and 1988, the import share of Other Asia increased from 0.6 percent to 3.9 percent, that of Africa from 0.2 percent to 2.0 percent, that of Latin America from 0.1 percent to 2.4 percent, and that of Southern Europe remained from 0.1 percent to 0.2 percent. Finally, China's import share was 4.1 percent in 1988; no data are available for 1963.

The commodity composition of Thai exports was substantially transformed during the period under consideration. The shares of nonfuel primary products declined continuously, from 96.5 percent in 1963 to 78.6 percent in 1973, to 72.7 percent in 1981, and again to 46.8 percent in 1987. In turn, the share of manufactured products increased from 2.5 percent in 1963 to 16.0 percent in 1973, to 25.5 percent in 1981, and to 51.6 percent in 1987 (see Table 9.7).

Among nonfuel primary products, the decline was concentrated in industrial materials, from 40.1 percent in 1963 to 10.0 percent in 1987. During this period, the export share of rubber fell from 20.2 percent to 6.9 percent and that of tin from 7.9 percent to 0.8 percent.

The export share of food and live animals decreased from 56.0 percent in 1963 to 36.3 percent in 1987. Within this commodity category, however, disparate changes are shown for some major commodities. While the share of rice declined from 36.3 percent to 7.6 percent between 1963 and 1987 and that of maize fell from 8.8 percent to 1.3 percent, increases from 1.8 percent to 6.9 percent were experienced in vegetables (mainly cassava used in animal feeding), from 1.5 percent to 3.1 percent for sugar and from 0.8 percent to 5.3 percent for fish.

Manufactured exports have come to be dominated by textiles, apparel and leather products and by engineering products. Between 1963 and 1987, the share of the former increased from 0.7 percent to 20.9 percent and that of the latter from 0.1 percent to 13.4 percent. Within the first group, textile fabrics and apparel are of importance; the second is dominated by the exports of parts and components for assembly abroad.

Thailand also exports a wide range of chemicals, with a combined share of 3.8 percent in 1987. Furthermore, it is a large exporter of gems (4.0 percent in 1987) which represent the bulk of the 'other industries' category (7.6 percent).

In the case of imports, the share of fuels increased from 9.6 percent in 1963 to 13.3 percent in 1987, while that of nonfuel primary products rose from 10.9 percent to 14.1 percent (see Table 9.8). In the latter case, industrial materials dominated the outcome (8.9 percent in 1987, compared with 3.4 percent in 1963) reflecting the raw material needs of Thailand's industrial development.

The import share of manufactured goods declined from 77.1 percent in 1963 to 68.2 percent in 1987. The decline was dominated by textiles, apparel and leather products, whose import share fell from 12.8 percent to 3.2 percent between 1963 and 1987. These changes occurred as Thai industry was increasingly able to provide for domestic needs.

Smaller changes occurred in regard to other industrial categories. Increases were observed in chemicals, iron and steel and other industries, while declines were experienced in wood products and furniture, paper and paper products, nonmetallic mineral products and engineering products.

PROSPECTS FOR THE FUTURE

The rate of economic growth for Thailand has been projected at 6.8 percent a year for the 1987–2000 period. This growth rate exceeds

Table 9.8 Commodity composition of imports: major product groups: Thailand (percent of total imports)

		1963	1973	1981	1987
Fuels	(SITC 3)	9.6	11.3	29.8	13.3
Nonfuel primary products		10.9	15.3	12.1	14.1
Food and live animals	(SITC 0)	6.3	3.3	3.1	4.7
Beverages and tobacco	(SITC 1)	1.1	1.0	0.7	0.5
Industrial materials	(SITC 2+4+68)	3.4	11.0	8.3	8.9
Manufactures	(SITC 5+6+7+8–68)	77.1	70.2	54.1	68.2
Other	(SITC 9)	2.4	3.3	4.0	4.4
Total		100.0	100.0	100.0	100.0
Manufactures (industrial classification)		73.2	69.8	52.8	66.6
Textile, apparel, leather	(ISIC 32)	12.8	4.9	1.8	3.2
Wood product and furniture	(ISIC 33)	0.2	0.1	0.1	0.1
Paper and paper products	(ISIC 34)	2.4	1.9	1.3	1.5
Chemicals	(ISIC 35)	12.8	16.6	12.5	16.3
Nonmetallic mineral products	(ISIC 36)	1.4	0.9	0.9	0.9
Iron and steel	(ISIC 37)	6.9	7.7	6.0	7.4
Engineering products	(ISIC 38)	35.9	36.8	29.3	35.4
Other industries	(ISIC 39)	0.9	0.9	0.9	1.9

Source: UN, COMTRADE data base.

that observed in 1981–7, and it is only slightly below the average rate of GDP growth in the postwar period (see Table 9.1).

With population projected to rise at an average annual rate of 1.6 percent a year, the 6.8 percent GDP growth rate would translate into a 5.2 percent annual rate of growth of per caput income. This would put Thailand among upper-middle-income countries according to the World Bank classification. With economic growth concentrated in the manufacturing sector, Thailand would join the ranks of the NICs.

For the projected growth rate to be reached, certain conditions need to be fulfilled, however. In particular, more savings would have to be generated to provide for a higher level of investment. While Thailand has a high rate of private savings, it needs to continue reducing the dissavings of the public sector.

There are some possibilities for raising revenues as Thailand has one of the lowest ratios of government revenues to GDP (16.2 percent in 1987) among lower-middle-income countries. Possible revenue sources include increasing taxes on oil, limiting income tax exemptions and raising indirect taxes.

More should be sought on the side of current public expenditures, however. There are possibilities for reducing overstaffing in the government and, most importantly, improvements need to be made in the state enterprise sector. This would involve lowering the deficits of loss-making enterprises and raising public sector tariffs. Furthermore, state enterprises should pay taxes in the same way as private enterprises and further steps should be taken towards privatization.

As far as public investments are concerned, there is a need for improvements in infrastructure, including transportation, energy and telecommunications. Also, the investments in the Eastern Seaboard region should continue while avoiding highly capital-intensive investments, such as the proposed steel mill.

Increasing the efficiency of private investment would require improvements in the incentive system. Export incentives need to stepped up while reducing import protection. In regard to export incentives, it should be ensured that all direct and indirect exporters receive rebates of duties and indirect taxes on their inputs; the system of export financing would need to be expanded; and the growth of trading companies should be speeded up.

In regard to import protection, the reforms should include reducing the level and the dispersion of tariffs, involving the introduction of a 25 percent tariff ceiling. At the same time, quantitative import restrictions should be phased out.

There is also a need for financial sector reform. The government should permit the establishment of new commercial banks, including foreign banks, so as to increase competition. At the same time, investment banking should be expanded, open-market operations in short-term instruments should be furthered, and the development of the bond market ensured.

In the case of investment incentives, the measures applied should be increasingly oriented towards the promotion of labor-intensive industries, and in the implementation of the 1983 guidelines export-oriented projects should be given priority.

Finally there is a need for a reform of the educational system. The expansion of secondary education should be oriented toward meeting middle-level manpower requirements; there is a need for vocational education in the areas of industrial technology and agriculture; and these areas should also receive emphasis in university education. At the same time, spending on R & D should be increased.

Bibliography

Balassa, Bela, et al., 1980. *Industrial Development Strategy in Thailand*. A World Bank Country Study. Washington, DC: World Bank.

Baldwin, W. Lee and W. David Maxwell, 1975. *The Role of Foreign Financial Assistance to Thailand in the 1980s*. Lexington, MA: D.C. Heath.

Bunge, Frederica M. (ed.), 1981. *Thailand: A Country Study*. American University Foreign Area Studies. Washington, DC: US Government Printing Office.

Devarajan, Shantayanan and Hector Sierra, 1985. 'Growth Without Adjustment: Thailand, 1975–82'. CPD Discussion Paper, no. 1986–5. Washington, DC: World Bank.

Dowling, John Malcolm, Jr, 1984. 'Income Distribution and Poverty in Selected Asian Countries'. Asian Development Bank Economic Staff Paper, no. 22. Manila: The Asian Development Bank.

Economist Intelligence Unit, 1984. *Thailand: Prospects and Policies*. Special Report, no. 161. London: The Economist.

International Bank for Reconstruction and Development, 1959. *A Public Development Program for Thailand*. Baltimore, MD: The Johns Hopkins University Press.

Jansen, Karel, 1984. 'Stability and Stabilisation in Thailand'. Working Paper No. 10, Sub-series on Money, Finance, and Development. The Hague: Institute of Social Studies.

Keyes, Charles F., 1987. *Thailand: Buddhist Kingdom as Modern Nation-State*. Boulder, CO: Westview Press.

Marby, Bevars D., 1979. 'The Development of Labor Institutions in Thailand'. Data Paper No. 112, Southeast Asia Program, Department of Asian Studies, Cornell University. Ithaca, NY: Cornell University.

Marzouk, G. A., 1972. *Economic Development and Policies: Case Study of Thailand*. Rotterdam, Netherlands: Rotterdam University Press.

Muscat, Robert J., 1966. *Development Strategy in Thailand: A Study of Economic Growth*. New York: Praeger.

Randolph, R. Sean, 1986. *The United States and Thailand: Alliance Dynamics, 1950–85*. Research Papers and Policy Studies 12. Berkeley, CA: Institute of East Asian Studies, University of California.

Silcock, T. H. (ed.), 1967. *Thailand: Social and Economic Studies in Development*. Canberra: Australian National University Press.

Terwiel, B. J., 1984. *Development Issues in Thailand*. Gaya, India: Centre for Southeast Asian Studies.

Vorasopontaviporn, Pornpen, 1985. 'The Impact of Trade Policies on Employment and Income Distribution in Thailand', *Economic Bulletin for Asia and the Pacific*, vol. 36, no. 1.

10 Conclusions

The Pacific Area developing countries attained high rates of economic growth in the 1963–87 period, the exception being the Philippines. Per caput incomes increased approximately five times in the East Asian NICs (six times in Singapore); among the East Asian NECs, they rose approximately three times in Indonesia, Malaysia and Thailand while the increase was less than half in the Philippines.

The excellent economic record of the Pacific Area developing countries is put into focus if comparisons are made with Latin American countries at comparable levels of industrialization. While the Latin American countries had generally higher levels of per caput incomes at the beginning of the period, they fell increasingly behind.

The superior growth performance of the Pacific Area developing countries finds its origin in relatively high levels of savings and of investment efficiency, which were aided by the policies applied. Savings were promoted by financial sector reform, while the generally outward-oriented policy stance of the countries in question contributed to the efficiency of investment.

The system of incentives applied entailed either no discrimination or limited discrimination against exports, the major exception being the Philippines. The share of exports in the GDP increased as a result, with export expansion involving a shift towards manufactured goods.

In particular, the Pacific Area developing countries relied to a considerable extent on export promotion in response to the external shocks of the 1973–81 period and beyond. They did not engage in excessive foreign borrowing which would have given rise to debt servicing problems (the Philippines being the major exception again).

This volume projects a continued favorable growth performance of the Pacific Area developing countries in the 1987–2000 period. The range of projections is 7–8 percent for the East Asian NICs and 6–7 percent for the East Asian NECs, except for the Philippines where the projected growth rate is 5 percent. These projections represent some deceleration compared with the 1963–87 period, but are generally an improvement compared with 1981–7.

The projections reflect the experience and prospects of individual countries. They also reflect the assumptions that, aided by their high investment shares, the East Asian NICs will make considerable progress in applying modern technology and that the East Asian NECs will follow in their footsteps in upgrading the product composition of exports.

As to the external environment, an assumption has been made that there will be no increase in protection in the developed countries. At the same time, to varying extents, policy changes in the Pacific Area developing countries would be necessary to attain the projected growth rates. These policy changes are summarized below.

In the case of *Hong Kong*, it has been assumed that the continuation of *laissez-faire* policies would be appropriate. While there are no signs that the Chinese government would change these policies, Hong Kong becoming part of China in 1997 introduces an element of uncertainty into the projections.

Some appreciation of the currency would be necessary in *Korea*, in view of its continued current account surplus which limits the growth of domestic consumption and investment. Lowering import protection would further reduce the current account surplus; it would at the same time contribute to the efficiency of resource allocation while allowing Korea to forgo the use of export incentives.

Korea also needs to further liberalize its financial system. This would involve greater interest rate flexibility, the elimination of directed credits and the increased presence of foreign banks. Capital markets would need to be promoted and mortgages and consumer credit liberalized. Finally, Korea needs investments in the physical and social infrastructure to raise living standards and to reduce regional inequalities.

Singapore would also need to appreciate its currency lest the current account surplus grow further and inflation threaten its economy. With appreciation, it would be possible to rely to a greater extent on domestic demand for economic growth.

Singapore has practically a free trade system and it welcomes foreign direct investment. At the same time, it would be desirable to give a greater role to private business in economic life. Technical education should also be upgraded.

Taiwan should eliminate quantitative import restrictions and reduce tariffs. It should appreciate its exchange rate in order further to reduce its current account surplus. The appreciation would have to be accompanied by appropriate steps to ensure increases in domestic investment and consumption. This would involve increased infrastructural investments, the liberalization of mortgage credits and the expansion of consumer credit.

There is a need, too, to liberalize money markets and to develop capital markets in Taiwan. Finally, the tax system should be reformed by eliminating the encouragement of savings while reducing the taxes which burden private investment and consumption.

In *Indonesia*, the growth projection reflects the assumption of stable, and eventually rising, oil prices as well as improvements in economic policies. Policy changes in agriculture, industry, international trade, the government budget and the financial sector would complement each other in contributing to rapid economic growth.

In agriculture, emphasis should be given to product diversification in Java and to exploiting the production potential of the outer islands. In industry, the gradual denationalization of state enterprises should be undertaken while streamlining the operation of the remaining state enterprises. Moreover, the focus of investment policy should be shifted from regulation to promotion and the local content program reduced in scope and rationalized.

There is further need for the liberalization of trade. Import bans and import quotas should be abolished and import licensing phased out over time. Also, the tariff structure should be rationalized, with the range of tariffs reduced and tariff levels lowered.

The deficit of the government budget should be reduced by lowering administrative expenditures and improving the tax collection effort. In the financial sector, an increasing role should be given to market forces in the determination of interest rates, and regulations on the money market as well as on the bond and stock markets should be liberalized.

In *Malaysia*, the first priority is to reduce the large government budget deficit. While some revenue-raising measures are possible through extending the coverage of the sales tax or transforming this into value added tax, the principal change should be a cut in expenditures. In addition, the public enterprise system should be reformed by privatizing firms in the competitive industrial sector, closing down firms that cannot be salvaged and improving efficiency in the rest.

Import quotas should be eliminated and tariffs reduced. In turn the duty-free treatment of imported inputs, enjoyed in the FTZs, should be extended to domestic enterprises which do not export all of their production.

The granting of pioneer status should be limited to export-oriented firms and pioneer status for other enterprises should not be renewed. Instead, reliance should be placed on cutting corporate profit taxes.

At the same time, contributions to the Employee Providential Fund should be reduced.

In the *Philippines*, too, cutting the government budget deficit is a primary consideration. This would necessitate reducing the number of government employees and economizing on current budgetary expenditures in general. There is a need, however, to increase infrastructural investments which requires an improved tax collection effort and higher value added taxes. In the public enterprise sector, the privatization of public trading companies should be completed, public enterprises in the competitive industrial sector privatized and financial controls instituted in regard to enterprises that remain in the public sector.

There is also a need to reduce import protection. At the same time, it should be ensured that all exporters receive tradable inputs at world market prices by allowing the duty-free entry of inputs for export production even if domestic substitutes are available. Exporters should also have access to export financing at internationally competitive rates.

Assistance should be provided to commercial banks that are basically sound, while encouraging the merger of those that cannot be saved. Also, the scope of operation of the Philippines National Bank would need to be reduced and its privatization completed. Finally, the Development Bank of the Philippines may play an important role in channeling institutional savings into long-term investment by the private sector.

Thailand also needs to reduce dissavings by the public sector. There are possibilities for raising revenues by increasing taxes on oil, limiting income tax exemptions and raising indirect tax rates, but emphasis should be given to lowering government expenditures by reducing overstaffing in the government and making improvements in the public enterprise sector. At the same time, there is a need for improvements in the infrastructure.

Import protection should be reduced by phasing out quantitative import restrictions while lowering and rationalizing tariffs. In turn, it should be ensured that all direct and indirect exporters receive rebates of duties and indirect taxes on their inputs; the system of export financing would need to be expanded; and the growth of trading companies speeded up. Export-oriented projects should also be given priority in providing investment incentives.

In the financial sector, the government should permit the establishment of new commercial banks, including foreign banks. In addition there is a need for the expansion of investment banking, an open market in short-term instruments should be established, and the development of the bond market ensured.

If appropriate policies are followed, the Pacific Area developing countries would thus maintain high economic growth rates until the end of the century. This, in turn, would permit them to move up on the international income scale.

Singapore and Hong Kong have already surpassed New Zealand, Ireland and Spain in terms of per caput income. By the end of the century, their per caput incomes would reach the present-day incomes of Canada and Denmark. At the same time, Taiwan would reach Singapore's and Hong Kong's present per caput income level, while Korea would approximate that of Spain, thereby moving into the industrial country group.

Among the NECs, Malaysia and Thailand would become NICs while the Philippines would rank higher among lower-middle-income countries. Finally, Indonesia would move from the lower-income to the lower-middle-income country group.

As a result of these changes, the relative importance of the Pacific Area developing countries would increase to a considerable extent during the rest of the century. This conclusion applies also to international trade, given the export orientation of the countries in question. Their development would thus further increase the weight of the Pacific area in the world economy.

Index

African developing countries 25, 26, 27
  trade with Pacific developing countries: Hong Kong 38, 39; Indonesia 132, 133, 134, 135; Korea 62, 63; Malaysia 155, 157; Philippines 173, 174, 175; Singapore 88, 89; Taiwan 111, 112, 113; Thailand 193, 194, 195, 196
Aquino, C. 164
Argentina
  debt 16, 17, 29
  education 21, 22, 24
  employment and unemployment 19, 20
  exports 6–11 *passim*
  GNP 29
  health 20, 21
  per caput income 2, 3
  policies 12–13, 14–15, 16
  savings and investment 4, 5
Asian developing countries 25, 26, 27
  trade with Pacific developing countries: Hong Kong 38, 39, 40; Indonesia 132, 133, 134, 135; Korea 62, 63; Malaysia 155, 156, 157; Philippines 173, 174, 175; Singapore 87, 88, 89; Taiwan 110–11, 112; Thailand 193, 194, 195, 196
Australia 25, 26, 27
  trade with Pacific developing countries: Hong Kong 38, 39; Indonesia 132–3; 134, 135; Korea 62, 63; Malaysia 153, 155, 156, 157; Philippines 171, 173, 174, 175; Singapore 87, 88, 89; Taiwan 110, 111, 112, 113; Thailand 191, 193, 194, 195

Brazil
  debt 16, 17, 29
  education 21, 22
  employment and unemployment 19
  exports 6–11 *passim*
  GNP 29
  health 20, 21
  per caput income 2, 3
  policies 12–13, 14–15, 16
  savings and investment 4, 5
Britain 73

Canada 25, 26, 27
  trade with Pacific developing countries: Hong Kong 38, 39, 40; Indonesia 132, 134, 135; Korea 62, 63; Malaysia 153, 155, 156, 157; Philippines 171, 173, 174, 175; Singapore 87, 88, 89; Taiwan 110, 111, 112, 113; Thailand 191, 193, 194, 195
chaebol (conglomerates) 56
Chiang Kai-shek 96
Chile
  debt 16, 17, 29
  education 21, 22, 24
  employment and unemployment 19
  exports 6–11 *passim*
  GNP 29
  health 20, 21
  per caput income 2
  policies 12, 14–15
  savings and investment 5
China 25, 26, 27
  Hong Kong 30, 42–3
  Singapore 74
  Taiwan ruled by 96
  trade with Pacific developing countries: Hong Kong 36, 38, 39; Indonesia 132, 133, 134,

207

135; Korea 60–2, 63;
Malaysia 155, 156, 157;
Philippines 173, 174, 175;
Singapore 87, 88, 89;
Taiwan 110, 111, 112;
Thailand 193, 194, 195, 196
China External Trade Development
 Council 99
Colombia
 debt 16, 18, 29
 education 22, 24
 employment and
  unemployment 19, 20
 exports 6–10 *passim*
 GNP 29
 health 20
 per caput income 2, 3
 policies 14–15, 17
 savings and investment 5
Cowperthwaite, Sir J. 32

Daewoo 101
debt, foreign 3, 16–17, 18, 29
 *see also under individual
  countries*
Development Bank of the
 Philippines 166–7, 179, 205
Development Bank of
 Singapore 80

economic growth 1–3, 28, 29, 202
 *see also under individual
  countries*
education 21–4
 *see also under individual
  countries*
employment 19
 *see also under individual
  countries*
Europe, Western 25, 26, 27
 trade with Pacific developing
  countries: Hong Kong 38, 39,
  40; Indonesia 132, 134;
  Korea 60, 62, 63;
  Malaysia 153, 155, 157;
  Philippines 171, 173, 174,
  175; Singapore 87, 88, 89;
  Taiwan 110, 111, 112, 113;
  Thailand 191, 193, 194, 195

European developing
 countries 25, 26, 27
 trade with Pacific developing
  countries: Hong Kong 38, 39;
  Indonesia 132, 133, 134, 135;
  Korea 62, 63; Malaysia 155,
  156, 157; Philippines 173,
  174, 175; Singapore 88, 89;
  Taiwan 111, 112;
  Thailand 193, 194, 195, 196
European socialist countries 25,
 26, 27
 trade with Pacific developing
  countries: Hong Kong 38, 39;
  Indonesia 132, 133, 134, 135;
  Korea 60–2, 63;
  Malaysia 155, 156, 157;
  Philippines 173, 174, 175;
  Singapore 88, 89;
  Taiwan 111, 112;
  Thailand 193, 194, 195
export promotion 12–13, 17, 28,
 202
 Indonesia 123–4
 Korea 47–8, 48–9, 51
 Malaysia 142–3, 146, 160
 Philippines 165
 Singapore 76–7
 Taiwan 96, 98–9
 Thailand 185–6, 199
exports 6–11, 202
 geographical composition 24,
  25, 28
 see also imports; trade; *and
  under individual countries*

GDP growth rates 4, 5
 *see also under individual
  countries*
GNP growth rates 29
government policies *see* policies;
 and under individual countries
Government of Singapore
 Investment Corporation 80
Griffith, J. 33

Haddon-Cave, Sir P. 32
Harbison-Myers index 21–4
health 20, 20–1

Index

higher education enrollment 21, 22–3, 24
Hon Sui Sen 78
Hong Kong 30–45
 balance of payments 36, 37
 debt 16
 economic growth 34–6;
  GDP 5, 34; GNP 29;
  industrial composition 34–35;
  per caput income 1–2, 34;
  projections 42–3, 206;
  trade 34, 35
 education 21–4, 31;
  technical 32
 employment and
  unemployment 19, 20
 entrepôt trade 30, 36
 Exchange Stabilization Fund 33
 exports 6–11 *passim*, 25;
  commodity composition 8–9,
  40–2; geographical
  composition 36–40
 future prospects 42–3
 health 20, 21, 31
 imports 26; commodity
  composition 42, 43;
  geographical composition 36,
  39, 41
 Industrial Development
  Board 32
 manufacturing 1, 30, 31
 policies 31–3; financial
  system 33; foreign direct
  investment 33; for future
  growth 43, 203; legal
  system 33; role of the
  state 31–2; shocks and
  responses 14–15;
  taxation 31
 population 30
 savings and investment 4, 5, 34,
  35, 36
 trade balance 27
 trade with other Pacific
  developing countries:
  Indonesia 132, 133, 134, 135;
  Korea 62, 63; Malaysia 155,
  156, 157; Philippines 173,
  174, 175; Singapore 87, 88,
  89; Taiwan 110, 111, 112,
  113; Thailand 193, 194, 195
Hong Kong Training Council 32
Hyundai 101

import substitution 11–12, 13, 16, 17
Indonesia 123
Korea 46, 47–8, 49
Malaysia 142, 144–6
Philippines 18, 164–5
Singapore 73, 76
Taiwan 96, 97–8, 99–100
imports 24–6
 see also exports; trade; *and under
  individual countries*
Indonesia 121–41
 balance of payments 130, 131
 debt 16, 18, 29
 economic growth 127–30;
  GDP 5, 128; GNP 29;
  industrial composition 128–9;
  per caput income 2, 127, 138;
  projections 137–8, 206;
  trade 128, 129
 education 22, 24, 127, 139
 employment and
  unemployment 19
 exports 7–11 *passim*, 25;
  commodity composition 8–9,
  135–6; geographical
  composition 130–3
 Foreign Capital Investment
  Law 125
 future prospects 137–9
 'Guided Economy' 121
 health 20, 21
 imports 26; commodity
  composition 136–7;
  geographical
  composition 133–5
 manufacturing 1, 123
 policies 18, 122–7;
  agriculture 122–3, 138;
  financial system 126–7, 139;
  foreign direct investment 123,
  125–6, 139; for future
  growth 138–9, 204;
  planning 122; private sector

(pribumi) 125, 138; shocks
and responses 14–15; state
enterprises 124–5, 138;
taxation 127, 139;
trade 123–4, 138–9
population 121, 127, 138
savings and investment 5,
129–30
trade balance 27, 28
trade with other Pacific
developing countries: Hong
Kong 38, 39, 40; Korea 62,
63; Malaysia 155, 156, 157;
Philippines 173, 174, 175;
Singapore 73, 74, 88, 89;
Taiwan 110, 111, 112, 113;
Thailand 193, 194, 195
infant mortality rates 20, 21
investment 4–6, 28, 202
see also under individual
countries

Jacoby, N. H. 103
Jamaica
debt 16, 18, 29
education 22, 24
employment and
unemployment 19, 20
exports 7, 8–9, 10
GNP 29
health 20, 21
per caput income 2, 3
policies 14–15, 17–18
savings and investment 5
Japan
foreign investment 149, 187
occupation of the
Philippines 164
Taiwan ceded to 96
trade 25, 26, 27; with Hong
Kong 38, 39, 40; with
Indonesia 132–3, 134–5; with
Korea 60, 62, 63; with
Malaysia 153, 155, 156, 157;
with the Philippines 171, 173,
174, 175; with Singapore 87,
88, 89; with Taiwan 110, 111,
112, 113; with Thailand 191,
193, 194, 195

Java 121
see also Indonesia
Jurong Industrial Estates 76
Jurong Town Corporation 80

Korea 46–72
balance of payments 60, 61
chaebol 56
debt 16, 17, 29
division of 46
economic growth 46, 57–60;
GDP 5, 57; GNP 29;
industrial composition 57–8;
per caput income 2, 46, 57;
projections 66–7, 206;
trade 58
education 21, 22, 24, 55–6
employment and
unemployment 19, 20
exports 6–10 passim, 25, 46–7;
commodity composition 8–9,
64–5; geographical
composition 60–2
Foreign Capital Inducement
Law 56, 60
future prospects 66–7
health 20, 21
imports 26, 46–7; commodity
composition 65–6; geographical
composition 62–4
manufacturing 49–50, 51, 101
National Project for Research
and Development 55
Office of Fair Trade 54
policies 12, 47–56;
agriculture 53; capital-intensive
industries 49–50; exchange
rate 47, 67; export
promotion 47–8, 48–9, 51;
Fifth Five-Year Plan 51–3;
financial system 48–9, 53–4,
67; foreign direct
investment 56; functional
approach 54–5; for future
growth 67, 203; import
liberalization 51, 52–3, 67;
import substitution 46, 47–8,
49; investment 50; promotion
of technology 55; shocks and

Index

responses 14–15; tariffs 53, 67
population 46, 67
savings and investment 4, 5, 46–7, 58–60
Science and Technology Development Law 53
Tariff Reform Act 53
Technology Development Promotion Act 55
trade balance 27
trade with other Pacific developing countries: Hong Kong 38, 39, 40; Indonesia 132, 133, 134, 135; Malaysia 155, 156, 157; Philippines 173, 174, 175; Singapore 87, 88, 89; Taiwan 110, 111, 112, 113; Thailand 193, 194, 195
Korea Trade Promotion Association (KOTRA) 48
Korean war 46
Krause, L. B. 80
Krung Thai Bank 185

Land Bank of the Philippines 166
Latin America
  developing countries compared with Pacific developing countries 1–29, 202; economic growth 1–3; exports 6–11; policies applied 11–18; savings and investment 4–6; social indicators 19–24; trends in trade 24–8
  trade with Pacific developing countries: Hong Kong 38, 39; Indonesia 132, 133, 134, 135; Korea 62, 63; Malaysia 155, 156, 157; Philippines 173, 174, 175; Singapore 88, 89; Taiwan 111, 112, 113; Thailand 193, 194, 195, 196
  see also under individual countries
Lee Kuan Yew 81
life expectancy rates 20, 21

literacy rates 21, 22–3, 24
Little, I. M. D. 103
Lucky 101

Malayan Federation 142
Malaysia 142–63
  balance of payments 153, 154
  Capital Investment Committee (CIC) 145
  debt 16, 18, 29, 160, 204
  economic growth 150–3; GDP 5, 150, 151; GNP 29; industrial composition 150–2; per caput income 2, 3, 150; projections 159–60, 206; trade 151, 152
  education 22, 24, 149
  employment and unemployment 19, 148
  exports 7–11 passim, 25, 143; commodity composition 8–9, 157–8; geographical composition 153–6
  Federal Industrial Development Authority (FIDA) 145
  free trade zones (FTZs) 146–7
  future prospects 159–60
  health 20, 21
  imports 26; commodity composition 159; geographical composition 156–7
  Investment Incentives Act 142, 143, 144, 146
  Labor Utilization Relief Act 144
  licensed manufacturing warehouses (LMWs) 146, 147
  manufacturing 142, 143–4
  Pioneer Industries Ordinance 142, 143
  policies 18, 143–50; agriculture 143; export promotion 142–3, 146, 160; financial system 149–50; foreign direct investment 149; for future growth 160, 204–5; investment incentives 144; New Economic Policy (NEP) 147–8; pioneer

status 143–4, 146, 160;
privatization 148–50;
promotion of heavy
manufacturing 147; public
enterprises 148, 160; shocks
and responses 14–15; tax
incentives 143–4;
trade 144–7, 160
population 142, 159
poverty eradication 147–8, 160
savings and investment 4, 5,
152–3
Tariff Advisory Board 144, 145
trade balance 27, 28
trade with other Pacific
developing countries: Hong
Kong 38, 39, 40;
Indonesia 132, 133, 134, 135;
Korea 62, 63;
Philippines 173, 174, 175;
Singapore 73, 74, 87, 88, 89;
Taiwan 110, 111, 112, 113;
Thailand 193, 194, 195
manufacturing
share in exports 6–11
share in GDP 1
*see also under individual
countries*
Mexico
debt 16, 17
education 22, 24
employment and
unemployment 19
exports 6–11 *passim*
GNP 29
health 20, 21
per caput income 2
policies 12–13, 13–16
savings and investment 4, 5
Middle East 25, 26, 27
trade with Pacific developing
countries: Hong Kong 38, 39;
Indonesia 132, 133, 134, 135;
Korea 60, 62, 63;
Malaysia 155, 156, 157;
Philippines 173, 174, 175;
Singapore 87, 88–9;
Taiwan 111, 112, 113;
Thailand 193, 194, 195

Multifiber Arrangement 41

NECs, Pacific
compared with Latin America:
debt 16, 18, 29; economic
growth 2, 3, 29;
education 22, 24;
employment and
unemployment 20;
exports 6–11 *passim*;
health 20, 21;
policies 14–15, 17–18; savings
and investment 4–6
growth 202–3
manufacturing 1
trade with other Pacific
developing countries: Hong
Kong 38, 39, 40;
Indonesia 132, 133, 134, 135;
Korea 62, 63, 64;
Malaysia 155, 156, 157;
Philippines 173–4, 175;
Singapore 88, 89;
Taiwan 110, 111, 112, 113;
Thailand 193, 194, 195
trends in trade 25, 26, 27, 28
see also Indonesia; Malaysia;
Philippines; Thailand
Netherlands 121
New Zealand 25, 26, 27
trade with Pacific developing
countries: Hong Kong 38, 39,
40; Indonesia 132, 133, 134;
Korea 62, 63; Malaysia 153,
155, 156, 157;
Philippines 171, 173, 174,
175; Singapore 87, 88, 89;
Taiwan 110, 111, 112, 113;
Thailand 191, 193, 194, 195
NICs, Pacific
compared with Latin America:
debt 16–17, 29; economic
growth 2–3, 29;
education 21–4; employment
and unemployment 19, 20;
exports 6–11 *passim*;
health 20, 20–1;
policies 11–17; savings and
investment 4, 5

growth 202–3
manufacturing 1
trade with other Pacific
 developing countries: Hong
 Kong 38, 39–40;
 Indonesia 132, 133, 134, 135;
 Korea 62, 63, 64;
 Malaysia 155, 156, 157;
 Philippines 171–3, 174, 175;
 Singapore 87, 88, 89;
 Taiwan 110, 111, 112, 113;
 Thailand 193, 194, 195
trends in trade 25, 26, 27, 28
see also Hong Kong; Korea;
 Singapore; Taiwan

Park Chung Hee 47, 50
People's Action Party (PAP) 75
per caput income 1–3, 28, 202
*see also under individual
 countries*
Peru
 debt 16, 18
 education 22, 24
 employment and
  unemployment 19, 20
 exports 7, 8–9, 10
 GNP 29
 health 20
 per caput income 2, 3
 policies 14–15, 18
 savings and investment 5
Philippines 28, 164–82
 balance of payments 171, 172
 debt 16, 18, 29, 166, 202
 economic growth 167–71, 202,
  206; GDP 5, 167, 168;
  GNP 29; industrial
  composition 167–8; 169; per
  caput income 2, 3, 167;
  projections 178; trade 168–9
 education 22, 24, 167, 179
 employment and
  unemployment 19, 20
 Export Incentives Act 165
 exports 7–11 *passim*, 25, 164;
  commodity composition 8–9,
  174–6; geographical
  composition 171–4

future prospects 178–9
 health 20
 imports 26; commodity
  composition 176–7;
  geographical
  composition 174, 175
 policies 17, 165–7;
  agriculture 165; financial
  system 166–7, 179; for future
  growth 178–9, 205;
  protectionism 164, 205;
  public sector 166, 178; shocks
  and responses 14–15, 18;
  trade 164–5, 179
 population 164, 178
 savings and investment 5,
  170–1, 178
 trade balance 27
 trade with other Pacific
  developing countries: Hong
  Kong 38, 39, 40;
  Indonesia 132, 134, 135;
  Korea 62, 63; Malaysia 155,
  156, 157; Singapore 87, 88,
  89; Taiwan 110, 111, 112,
  113; Thailand 193, 194,
  195
Philippines National Bank 166–7,
 179, 205
physician/population ratio 20, 21
policies 11–18, 28–9
 necessary for future
  growth 203–6
*see also under individual
 countries*
'positive non-interventionism' 32
Psacharopoulos index 22–3, 24

Raffles, Sir T. S. 74

Sabah 142
see also Malaysia
Samsung 101
Sarawak 142
see also Malaysia
savings 4–6, 28, 202
*see also under individual
 countries*
Scitovsky, T. 101

secondary school enrollment 21, 22–3
shocks, external, and responses to 13, 14–15, 17–18
SIMEX 83
Singapore 73–95
  balance of payments 85–7
  Central Provident Fund 80
  Control of Manufacturing Ordinance 75
  Economic Development Board (EDB) 75–6, 78, 79
  economic growth 83–7; GDP 5, 83; GNP 29; industrial composition 83–4; per caput income 1–2, 83, 202; projections 92, 206; trade 84
  education 22, 24, 77, 78–9
  employment and unemployment 19, 20, 74, 77
  entrepôt trade 73, 74
  Export Credit Insurance Corporation 77
  exports 6–11 *passim*, 25; commodity composition 8–9, 89–91; geographical composition 87, 88
  Federation of Malaysia 73, 76, 142
  future prospects 82
  health 20, 21
  imports 26; commodity composition 91–2; geographical composition 87–9
  Industrial Expansion Ordinance 75, 82
  manufacturing 73, 74, 82
  Pioneer Industries Ordinance 75, 81–2
  policies 12, 74–83; export expansion 76–7; financial system 73, 74, 82–3; foreign direct investment 73–4, 81–2; for future growth 92, 203; high-technology industries 78–9; import substitution 73, 76;
  industrialization 74–6; public enterprises 80–1; shocks and responses 14–15; training schemes 77, 78–9; wages 79–80
  population 73, 74, 92
  savings and investment 4, 5, 80, 84–5
  surplus 17, 29
  Technical Education Department 77
  trade balance 27
  trade with other Pacific developing countries: Hong Kong 38, 39, 40; Indonesia 132, 133, 134, 135; Korea 62, 63; Malaysia 153–5, 156, 157; Philippines 173, 174, 175; Taiwan 110, 111, 112, 113; Thailand 193, 194, 195
social indicators 19–24
Spain 164
Suharto, President 121, 122, 126

Taiwan 96–120
  aid 103–4
  balance of payments 108–10
  economic growth 106–10; GDP 5, 106; GNP 29; industrial composition 107; per caput income 2, 96, 106; projections 115–16, 206; trade 106–7
  education 22, 24, 104
  employment and unemployment 19, 20
  exports 6–10 *passim*, 25, 96; commodity composition 8–9, 113–15; geographical composition 110–11
  future prospects 115–17
  health 20, 21
  Hsinchu science-based industrial park 102–3
  imports 26; commodity composition 115, 116; geographical composition 111–13

Index

Investment Encouragement
  Law 100–1
manufacturing 1, 98, 100, 101–2
policies 12, 97–106;
  agriculture 100; Central Bank
  borrowing 106; currency
  reform 97; exchange rate
  system 97–8, 116; export
  expansion 96, 98–9; financial
  system 104–6, 117; for future
  growth 116–17, 203–4;
  high-technology
  industry 102–3; import
  liberalization 99–100; import
  substitution 96, 97–8, 99–100;
  industrial parks 101, 102–3;
  land reform 97;
  planning 103; public
  sector 102; shocks and
  responses 14–15
population 96, 116
savings and investment 4, 5,
  107–8
surplus 17, 29
trade balance 27, 28
trade with other Pacific
  developing countries: Hong
  Kong 38, 39, 40;
  Indonesia 132, 133, 134, 135;
  Korea 62, 63; Malaysia 155,
  156, 157; Philippines 173,
  174, 175; Singapore 87, 88,
  89; Thailand 193, 194, 195
Thailand 183–201
  balance of payments 191, 192
  debt 16, 18, 29
  economic growth 188–91;
    GDP 5, 188, 188–9;
    GNP 29; industrial
    composition 189–90; per
    caput income 2, 3, 188;
    projections 197–8, 206;
    trade 189, 190
  education 22, 24, 199
  employment and
    unemployment 19
  exports 6–11 *passim*, 25;
    commodity composition 8–9,
    196–7; geographical

composition 191–4
future prospects 197–9
health 20
imports 26; commodity
  composition 197, 198;
  geographical
  composition 194–6
manufacturing 183, 184–5
policies 184–8;
  agriculture 184; Eastern
  Seaboard Program 186, 199;
  export promotion 185–6, 199;
  financial system 187–8; 199;
  foreign direct investment 187;
  for future growth 198–9,
  205–6; import protection 185,
  199; private sector 184–5, 187;
  shocks and responses 14–15,
  18; state enterprises 186–7
population 183, 198
savings and investment 5,
  190–1, 198
trade balance 27
trade with other Pacific
  developing countries: Hong
  Kong 38, 39, 40;
  Indonesia 132, 134, 135;
  Korea 62, 63; Malaysia 155,
  156, 157; Philippines 173–4,
  175; Singapore 88, 89;
  Taiwan 110, 111, 112, 113
trade, trends in international 24–8
see also exports; imports; *and
  under individual countries*

unemployment 19–20
*see also under individual
  countries*
United States
  Philippines as colony 164
  trade with Pacific developing
    countries: Hong Kong 36–8,
    39, 40; Indonesia 132, 133,
    134; Korea 60, 62–3;
    Malaysia 153, 155, 156, 157;
    Philippines 164, 171, 173,
    174, 175; Singapore 87, 88,
    89; Taiwan 110, 111, 112–13;
    Thailand 191, 193, 194, 195

Venezuela
- debt 16, 17, 18, 29
- education 22–3, 24
- employment and unemployment 19, 20
- exports 7, 8–9, 10
- GNP 29
- health 20, 21
- per caput income 2, 3
- policies 14–15, 17
- savings and investment 5

Vietnam 110–11
Vincent, D. P. 53